Pragmatism and the Reflective Life

Pragmatism and the Reflective Life

Stuart Rosenbaum

LEXINGTON BOOKS

A division of
ROWMAN & LITTLEFIELD PUBLISHERS, INC.
Lanham • Boulder • New York • Toronto • Plymouth, UK

Published by Lexington Books
A division of Rowman & Littlefield Publishers, Inc.
A wholly owned subsidary of The Rowman & Littlefield Publishing Group, Inc.
4501 Forbes Boulevard, Suite 200, Lanham, Maryland 20706
http://www.lexingtonbooks.com

Estover Road, Plymouth PL6 7PY, United Kingdom

British Library Cataloguing in Publication Information Available

Library of Congress Cataloging-in-Publication Data

Rosenbaum, Stuart E.
  Pragmatism and the reflective life / Stuart Rosenbaum.
     p. cm.
  Includes bibliographical references and index.
  ISBN 978-0-7391-3237-1 (cloth : alk. paper) — ISBN 978-0-7391-3239-5
(electronic)
  1. Ethics. 2. Pragmatism. I. Title.
  BJ1031.R66 2009
  171'.2—dc22   2009010585

Printed in the United States of America

To my grandfather, Thomas Carleton Colwell, and my father, Earl Vernon Rosenbaum, for their help along life's way

Contents

Preface

I came to American philosophy comparatively late in my academic career. Only after I had been teaching philosophy for several years did I begin to read around among the American philosophers. I am grateful to Richard Rorty for providing the stimulus—an NEH summer seminar at Princeton University—that stirred my interest in American philosophy. I had a slow start of it, but Rorty's *Philosophy and the Mirror of Nature* I found especially challenging to my analytic propensities; at the same time it invited me to revisit the submerged dimensions of sentiment I had reluctantly come to believe irrelevant to real philosophy. I had deluded myself into believing that the pursuit of truth was an intellectual pursuit that would tolerate no interference from the heart.

The American tradition, in virtually all of its prominent personalities, let me see that philosophy need not be solely an intellectual pursuit but that it should enable, in Dewey's words, a "recovery of philosophy" for human life. The American tradition lets us be whole persons; it invites our joys and sorrows, our loves and hopes, and our physical and psychological needs to be fully integrated into proper philosophical inquiry. Within the American context literature and art become acutely relevant to the practice of philosophy. William James and John Dewey make this inclusive spirit—a determination to respect philosophically all varieties of human creativity—explicit repeatedly throughout their philosophical work. In James's "The Moral Philosopher and the Moral Life," philosophers become "statesmen" whose primary tools are "novels and dramas of the deeper sort, . . . sermons, . . . books on statecraft and philanthropy and social and economical reform."[1] James's academic training was in medicine and psychology, and he aspired as a youth to become an artist; his philosophy respects the whole person he himself became. And John Dewey made aesthetics the cornerstone of his entire philosophical perspective; for Dewey, the creativity evident in artistic activity was the key to understanding what life was about—and what philosophy should be about.[2] I especially appreciate the closing sentences of the second chapter of Dewey's *Art as Experience*:

> Ultimately there are but two philosophies. One of them accepts life and experience in all its uncertainty, mystery, doubt, and half-knowledge and turns that experience upon itself to deepen and intensify its own qualities—to imagination and art. This is the philosophy of Shakespeare and Keats.[3]

The autobiographical dimension to this book comes in its account of how one might move from the intellectualist enterprises of most current philosophy toward a more integrated style of inquiry that seeks greater unity of head and heart. In this way, the book stands in gentle opposition to the spirit of Richard Rorty's essay, "Trotsky and the Wild Orchids." My own metaphorical Trotsky has always been my conviction that there is a truth to life that transcends individuals' idiomatic efforts to give their lives form and substance; I got this "Trotsky" during my youth from my grandfather and from the Southern Baptist church I grew up in on the meager outskirts of Dallas, Texas. My own metaphorical Wild Orchids has been a love of literature and poetry that refused to leave me even as I trekked determinedly through the landscape of analytic philosophy. Richard Rorty, through his gentle yet insistent disavowals of the goals of analytic philosophy, gave substance to my desire to bring together in thought my own metaphorical Trotsky and my own metaphorical Wild Orchids. This book is a partial account of my effort. (I do agree with Rorty that there *need* be no harmony between individuals' "Trotskys" and their "Wild Orchids," but I hope such harmony is possible, and I hope too that this book may be a small example of that possibility.)[4]

The book is about pragmatism and especially about pragmatism's moral perspective. This focus will be puzzling to many who take morality seriously, for many see pragmatism as being a particularly degraded form of intellectual perspective, one that *could not* yield any fulsome understanding of morality. I disagree. Maybe because of my late introduction to it, I see pragmatism as a compelling development out of the context of Western intellectual history. As American democracy has proven to be, in principle at least, a particularly attractive development on the world's social and political scene, so American pragmatism will prove to be a particularly attractive development on the world's intellectual scene. Since I have this conviction, I have had mixed feelings about using the term "pragmatism," precisely because it has appeared to many serious intellectuals to be an effort to read into the intellectual world the kind of "bottom-line" mentality characteristic of American corporate and political life. As John McDermott has put this point, "if Richard Nixon was a pragmatist, then the rest of us are called to be something different, something better."[5] Unfortunately the intellectual content of the American pragmatist tradition has become a caricature, a straw man, for those who want to make their own "ideological hay."

The best way to displace the caricature and the straw man is to offer engagement with the real thing. American intellectuals need to find again their own intellectual tradition; they need to engage the primary sources of American intellectual life if they are to understand the content of American pragmatism. In this volume I have chosen to respect the distinction between the caricature of pragmatism and the real thing partly by giving up the adjective "pragmatic" to popular caricature and reserving the adjective "pragmatist" for what I conceive as the real thing. Whenever I write about the content of the American tradition of pragmatism, I use the adjective "pragmatist," and I have shunned entirely the use of "pragmatic"; I give over the term "pragmatic" to descriptions of more or less shady politicians and businesspeople, and generally to "bottom-line" mentalities. And of course I hope this volume may supply some motivation once again to engage primary sources in the American pragmatist tradition.

In addition to Richard Rorty, two other contemporary philosophers have been greatly significant in my personal development. One is Richard Bernstein, the "Tigger" of contemporary American philosophy in contrast to Richard Rorty's "Eeyore." Bernstein exudes the intensely ecumenical character of the American tradition, not only in the intellectual perspectives he takes but also in the breadth of his interests. The other is Ernest Sosa, my dissertation mentor, who taught me in ways of which I am sure he was unaware that, in the words of Emerson, "character is higher than intellect"; I am grateful for his manifold example. Also important to me have been members of the Society for the Advancement of American Philosophy and especially John McDermott, friend and colleague ninety miles to the south whom I see too infrequently. Duane Cady has been a friend and helpful professional colleague since our time in graduate school, as has my philosopher brother, Stephen. I am grateful to Bob Baird, Bill Cooper, and Bud Duncan for their constancy as colleagues in the Baylor philosophy department. Finally, I appreciate Baylor University's patient confidence in granting me time for research and writing, especially a sabbatical leave during which I was able to complete the manuscript, and also Amy Antoninka who assisted my writing and research on a summer research grant from Baylor University.

NOTES

1. William James, *The Will to Believe and Other Essays in Popular Philosophy* (Mineola, N.Y.: Dover Publications, 1956), 210.

2. See Dewey's *Art as Experience* in *The Later Works, 1925–1953*, ed. Jo Ann Boydston (Carbondale: Southern Illinois University Press, 1989).

3. *Art as Experience (1934)*, vol. 10 of *The Later Works, 1925–1953*, ed. Jo Ann Boydston (Carbondale: Southern Illinois University Press, 1989), 41.

4. Rorty's autobiographical essay appears in *Philosophy and Social Hope* (London: Penguin Books, 1999), 3–20. All philosophers and aspiring philosophers should read this essay; as a description of philosophical psychology it is unmatched.

5. "Pragmatic Sensibility: The Morality of Experience," in *New Directions in Ethics*, ed. Joseph DeMarco and Richard Fox (New York: Routledge & Kegan Paul, 1986), 114.

1

—⁓⁓—

Introduction

A number of books seek to explain pragmatism and its treatment of particular issues in philosophy. In addition, many predispositions about what pragmatism is as well as what is wrong with it are popular in current philosophical culture. A book not only about pragmatism but also about morality multiplies difficulties. When it comes to morals—to leave philosophical issues out of account—almost everybody thinks they are expert, and frequently individuals' religious views settle important moral issues for them. Is abortion permissible? Is gay marriage permissible? Other "hot button" moral issues get regular attention in public media venues, and commentators promulgate popular or acceptable views about such issues.

I believe that American pragmatism offers benefits unavailable in other sectors of intellectual culture, especially in philosophy, and enables the kind of thought about morality that empowers, uplifts, and integrates communities and individuals, no matter how different from one another those communities or individuals may appear. Finding the strands of pragmatist tradition that have this benefit requires staking out claims in different intellectual directions. Most of the claims I set out here are controversial, and I try to set as much context for them as possible in a brief space so that they seem plausible. I do not expect conversions to pragmatism nor to ways of thinking about morality or religion consonant with it; I do hope to set a context for American pragmatism that gives a positive tone to its moral and religious perspectives.

PRAGMATISM VERSUS ANGLO-EUROPEAN PHILOSOPHY

Pragmatism, considered as an American intellectual phenomenon, has much in common with ways of thinking about morality and religion that are current in parts of the world that have not been influenced by Anglo-European philosophical traditions. Pragmatism is comfortable with moral and religious traditions that do not trace their sources to those Anglo-European traditions. Along, for example, with strands of African, Chinese, and Russian thought, the American pragmatist tradition celebrates human unity with the natural world and accommodates that unity in its thought about morality and religion. The tendency of pragmatism to cohere with non-European traditions of thought is evident in many representatives of the American intellectual tradition, from the earliest to the most recent. Roger Williams and Jonathan Edwards, in some tendencies of their thought,[1] are examples of early representatives and Hilary Putnam and Richard Rorty are contemporary representatives. What is common among these representatives of the American tradition I try to express in the following chapters.

My purpose, however, is not to trace the historical development of views prominent in the pragmatist tradition; nor is it to make any comparative study of it with other traditions.[2] Here I trace a path into the pragmatist tradition of thought from the Anglo-European traditions that have become dominant in the philosophical world not only of Europe and Britain but also of America. My central concern is to show how one may move conceptually from Anglo-European traditions of thought toward pragmatist traditions of thought, especially about issues of morality and religion.

The intellectual habits of analytic philosophy tend to be largely dominant on the American philosophical scene, and they are particularly so in thought that focuses on morality and religion. Philosophers typically seek to understand the conceptual content of the ideas of rightness and goodness, and they also typically debate the strengths and weaknesses of deontological, consequentialist, and virtue theories of morality. When issues of religion are the center of attention, traditional Western religious ideas are usually the focus of philosophical thought. Usually an understanding of God as the Being than which no greater can be conceived, an account given explicitly by St. Anselm, is taken for granted and the consequences of this understanding are explored in detail, along with its implications for the problem of evil, the powers of God, and the relation of God to humanity.

Pragmatist alternatives to these traditional theories of morality and religion suffer a bad reputation for several reasons. Prominent among those reasons is the fact that pragmatists do not seek conceptual universality, conceptual necessity, or a priori knowledge. Instead, pragmatists see humans as thoroughly embedded in their natural world, and this embedding includes their concepts and their ability to manipulate those concepts. Conceptual universality, necessity, and a priori knowledge, the primary goals of analytic philosophers, are not goals for pragmatists because pragmatists do not regard those things as separable in thought from the widest possible human agreement about how to use ideas of morality and religion to seek better lives for individuals and communities. Pragmatists believe that the significance of all ideas, especially ideas of morality and religion, is their fruitfulness for individuals and communities. In maintaining their commitment to fruitfulness, as opposed to conceptual necessity and universality, pragmatists open a gulf between themselves and traditional, analytic philosophers. Consequently, an issue prominent in following chapters is how to understand this gulf between conceptual universality and the wide fruitfulness of ideas that pragmatists seek. And, of course (following the metaphor), one also faces eventually the issues of how to bridge the gulf or of how to choose intellectual life on one side of it in preference to life on the other side of it. Once these alternatives come clearly into focus, one faces difficult problems of choice.

The gulf between conceptual universality and the widest possible fruitfulness of ideas is fundamental to understanding the tension between pragmatists and analytic philosophers, because this gulf means that those on different sides of it focus on different intellectual goals. These diverse goals are, on one side, precision and justification, and on the other side, understanding and explanation; those focused on conceptual universality focus on the first two of these goals, while those concerned with fruitfulness focus on the latter two. Since their intellectual goals are different, one might suppose that there need be no real tension between the two perspectives, and that perhaps pragmatists and analytic philosophers might live and work together as happily as do sociologists and physicists, or historians and biologists. Unfortunately, the interactions between pragmatists and analytic philosophers are usually not as happy as those between sociologists and physicists, historians and biologists. This absence of accord in their intellectual relationships results from the fact that each side believes it has trenchant, perhaps definitive, critiques of the other side; thus pragmatists think they understand where analytic philosophers go awry, and analytic philosophers think they understand where pragmatists go awry. Attempting to adjudicate this kind of philosophical disagreement inevitably lands in serious controversy.[3]

I am not reticent about my sympathies. I believe that when intellectual historians of the future write about twenty-first-century philosophy they will see it as expressing a definitive turn, in the American intellectual context, toward pragmatism. Though I add that the turn I foresee will be not just toward an American intellectual tradition, but rather toward a wider range of perspectives—African, Chinese, and Russian, for example—each cohering with basic perspectives of the tradition of pragmatism that has roots in the American context. There is genuine cosmopolitanism in the tradition of pragmatism; there is continuity between the moral and religious perspectives of pragmatism and the moral and religious perspectives of many non-European traditions of thought about morality and religion. This genuine cosmopolitanism in American pragmatism I hope will come definitively into the future of American life; a genuinely cosmopolitan perspective, an inclusive, ecumenical perspective, is integral to pragmatism. Scholars and philosophers who focus on American philosophy have only begun to elaborate its cosmopolitan, inclusive, and ecumenical commitments.

Central to my efforts to elaborate those commitments here are the character and work of John Dewey. Other thinkers in the American tradition are important and provide helpful nuances to the commitments I find in Dewey's work. Dewey is central to what follows because he is acutely attuned to the compelling character of the search for universality and transcendence that is inseparable from traditional Anglo-European philosophy and contemporary analytic philosophy. Though Dewey understands well the compelling character of that search, he also understands well its "Achilles heel," its effort to separate humanity from its home in the natural world. Dewey, in reaction against long-standing traditions of Western thought that seek transcendence for humanity, brings humanity back to the natural world. In Dewey's thought and in pragmatism generally, ideas and concepts are as much the result of human interactions with nature as are the provisions humans wring out of nature—plants and animals, for example—for sustenance of their lives.

If one follows Dewey and pragmatism generally in appreciating the Achilles heel of the philosophical search for conceptual universality, then one needs to explain what thought about morality or religion can be apart from that search. What is moral philosophy apart from the effort to find some conceptual guarantee that one way of thinking about morality is rationally preferable to others? What might Dewey and pragmatism offer as substitutes for this conceptual task of the Western philosophical tradition? How might pragmatism enable what Dewey thinks of as the "recovery" of philosophy?[4] What lies on the natural, human side of philosophical thought, on the side that shuns efforts to transcend the natural world and that supports individuals and communities in their efforts to find better futures?

THE REFLECTIVE LIFE

Dewey's answer to these questions comes in his 1932 *Ethics* with the idea of the reflective life. The idea of the reflective life is integral to Dewey's effort to provide what he calls "a working theory of morality."[5] What he means by a working theory of morality is a theory that enables serious thought about morality but stops short of the search for conceptual universality. A working theory in this sense makes use of all the resources of human intellectual life and in particular of the resources of science. These resources may be biological; they may be sociological; they may be psychological or anthropological; generally, they are any resources that might illuminate human moral practices, but they do not include efforts to find or justify universality of conceptual content. The idea of the reflective life and how it may provide a working theory of morality are central concerns of this book.

Dewey does not offer a systematic account of the reflective life; one does not find anywhere in his corpus a theoretical account of what that kind of life is. One must discern its content almost by osmosis; reading carefully through Dewey's works, one finds that the central content of the idea emerges naturally from familiarity with his values and his fundamental intellectual commitments. Here I provide a brief preliminary account.

THE REFLECTIVE LIFE: A PRELIMINARY ACCOUNT

The reflective life is a life that might be lived by anyone in any station of life; it is evident in people so deeply rooted in who they are that they immediately command respect, simply in virtue of being themselves. Such people may be musicians, historians, laborers, union members, farmers, politicians, or even philosophers. No particular activity of life or career pursuit is needed to be the kind of person who lives the reflective life. Examples of those who live the reflective life may be living persons, persons from the historical past, or characters of art, fiction, or poetry.

The immediate contrast Dewey draws in introducing the idea of the reflective life is the contrast between living reflectively and living in accord with custom or convention. This distinction, or one to the same effect, is made in every human community, no matter what may be its location in time and place. The idea of this distinction is humanly universal; wherever there are humans and communities, there is this distinction. This universality of the distinction is evidenced scientifically, through observation of humans and their communities; it is not a product of philosophical analysis.

Those individuals who manage to live the reflective life in their communities attract from their fellows the respect that is largely the point of living in community with others. The respect these individuals attract tends to endure and grow because it issues from habits of life and character that become stronger as one grows older, and it reinforces itself in all those dimensions of relationship that are a normal part of everyday life. In most human cultures, the elders are those who live such lives; they are the wise, those whom the adolescent, the immature, or the less gifted seek to emulate in their own actions and characters.

The reflective life appears in different historical and cultural traditions under different labels. *Wisdom* is the label that has been most prominently associated with reflective living in Western culture. Those whom we think of as wise are among those who live the reflective life. In other traditions, this kind of life appears in other guises. For the Confucian tradition, the *shengren* are cultural analogues of the wise; for the Hindu tradition, the *Brahmin* are cultural analogues of the wise; for the Muslim tradition, there are the *imam*; for the Buddhist tradition, the *Bodhisattvas*; and Native American tradition tells of the *shaman*. Each cultural tradition has its own way of speaking about those who are wise, those who live the reflective life in their own communities.

The reflective life is attractive in any tradition under any label; it is a life that brings to those who live it respect and honor in their communities. Living a reflective life and living it more fully and more intensely, and enabling others also to live it, are compelling goals in any cultural context. These goals are definitive forces even in the Western tradition that, unlike American pragmatism or those other cultural traditions, seeks necessity and universality of conceptual content.

Anglo-European philosophers typically think of wisdom as a kind of knowledge, a conceptual knowledge that one might apply in one's life. When Socrates seeks from Euthyphro, his interlocutor in Plato's *Euthyphro*, an account of piety, he seeks to elicit an account that might be grasped intellectually and then applied. For this model of wisdom, wise action and practice depend on antecedent knowledge of the content of concepts. One must know what piety *is* in order to be pious. Likewise, one must know what justice *is* in order to be just; one must know what knowledge *is* in order to have knowledge; and one must know what courage *is* in order to be courageous. This Platonist tradition to which all Western intellectuals are heirs requires characterizing theoretically what is desirable in practice as a condition of engaging in successful practice; one must have theoretical knowledge of rightness and goodness in order to do right and be good. Thus, the real business of philosophy in this Western, Platonist tradition is to discover the conceptual knowledge that in principle precedes successful living.

A large alternative to this Western and Platonist way of thinking about successful living appears in American pragmatism. Dewey's working theory of morals seeks to characterize successful living as a practice that does not need the antecedent knowledge of theory that motivates the traditional Western and still Platonist tradition. The idea of the reflective life is Dewey's scientific surrogate for the moral theories of that Platonist tradition. Dewey turns away, as do pragmatists generally, from the Platonist-inspired idea that clarity of thought or understanding about concepts must precede successful living; pragmatists reject the idea that wisdom, right action, or good character requires antecedent understanding of conceptual content.

For Dewey and for pragmatists generally human communities and practices precede understanding and theory. Theorizing is itself a human practice, and as a practice it has particular conventions, goals, and standards rooted in sustaining cultures. The independence of all culture that is implicit in efforts to discover precise conceptual content apart from cultural conditions becomes irrelevant for the pragmatist understanding of humans as fully historical creatures of time and circumstance. For this pragmatist understanding of human phenomena, theorizing can never achieve its Platonism-inspired goal of transcending all human culture.

When Dewey speaks of the reflective life, he is speaking of a way of living that is possible for any human in any time or circumstance, but he speaks, again, scientifically rather than philosophically. He offers no conceptual analysis of the idea of the reflective life, and one must give account of that idea apart from resort to tools of conceptual analysis. The human tools relevant to understanding how to think about the reflective life are the tools of science: observation, experience, hypothesis, and test. These tools of science need not be elaborated philosophically in an effort to explain what *proper* scientific method is. The method of science, in the relevant sense, is not unified in any systematic way. As practices oriented around producing better ways of knowing, and thus better ways of living, have developed in various contexts, they have led to conceptions of method in science that resemble one another, but to no essential core of method that must be present in order to qualify as properly scientific.[6]

Just as Dewey understood and interacted with influential Western theories of morality, I too shall express an understanding of contemporary theories of morality and interact critically with those theories. My reason for entertaining and interacting with such theories is to express my own rationale for turning toward a pragmatist perspective about issues of morality. Seeing how one can circumscribe the prospects of philosophical moral theory may yield significant motive for investigating the pragmatist understanding of morality centering about the idea of the reflective life. Understanding that the philosophical search for conceptual universality is unlikely to yield progress may motivate fuller consideration of this alternative rooted in the American pragmatist tradition.

PRAGMATISM'S HUMAN GOAL: ECUMENISM

What is at stake in pragmatists' philosophical work is more than an understanding of how humans are continuous with their natural world, more than an effort to resist an understanding of humans as "resident aliens" who must patiently await the coming of another world. These "negative" goals are certainly real in pragmatism, but pragmatists think of them as secondary to the cosmopolitan, egalitarian, and democratic future they hope may become possible for all humanity. This large vision of ideal possibility—a democratic future for all humanity—was real in the character and work of John Dewey; it was also real in many others in the American tradition, especially in William James, and in the earliest years of the American experiment also in Roger Williams. This vision of ideal possibility is the largest motivating force behind the work of the American pragmatists.

The continuing need for ecumenical perspectives, as a way of realizing the democratic prospects for humanity, is evident in many ways apart from pragmatists' commitment to democratic ideals. A quick look at the twentieth century's last World Congress of Philosophy makes this point.

The twentieth century's last World Congress of Philosophy, held in Boston during the summer of 1998, invited philosophers to reflect about the role of philosophy in globally diverse cultures. In their introduction to the twelve-volume *Proceedings* of the Congress, the editors note that at one session distinguished senior philosophers spoke on the topic, "what we have learned in philosophy in the twentieth century." By the editors' account,

> [Three] analytic philosophers said they had come to appreciate the worldwide reach of philosophy; another said nothing about the topic, presumably because that is not a philosophic question for his kind of analysis; another philosopher reminded the others that they all assumed that analytic philosophy is all there is and noted the importance of Heidegger for global philosophy; and finally a Muslim philosopher pointed out that none of the speakers recognized the philosophic traditions of all the other world cultures and yet it is precisely those other philosophic traditions that are growing and burgeoning in educational institutions around the world. The last speaker was cheered.

The editors reflect about this session that

> [w]hile one might be tempted to regard that session as a sad instance of Western cultural blindness, a much more productive perspective would see it as a transition to a much more encompassing and . . . inclusive vision of philosophy. Western thinkers have grown accustomed to thinking that the phi-

losophy of the twentieth century belonged exclusively to them. Now they realize that their comfortable expectations no longer hold.

The inclusive vision the editors are tempted to hope for is indistinguishable from the large democratic and ecumenical goal of the American pragmatist tradition. Furthermore, that inclusive vision is encouraged by developments in the very tradition of analytic philosophy that seems to so many other cultures to be blind to their own traditions. These encouraging developments are the focus of my third chapter.

Pragmatism's inclusive and ecumenical vision is rooted in ways of thinking about value very different from the ways of thinking about it embedded in Enlightenment and contemporary analytic philosophy. Pragmatists think of value as rooted in particular individuals and communities rather than in the abstraction that is presumed by moral philosophers.

Contemporary analytical method in thinking about moral value typically involves an effort to arrive at conceptual generalities or abstractions that fit moral experience. The fit in question is supposed to enable and justify judgments about particular cases in virtue of generalizations that apply to them. Particulars, and judgments about them, are thought of as useful for their illumination of general rules or laws that may then be applied to achieve successful action or practice. In this way, the Platonist perspective that requires illumination of the intellect as a condition of successful living finds expression in classical and contemporary moral theory. Whether one thinks of Aristotle, Kant, Mill, Rawls, or more eclectic philosophers, their goal is usually to achieve a conceptual generality that may be applied in particular cases of action or practice. The pragmatist tradition abandons this pervasive and analytical philosophical perspective and instead makes human practices primary in thinking about value; pragmatists abandon the characteristic philosophical search for conceptual necessity and universality.

Their abandonment of the search for necessity and universality makes possible for pragmatists a deep commitment to the values of democracy, and to a cosmopolitan and egalitarian ecumenism.

PRAGMATISM

Chapter 2 is an effort to carve out a conceptual space for pragmatism within historical traditions of philosophical thought; it seeks to describe the tradition of pragmatism as one kind of development out of the classical empiricism of the British tradition, and it seeks to show that developments in American thought conflict in irreconcilable ways with basic commitments of traditional Western, and now analytic, philosophy. This chapter focuses on one way of understanding pragmatism, one way of seeing how it is different from, and irreconcilable with, the Platonist-inspired tradition of conceptual inquiry that still dominates philosophy. After characterizing pragmatism in a general way, I make use of Charles Sanders Peirce's understanding of belief in order to elaborate that characterization. Finally I explain in a preliminary way, though I come back to the issue at various places throughout the book, how the gulf between pragmatism on one side and Platonist-inspired traditions on the other cannot be bridged; in a distinct way, these two traditions are incommensurable.

MORAL THEORY

Chapter 3 argues that moral theory fails when it is understood as a quest for conceptual universality that might enlighten the projects of living. Contemporary understandings of morality as an institution capable of being brought into sharp theoretical focus through careful analysis of moral concepts are inadequate to the institutions of morality. Not only are they inadequate but also they are ethnocentric in not taking seriously the moral institutions, traditions, and contexts of other cultures. Although this failure among analytic moral philosophers to embrace an ecumenical perspective is significant, this third chapter focuses on specific theoretical failures within prominent moral theories. Exhibiting the limited prospects for moral theory may encourage thinking about morality as a cultural institution embedded in human practices.[7]

Although I argue in this third chapter that traditional moral theory is limited, I want to acknowledge here the abiding idealism among Western moral philosophers. Most of those philosophers have been idealistic, many to the point of obsession. Concern to live well, to relate well to one's neighbors, and to arrive at modes of institutional function that serve large human goods has been pervasive among Western philosophers. When Karl Marx sat in the British library writing *Das Kapital*, he did so out of personal commitment to large social ideals, and the history of twentieth-century communism is largely a history of the vicissitudes of Marx's ideals. When Jonathan Edwards toiled over his sermons and treatises amid the gentle chaos of his households in Northampton and Stockbridge, he did so out of commitment to a demanding religious ideal, and the history of Protestantism since 1750 is largely a history of the vicissitudes of Edwards's religious thought. Many individuals seek in their lives, as did Marx and Edwards, to realize social or personal ideals that give meaning to their lives beyond the nourishing and resting, the getting and spending that frame daily living.

The history of philosophy is a symptom of the realization that ideals, of the sort to which Marx and Edwards were committed, are vital for humanity. Moral philosophy, seen from the perspective of pragmatism, is the history of efforts to systematize ways of thinking about such ideals, ways that have come to seem fundamental in Western philosophy to all serious thought about them. Thus Aristotle, Kant, and Mill, to mention obvious examples, embrace different understandings of moral ideals and seek to show how their understandings are rooted in permanent, ontological fact. From this perspective, Aristotle's moral philosophy rests on a teleological ontology, an understanding of the proper end of each natural kind, among which humans are the most important because of their rationality; Kant's moral philosophy rests on an ontology of human reason and of its scope and limits; and Mill's moral philosophy rests on a psychological ontology, an understanding of the essence of the human psyche. Each of these perspectives—and more might be mentioned—seeks a unitary account of what is ideal in human life and in human society. Conceptual universality and clear implications for human behavior are the goals of these historically important theories of morality. Contemporary philosophers committed to these perspectives are fixtures in American colleges and universities.[8] Alternatives to these ways of thinking about ideals get little attention within academic moral philosophy.

The common ideals of happiness, justice, equality, fraternity, respect for duty, responsible behavior, and goodness of character are motivations for the theorizing of moral philosophers. Realizing those ideals in human communities, however, apart from the question of their intellectual foundations, is fraught with many kinds of difficulties. These difficulties include not only conflicting cultural traditions and engrained habits of thought and action, but also conflicting accounts of ontology that may appear incompatible with these, or any, moral ideals. (Mechanistic materialism is an example of a conflicting ontology that is usually thought incompatible with moral ideals.) Difficulties like these inspire the efforts of moral philosophers to bring overpowering stature to one of these moral theories and its supporting ontology. The goal of moral theory, in its dominant analytic guise, is to overcome intellectually the inertia of entrenched cultural traditions and of engrained habits of thought and action, and to overcome also those ontological perspectives that are incoherent with any moral ideals.[9]

Pragmatists do not share the confidence of many philosophers that moral theory might bring closer a realization of moral ideals. Pragmatists think that no moral theory or argumentative strategy is capable of overcoming cultural traditions and engrained habits largely because they believe that the moral theories and argumentative strategies are themselves as much creatures of cultural conditions as are the traditions and habits theorists might like to use their theories and strategies to overcome. When Jeremy Bentham and John Stuart Mill, for example, argued for utility as the source of morality in order to get intellectual leverage against social practices prevalent in nineteenth-century British society, their egoistic ontology of human psychology, the foundation of their moral theory, was as much a consequence of British intellectual culture as were social practices they sought leverage against.[10]

In holding that theory and argumentative strategy have roots in human culture, pragmatists reject the intellectual aspirations of Western moral philosophers. Those philosophers have, on this pragmatist understanding, no rational strategy, no intellectual "trump card," that might lift them above their own cultural traditions; they have no way to achieve rational autonomy over or against their own or any culture. What moral philosophers hope for—rational vindication of a special ideal or ontology—they have no resources to justify beyond the ordinary resources available to any interested person. Recourse to reason or to the nature of persons or to the nature of God does not enable transcendence of cultural traditions of thought about reason, personhood, or God. Many individuals of breadth and experience are aware that there are different cultural traditions of thought about these issues. Pragmatists, in accepting the cultural and historical contexts that circumscribe human rationality, assert their refusal to be illegitimately ethnocentric.

The ethnocentrism pragmatists reject is the kind that privileges philosophy as a source of rational adjudication for disputes about morality and social practice. The hope of philosophers to rise above tradition and to use reason as the ultimate tool for subjecting custom and tradition to its unifying power is empty.[11] The kind of ethnocentrism that acknowledges its own cultural roots is different from this rational, imperialistic variety. Richard Rorty's pragmatism embraces an ethnocentrism that admits its own cultural roots; its difference from the ethnocentrism of typical moral philosophers is its acknowledgment of its own cultural roots.[12] This pragmatist ethnocentrism hopes to persuade proponents of different cultural traditions to embrace its values, or approximations of its values, by appeal to the consequences of doing so. Pragmatist ethnocentrism is not imperialistic because it is not rationalistic; it does not believe in its intellectual superiority but in its attractiveness as it is realized in human communities.

According to pragmatists, the fault of moral theorists and philosophers generally is their misplaced confidence in the power of thought to transcend culture. Pragmatists on the contrary see reason as a tool that enables humans, when they use it well, to deal effectively with concrete problems. Pragmatists acknowledge that, apart from concrete problems and needs, reason may become a source of deep insight and aesthetic pleasure, and for many philosophers and mathematicians, such insight and pleasure detaches reason from the concrete problems that ordinarily occasion its use. This insight and pleasure in the use of reason, however, does not legitimate endowing reason with any power to transcend culture. Reason, pragmatists think, is as much a creature of culture and tradition as is etiquette, and it has precisely as much ontological power as does etiquette.[13]

This modest understanding of reason as part of human culture has been responsible for much misguided criticism.[14] Many thinkers have seen moral and conceptual relativism veiled behind pragmatism's commitment to egalitarianism. Such criticisms I believe are groundless,[15] and this third chapter explains how they are so.

THE REFLECTIVE LIFE

Chapter 4 focuses on Dewey's distinctive way of thinking about the deeply rooted hopes that have motivated moral philosophers, scientists, social workers, law enforcement officials, priests, educators, and many others. The central idea in his account of this distinctive way to think about moral value is the idea of the reflective life. The reflective life in Dewey's account of it is a life lived out of a particular context of moral and social traditions and also lived toward significant ideal ends. The reflective life is a life of autonomous thought and action that respects the cultural context in which it comes to maturity and it is a life that seeks also to realize specific ideals of personal and social aspiration. The ideas central to the reflective life in Dewey's work are those of autonomy, community, and ideality. Clarifying and elaborating the idea of the reflective life is the main task of chapter 4.

This idea of the reflective life is vague, but in the context of Dewey's treatment it becomes vivid and compelling. The reflective life contrasts with a life lived in accord with custom. Almost all individuals feel their individuality in such a way as to require deliberation about how they should respond to their culture's moral expectations. If one's country goes to war, for example, then one may expect to exercise some judgment about how to participate in the country's commitment to war; sometimes one expects even to decide about whether to participate at all in the country's military commitment. Other examples of the need for independent judgment come immediately to mind. The ubiquity of such personal situations and the ordinary need for deliberate decisions about them reinforces the distinction between customary expectation and what one ought to do. To live reflectively is to live in awareness of this tension between the community's expectations and one's own autonomy.

When Dewey speaks about the reflective life he speaks about an understanding of the business of living that is shared, at least to the extent that one is able to judge of such things, by virtually every human on the planet. No theory need be called upon to justify this distinction between the reflective life and life in accord with custom, for the distinction itself is as much embedded in human experience as is the distinction between oneself and others. The distinction is philosophically innocent, and requires no theorizing in its defense. One may assume the distinction as a cornerstone of thought about morality that is as near universal as one might hope to get without drawing on distinctions—the a priori/a posteriori or the necessary/contingent distinctions, for example—rooted in Western philosophy; it is an observational generalization about human life as innocent philosophically as is the observation that humans, like chickens, are bipeds.

The issue that remains after accepting this uncontroversial distinction between reflective living and living in accord with custom, however, is the issue whether it holds any philosophical interest. If one is not seeking to justify a particular account of right action, of the good life, or of associated ideas, then how might one elaborate an understanding of the reflective life to clarify its usefulness generally in thinking about living well, living harmoniously with others, or living toward better institutions? How might the idea of the reflective life serve as anything remotely like a surrogate for philosophical moral theories? Chapter 4 suggests answers to these questions about the idea of the reflective life.

MORAL IDEALS

Chapter 5 takes up the issue of moral ideals. Integral to reflective living is living toward significant ideals, ideals of personal aspiration and ideals of human institutions. Such ideals may be more or less idiomatic and they may be more or less universal in scope. The ideals of justice, goodness, rightness, duty, responsibility, and community solidarity are more extensive in scope than those of financial success, popularity, political success, or being reliably fashionable in one's style of dress. The more extensive ideals are those that have motivated moral philosophy.

The philosophical problem about ideals derives from the fact that they beckon from beyond the status quo. Ideals transcend personal dimensions of habit and character and enable us to see individuals' defects and foibles; they transcend the social institutions that do not measure up to them, and they enable us to see how those institutions might be better. Individuals seem, in short, to have two kinds of awareness: the kind that enables them to see clearly what their conditions are and the kind that enables them to see clearly what their conditions might more ideally be. A strong philosophical temptation, one largely dominant in Western philosophy, is to think of these kinds of awareness as something like experience on one side and intuition or reason on the other, the latter enabling awareness of transcendent ideals against which we may measure and judge realities of experience. But pragmatists do not believe, as I have already urged, that persons have a capacity of knowing—reason or intuition—that enables them to appropriate ontologically transcendent ideals. The very idea of ontological transcendence, even the very idea of ontology, is largely foreign to pragmatism.[16] Pragmatists are largely committed to a unitary way of thinking about the natural world that does not admit ontological gaps; and they observe that alleged ontological gaps turn out to be invitations for clever people like Emerson, Nietzsche, or Dewey to fill them with the ordinariness of experience and culture. Just as biologists and philosophers of science reject "God of the gaps" strategies of explanation for biological phenomena, pragmatists likewise reject "ontology of the gaps" strategies for all human phenomena. And pragmatists are aware too of the ubiquity of ontology of the gaps strategies in the history of Western thought, especially in moral philosophy.

What can ideals be? How may pragmatists preserve anything remotely like the kinds of dual awareness that enable judgments of comparison between the status quo of individuals and societies on one hand and the more ideal conditions all agree are worth striving toward on the other?[17] One conclusion of chapter 5 is that pragmatists may preserve the dual awareness that enables these judgments of comparison, and they need not resort to special cognitive skills or ontological transcendence in order to explain it.[18]

A pragmatist way of preserving the dual awareness implicit in moral thought requires respect for the particularity of individual moral situations. This particularity has dimensions both culturally local and psychologically individual. Finding a way to speak about ideals in the fullness of their particularity is finding a pragmatist account of ideals. The account of ideals suggested in chapter 5 views them as concrete, particular realities rather than as abstract realities. Ideals are as particular and concrete as the humans who have them, deliberate about them, and live in accord with them. Since they are such concrete realities, ideals are philosophically unproblematic; they give rise to no epistemological or ontological issues and they are fully functional as ideals in the situations that elicit appeal to them. The pragmatist understanding of ideals follows the strongly suggestive remarks of William James that they are our "saints." That our saints *are* our ideals is a conclusion implicit in canonical sources in the pragmatist tradition of thought, especially in the work of William James and John Dewey; chapter 5 makes this case and spells out consequences of this way of thinking about them.

DELIBERATION IN THE REFLECTIVE LIFE

Chapter 6 focuses on deliberation and action. Who one is in the fullness of one's individuality finds expression on every occasion of choice. This individuality in actions and choices means there are no ways to characterize what acting and choosing are *in themselves*. Philosophers typically write and think as though it might be possible to explain what acting or choosing *is* in a general and comprehensive way apart from the diverse individuals who act and choose; they seek conceptual necessities about action and choice. However, the elusiveness of an adequate philosophical account of practical reasoning and of deliberation, because of the individuality in acting and choosing, undermines the philosophical effort to achieve conceptual precision about action and choice. Given the particular individuals in diverse cultures, along with their idiomatic ways of appropriating their situations, nothing of *conceptual* generality is available to philosophical effort. Choosing what to do or to believe is an idiomatic process that mirrors the diverse individuals in diverse communities seeking their individual futures.

Furthermore, being a reflective individual is making one's way toward a future in self-conscious awareness that one's future depends not only on what one chooses but also on who one is, and that one's personal identity is always in the making as one chooses. In this respect, pragmatist thought about choice and action takes seriously Hume's acute observation: "For my part, when I enter most intimately into what I call *myself*, I always stumble on some particular perception or other, of heat or cold, light or shade, love or hatred, pain or pleasure. I never can catch *myself* at any time without a perception, and never can observe anything but the perception."[19] Hume's observation is a baseline assumption for thinkers in the pragmatist tradition, and they add to Hume's observation the further existential observation that one's individuality is continually in the making in ongoing responses to one's environment. This surfeit of individuality and particularity that is characteristic of pragmatist thought undermines customary philosophical goals about choice and action.

To belabor a point already made, philosophers nonetheless characteristically seek more than tentative, contingent generalizations that future inquiry may replace; they are, after all, those whose professional lives begin in the seeking of certainty and include efforts to undermine mistaken claims to certainty in order to replace them with worthier candidates. The quest for certainty is a cultural habit of great inertia. Nevertheless, pragmatism acknowledges the ecological and cultural conditions in which humanity flourishes, and these conditions militate against the historical inertia of philosophy. When one accepts the local, the historical, and the biological dimensions of human life, then one accepts too the contingency and tentativeness of every generalization, of every result of inquiry.

The question for chapter 6 is how to make one's way reflectively and deliberately toward a meaningful future. Abandoning the quest for certainty is not abandoning a quest for meaning in one's own life and in the life of one's family and community. The question has two parts: The first: May anything of conceptual generality be said about decisions about action or belief? The answer given here is no. The second: How may one seek a meaningful future short of the quest for conceptual necessities about action and choice? Chapter 6 focuses on the first question. The second question is the focus of chapter 7.

EDUCATION FOR THE REFLECTIVE LIFE

Chapter 7 addresses the question of how to seek meaningful futures while avoiding quests for certainty; this question is the more difficult of the two and requires some reconstruction of thought about our understanding of humans as biological organisms. Fortunately, a path toward this reconstructed understanding of humanity is well marked by fellow laborers in the pragmatist tradition.

Well-known among scholars of the American tradition in philosophy is the fact that John Dewey gave pride of place among his intellectual concerns to institutions of education. These are the institutions, as he explained in *Democracy and Education*, that bring coherence and solidarity to communities and that open toward futures of hope and possibility.[20] These are the institutions that bear the burden of preserving and conveying what is of value from the past as well as of striving toward more meaningful futures; and their burden in these respects may become greater as we turn gradually away from our quests for certainty. Our institutions of education are the identifiable ways we seek to manage the unfolding of our individual and community futures.

All the ways we convey the values of our past and all the ways we exhibit our values in the present are strategies of education. All institutions of human culture function to convey, to exhibit, to sustain, or to undermine our values; values just are, functionally speaking, the vicissitudes of human institutions as they wax and wane in their cultural settings. A pragmatist understanding of value acknowledges this fact. Acknowledging this fact means putting human institutions at the center of thought about value; it means making those institutions' structures, operations, and goals a focus of deliberate thought. To belabor a point already made and to be relied upon throughout this volume, traditional philosophical issues about values, about their nature and justification, become distractions from the thought about value encouraged by a turn toward the tradition of pragmatism. Institutions of education—and these include all human institutions whether or not we think of them as educational—are conveyances of values. The human community, and perhaps especially the American community, needs to be more deliberate and thoughtful about the symbiotic relationship between institutions and values. Chapter 7 acknowledges the role of institutions in our understanding of value.

Value is embedded in all of life and in all institutions. This fact about value, its ubiquity in experience, grounds pragmatist thought about value. The most remote, arcane, and radical seeming ideals have their locus in experience just as do the more ordinary ideals expressed in the inertia of custom and tradition. Pragmatist thought about education acknowledges this fact. Determined attention to its phenomenology is the hallmark of pragmatists' attention to the moral life. The value humans need in order to do the work of living is value already written in their experience; it is written in the human past, in human cultures and traditions, and written as well in hopes for more satisfying futures. The philosophical task of pragmatism is to turn toward human institutions, toward the values they embody, and to seek their betterment. Chapter 7 reinforces in detail this way of thinking about value and education, and it makes concrete suggestions about how to move toward a better future.

FROM THE REFLECTIVE LIFE TO ECUMENISM

Chapter 8 arrives at last at the issue of ecumenism. The promise of pragmatism's reflective life is the promise of inclusiveness. Such inclusiveness is nothing short of the democratic ideal that was rooted in John Dewey's personal character, in his New England Congregationalist religion, and in his entire intellectual life. This inclusiveness holds together in thought the most compelling ideals of the American democratic experiment and the most compelling ideals of Western Christianity. Both sets of ideals are admittedly ethnocentric, and neither is somehow essentially imperialistic, in spite of the checkered historical record of each. (The role of the idea of manifest destiny in American history, and the role of various inquisitions, crusades, and conquests in Catholic and Christian history are parts of this checkered historical record.)

Bringing to the fore a pragmatist way of thinking about the ideals of democracy and Christianity enables a way of thinking about those local, concrete, and particular ideals that gives them power beyond the contexts that originally engendered and still empower them. This power, however, is independent of intellectual or political effort to justify or impose them on individuals and cultures that rely on different sets of ideals. The imperialism implicit in analytic philosophy and identified by the editors of the *Proceedings of the 1998 World Congress of Philosophy* Americans should avoid. A pragmatist way of thinking empowers ideals without seeking philosophically to justify them or politically to impose them; the strategies of philosophical justification and political imposition are some of the imperialistic strategies pragmatists avoid. Local, concrete, and particular ideals may be as psychologically universal as are biological needs. Giving voice to such local and particular ideals, ideals that may be nevertheless psychologically universal, becomes possible, natural, and compelling within the intellectual traditions of American pragmatism.

Many recent thinkers have challenged the impetus of the classical American pragmatists, especially James and Dewey, toward democratic and Christian inclusiveness, the sort of inclusiveness that hopes for coherence and harmony among diverse communities. Richard Rorty, a neopragmatist, has apparently turned reluctantly away from this classical pragmatist ideal of inclusiveness. For Rorty, realism about human psychology and culture encourages a rigid public-private distinction, a distinction Rorty believes is justified prudentially for most individuals; in respecting that distinction, individuals agree not to impose their own private, usually religious, commitments on others and in return individuals are entitled to be left alone to practice those commitments to the extent that they are not impositions on others who do not share them. Mill's treatment of these issues in *On Liberty* is a significant influence on Rorty's thought.[21] Nevertheless, the gap between the classical pragmatists' commitment to inclusiveness and Rorty's realism about human dispositions toward different others is palpable to those familiar with the thought of these American intellectuals.

The suggestion of the last chapter of this volume is that the classical pragmatists' optimistic commitment to inclusiveness may survive, and perhaps prosper, beyond the more realistic and almost Nietzschean pessimism that seems characteristic of Rorty's thought. A condition, however, of the potential to prosper of the classical commitment to inclusiveness is taking seriously the concrete and particular understanding of ideals that comes to the fore in chapter 5. That pragmatist understanding of ideals illuminates the potential for all humans in all cultural circumstances to gain access to the pragmatist ideal of the reflective life.

NOTES

1. Perry Miller has written about both of these early American intellectuals in ways that exhibit their congeniality toward what has become the pragmatist tradition of American intellectual culture. See his "Edwards and Emerson," in *Errand into the Wilderness* (Cambridge, Mass.: Harvard University Press, 1956), 184–203; and *Edwards* (New York: William Sloane Associates, 1949). See also Miller's *Roger Williams* (Indianapolis: Bobbs-Merrill Company, 1953).

2. I mention here two books that make a good start at exhibiting the relationships between American traditions and those of other non-Western intellectual cultures: Scott Pratt, *Native Pragmatism: Rethinking the Roots of American Philosophy* (Bloomington: Indiana University Press, 2002); and David Hall and Roger Ames, *The Democracy of the Dead: Dewey, Confucius, and the Hope for Democracy in China* (Chicago: Open Court Press, 1999).

3. Richard Bernstein is more optimistic about these divisions than I am here. See his "Pragmatism, Pluralism, and the Healing of Wounds," in *Pragmatism: A Reader*, ed. Louis Menand (New York: Vintage Books, 1997), 382–401.

4. See Dewey's "The Need for a Recovery of Philosophy," reprinted in Louis Menand, ed., *Pragmatism: A Reader* (New York: Vintage Books, 1997), 219–32.

5. John Dewey, *Ethics (1932)*, vol. 7 of *The Later Works, 1925–1953*, ed. Jo Ann Boydston (Carbondale: Southern Illinois University Press, 1989), 176.

6. Thomas Kuhn's 1961 *The Structure of Scientific Revolutions* is the classical source for this view, but it is a view that Dewey had embraced as early as the 1890s and that he expresses distinctively in his 1929 Gifford Lectures published as *The Quest for Certainty*; see John Dewey, *The Quest for Certainty (1929)*, vol. 4 of *The Later Works, 1925–1953* (hereinafter LW), ed. Jo Ann Boydston (Carbondale: Southern Illinois University Press, 1989).

7. Kwame Anthony Appiah's *Cosmopolitanism: Ethics in a World of Strangers* (New York: W. W. Norton, 2006) argues strongly for this understanding of morality as an institution of human cultures.

8. Some examples of contemporary Aristotelians are Alasdair MacIntyre (University of Notre Dame) and Martha Nussbaum (University of Chicago). Contemporary Kantians are Richard Eggerman (Oklahoma State University) and Robert Louden (University of Southern Maine). Contemporary utilitarians are Henry West (Macalester College) and Alasdair Norcross (University of Colorado). A concise account of these ontological entanglements of traditional Western moral theory, as well as a concise pragmatist response to them, appears in Richard Rorty's "Ethics without Principles," *Philosophy and Social Hope* (New York: Penguin Press, 1999), 72–90; see especially 84.

9. Any good history of philosophy provides accounts of the cultural contexts within which prominent moral philosophers worked, and those philosophers themselves customarily make clear their motivations. Plato and Aristotle provide this information, as do Kant, Bentham, and Mill. For an interesting discussion of the concepts of morality that have mainly interested philosophers—rightness, goodness, justice, and so on—see Kwame Anthony Appiah's *Cosmopolitanism*, cited in note 7 above.

10. An account of the historical roots of such intellectual phenomena as moral theories appears in C. S. Peirce's "Evolutionary Love," *The Collected Papers of Charles Sanders Peirce* (Cambridge, Mass.: Harvard University Press, 1960), 6.289. Also in this same vein, recent discussions of the Scopes "monkey trial" of the 1920s make clear that William Jennings Bryan's motivation for objecting to Darwinism was not its support of naturalistic ontology but rather its apparent endorsement of the kind of social Darwinism that abandoned Christian social values. See, for example, Marilyn Robinson, "Hallowed Be Your Name," *Harper's Magazine* 313, no. 1874 (July 2006); her essay is an excerpt from a longer essay in the spring 2006 issue of *The American Scholar*.

11. Hilary Putnam, in "How Not to Solve Ethical Problems," suggests that the metaphor of problem and solution is too dominant in thought about moral problems. He suggests instead focus on the metaphors of adjudication and reading, and he uses the example of the Supreme Court's 1973 *Roe v. Wade* decision as adjudication rather than solution and the example of various readings of Hamlet. These metaphors, he suggests, might be more helpful to philosophers than that of problem and solution. See *Realism with a Human Face* (Cambridge, Mass.: Harvard University Press, 1990), 179–92.

12. See again Rorty's "Ethics without Principles," *Philosophy and Social Hope* (New York: Penguin Books, 1999), 72–90.

13. For a pragmatist account of this aesthetic dimension of reason, see again John Dewey, *The Quest for Certainty* LW4:87–111. See also Larry A. Hickman, "Dewey's Theory of Inquiry," in *Reading Dewey: Interpretations for a Postmodern Generation*, ed. Larry A. Hickman (Bloomington: Indiana University Press, 1998), 166–86.

14. Bertrand Russell's treatment of pragmatism in his *A History of Western Philosophy* is not untypical. See *A History of Western Philosophy* (New York: Simon and Schuster, 1977), 811–27.

15. For a concise account of how these misguided criticisms might be turned aside by pragmatist sympathizers, see my "Morality and Religion: Why Not Pragmatism," in *Pragmatism and Religion: Classical Sources and Original Essays*, ed. Stuart Rosenbaum (Champaign: University of Illinois Press, 2003).

16. See the variety of opinions regarding what exactly comprises Dewey's metaphysics. For example, see Raymond Boisvert, *Dewey's Metaphysics* (New York: Fordham University Press, 1988); Gary Calore, "Towards a Naturalistic Metaphysics of Temporality: A Synthesis of John Dewey's Later Thought," *The Journal of Speculative Philosophy* 3, no. 1 (1989): 12–25; Morris Raphael Cohen, "Some Difficulties in Dewey's Anthropocentric Naturalism," *Philosophical Review* 49 (1940): 196–228; William Ernest Hocking, "Dewey's Concepts of Experience and Nature," *Philosophical Review* 49 (1940): 228–44; Martin Hollis, "The Self in Action," in *John Dewey Reconsidered*, ed. R. S. Peters (London: Routledge and Kegan Paul, 1977); Sholom J. Kahn, "Experience and Existence in Dewey's Naturalistic Metaphysics," *Philosophy and Phenomenological Research* 9 (1948): 316–21; Richard Rorty, "Dewey's Metaphysics" in *New Studies in the Philosophy of John Dewey*, ed. Steven M. Cahn (Hanover, N.H.: University Press of New England, 1977); and George Santayana, "Dewey's Naturalistic Metaphysics," *Journal of Philosophy* 22 (1925): 673–88.

17. I assume here without argument that reductive strategies, efforts to make awareness of ideals a simple and ontologically innocent—because it is merely emotional—matter of fact, as did the Logical Positivists, are not viable. For reinforcement of this view, see Dewey, *A Theory of Valuation*, LW13:189–254.

18. Some thinkers have argued recently that pragmatism in fact invites recourse to ontological transcendence as a way of accounting for this dual awareness. See Robert Roth, *Radical Empiricism: An Alternative* (New York: Fordham University Press, 1998); also Victor Kestenbaum, *The Grace and the Severity of the Ideal* (Chicago: University of Chicago Press, 2002).

19. David Hume, *A Treatise of Human Nature*, ed. L. A. Selby-Bigge (London: Oxford University Press, 1888), 256.

20. John Dewey, *Democracy and Education*, vol. 9 of *The Middle Works, 1899–1924* (hereinafter MW), ed. Jo Ann Boydston (Carbondale: Southern Illinois University Press, 1988).

21. For more information on the public-private distinction in Rorty, see David Hollenbach, "Civil Society: Beyond the Public Private Dichotomy," *The Responsive Community* 5, no. 1 (Winter 1994–1995), 16; Richard Rorty, *Contingency, Irony, and Solidarity* (Cambridge: Cambridge University Press, 1989), esp. xii–xv and 60–94; *Philosophy and Social Hope*, 50; *Objectivism, Realism, and Truth* (Cambridge: Cambridge University Press, 1991), 199.

2

—⁓—

Pragmatism

Misconceptions and caricatures of pragmatism abound in intellectual culture. John McDermott has said that Richard Nixon was called a pragmatist, and that if Richard Nixon was a pragmatist, then we have a moral responsibility to be something else.[1] McDermott himself is a pragmatist, however, and he believes, with most scholars of pragmatism, that there is much more to pragmatism than calculating and seeking one's advantage in the way apparently characteristic of Mr. Nixon's political life. I do not want to begin here, however, by trying to combat misconceptions and caricatures. Since I believe that pragmatism, in spite of much misunderstanding and misreading, is one of the noblest developments in Western intellectual history, I begin my account with some commentary about a profoundly idealistic statement from John Dewey. Dewey's "Creative Democracy: The Task Before Us" explains to those present at his eightieth birthday celebration the content of his life work; it is a compact statement that deserves many readings, for it captures the heart of pragmatism's moral and social idealism. I quote two passages.

The first passage explains the central values of democracy. The second passage explains pragmatism's difference from other Western philosophies. The first passage:

Democracy is a way of life controlled by a working faith in the possibilities of human nature. Belief in the Common Man is a familiar article in the democratic creed. That belief is without basis and significance save as it means faith in the potentialities of human nature as that nature is exhibited in every human being irrespective of race, color, sex, birth and family, of material or cultural wealth. This faith may be enacted in statutes, but it is only on paper unless it is put in force in the attitudes which human beings display to one another in all the incidents and relations of daily life. To denounce Nazism for intolerance, cruelty and stimulation of hatred amounts to fostering insincerity if, in our personal relations to other persons, if, in our daily walk and conversation, we are moved by racial, color or other class prejudice; indeed, by anything save a generous belief in their possibilities as human beings, a belief which brings with it the need for providing conditions which will enable these capacities to reach fulfillment. The democratic faith in human equality is belief that every human being, independent of the quantity or range of his personal endowment, has the right to equal opportunity with every other person for development of whatever gifts he has.[2]

This passage expresses what Dewey thinks of as the central values of democracy, and it expresses as well his own personal values. The passage shows why Dewey is known as "the philosopher of democracy." The idealistic tone of the passage is evident, if perhaps muted a bit by Dewey's demure prose style. The values evident in the passage are at the heart of the American democratic experiment. Can such idealistic values, or some approximation of them, be realized in human society? The effort to realize those values is the whole point of the American political tradition. Such values do not now pervade American culture; they did not do so when Dewey wrote those words. Those values are ideals; they are worthy of commitment; and Dewey spent his entire intellectual life trying to find ways to give them life in human communities, and especially in the American democratic community. This statement of Dewey's commitment to democratic ideals is inseparable from his commitment to pragmatism. Any account of pragmatism or its values that does not take with utmost seriousness the radical idealism evident in this passage cannot do it justice. I come back to this passage and to these values of democracy in chapter 8.

Consider now the second passage:

Since my adult years have been given to the pursuit of philosophy, I shall ask your indulgence if in concluding I state briefly the democratic faith in the formal terms of a philosophic position. So stated, democracy is belief in the ability of human experience to generate the aims and methods by which further experience will grow in ordered richness. Every other form of moral and social faith rests upon the idea that experience must be subjected at some point or other to some form of external control; to some "authority" alleged to exist outside the processes of experience.

This passage, like many in Dewey's work, one might pass by without appreciating its significance. The passage is worth attention here because it expresses the central intellectual commitment of the pragmatist tradition, the idea that experience itself is the source of its own guidance; experience itself is the source of aims and methods, principles, goals, and ideals that may yield better experience and better institutions. Experience does not need the guidance of external authority; it needs no external control to achieve betterment. (The almost technical term in the pragmatist tradition for betterment is "amelioration," and I shift to that term in deference to its typical use.)

The history of Western philosophy, however, is a history largely of efforts to find an external authority to control experience and guide it where it should go—to whatever amelioration is possible for human lives and institutions. Plato called upon the Forms for this purpose; Aristotle called upon the human *telos* to justify behavior and practice; Descartes called upon God to underwrite all human institutions; Kant called upon Pure Practical Reason to control behavior; and Mill called on an ontology of egoism to support his utilitarianism. This brief account of these important thinkers of course does not do them justice; each is far more important than these superficial remarks intimate. However, this brief account is all I need to exhibit the contrast between Dewey's commitment to experience as the source of its own guidance and characteristic moral theories of the Western tradition. This refusal to resort to efforts to discover external controls in order to achieve the betterment of experience is a central commitment of pragmatism, and Dewey in this compact essay captures perfectly that refusal. Dewey's entire life work is an effort to explain how experience can be a guide to its own betterment, its own amelioration. Needless to say, those who find necessary an external source of control react badly to Dewey's commitment. Some who react badly to this commitment I address in later chapters. For now, I provide a basic explanation of pragmatism.

PRACTICE EMPIRICISM

Pragmatism has roots in the empiricism of the classical British empiricists. That classical empiricism, however, is modified in the American intellectual context. The spirit of the American pragmatists is radically empiricist in that it seeks the fullest possible respect for human experience in all of its dimensions.[3] The various dimensions of human experience are, in pragmatism, the roots of all of human life, including human intellectual life. Thus the pragmatic tradition respects, though it greatly augments, the classical empiricist idea that all ideas originate in experience. Pragmatism's radical empiricism differs from classical empiricism in definitive ways. I consider here three of those ways.

The first definitive difference from classical empiricism is that pragmatism accords no pride of place to problems of epistemology and metaphysics; these problems and ways of thinking about them fall naturally into place as dimensions of the humans who are agents in specific communities. Pragmatists do not address in any special way the philosophical problems of knowledge and skepticism that loom large for Enlightenment thought. Knowing is, for pragmatists, just one way humans engage their world— it is a mode of practice—and it has no greater priority for human life than do loving, hoping, fearing, and other ways humans engage their world. Pragmatists do not have what philosophers have become accustomed to calling a "theory of knowledge"; they are not classical empiricists and they are not rationalists, nor are they skeptics. In pragmatism, knowing is simply a way of being human. Pragmatists take for granted the various practices of knowing, along with the claims and assertions that emerge from them, as a natural part of human life. Questions about *real knowledge* or *real truth* are contextualized within a particular practice. In this way, pragmatists refuse to enter Hume's study and to worry there with him about how or what they really know; they do, however, cheerfully join Hume in his goings about in the world, for they believe that those real-world goings about are a better measure of knowing than anything that might happen in Hume's study. Pragmatism's empiricism is radical, and it is centered on ordinary human practices. Does my black Lab have an ear infection? Are there quarks? Can one be both paranoid and have bipolar disorder? How far has the magnetic North Pole moved in the last decade? Such questions are answered in the context of traditions of practice; veterinarians, physicists, and psychologists are trained in the context of disciplinary traditions to give answers to such questions, and their answers constitute knowledge. Part of pragmatism is making this point about the activity of human knowing.

Pragmatism's empiricism is radical in that it does not discriminate among experiences to determine which are legitimate and which are not; and pragmatism's empiricism is deeply respectful of practices rooted in diverse institutions. Pragmatism may be thought of as practice empiricism, where the empiricism in question is not discriminatory toward any kind of experience; experiences (of all kinds) and practices (of all kinds) are central to pragmatist intellectual life. In consequence, pragmatists do not react well to invitations to sit with Hume in his empiricist and skepticism-producing study because they think something quite odd happens there.

The odd thing that happens in Hume's study can be appreciated only from the historical perspective that sees it as a development of the Cartesian culture of philosophy. Since pragmatists see all phenomena, even sophisticated intellectual phenomena, as fully embedded within cultural and ecological contexts, they think that understanding such phenomena requires understanding those contexts. This respect for cultural context is *the second definitive difference* between pragmatism and classical empiricism. Pragmatists think that understanding the Cartesian culture of philosophy, its historical sources and its various avenues of development, enables one to see that culture as conditioned by traditions and ways of thinking different from those that embed contemporary life, and that consequently may not be significant for contemporary life.[4] Another way to express this characteristic of pragmatism is to say that it takes for granted the genealogical perspectives usually associated with the thought of Friedrich Nietzsche.

Nietzsche's genealogy presents morality, whatever guise it takes in moral theory, as an outcome of the intersection of specific human needs with opportunities of circumstance and culture. The details of Nietzsche's genealogy do not matter here;[5] what matters is his insistence that all phenomena of culture, even the most sophisticated of intellectual phenomena, including moral thought, are rooted in need and in cultural possibility.

Pragmatists exploit this insight frequently associated with Nietzsche,[6] and they augment it with the Darwinian perspective that sees humans as animals with specific environmentally appropriate skills. Knowing is one of these skills; it is a natural activity that needs no distinctively philosophical effort in order to understand it. Knowing is not a mysterious activity that requires special ontological equipment; it is a natural part of life in humans' typical ecological and cultural settings. To appreciate this understanding of knowing is to transcend the need for a philosophical theory of knowledge; it is to transcend the need to know, for example, whether knowledge is true, justified belief or is instead something else, perhaps indefeasible, true, justified belief or the proper function of one's cognitive faculties. The classical pragmatists, including Charles Sanders Peirce, William James, and John Dewey, understood the human contexts for various activities of knowing, and saw that philosophical understandings of many basic concepts—knowledge, justification, duty, goodness, value, and so on—were too constrained in not appreciating natural contexts for intelligent human activities. To appreciate this pragmatist idea is part of becoming empowered to turn intellectual effort toward issues of greater moment for contemporary culture.

In *The Quest for Certainty*, his 1929 Gifford Lectures, John Dewey took up what he believed to be the largest intellectual problem bequeathed to philosophers of his own generation by Enlightenment thinkers such as Hume and Kant. That problem was finding a place for value in a world of fact. I cannot reprise here Dewey's genealogy of this problem, his comprehensive effort to provide an account of the settings of intellectual culture that gave birth and life to the problem of how to find a place for value in the mechanical world of Newtonian science. Suffice it to say that Dewey did provide a comprehensive account of the birth and growth of that issue for Enlightenment thinkers; he did so in such a way that the problem appeared, like any finite creature, to come to life, to grow to maturity, to decline into old age and finally death. Nietzsche's pronouncement of the death of God may yield an apt analogy for the problem of the place of value in a world of fact. As God, in Nietzsche's account, perished though few noticed the event, so the problem of the place of value in a world of fact perished, though again few noticed the event.

To notice the event, to become aware that the problem of the place of value in a world of fact perished, is to become empowered to address issues about values in an intelligent way apart from typical philosophical concerns about whether there really are values and if so what their nature and source might be. For Enlightenment thinkers and for later analytic philosophers, values are commands of God, dictates of reason, logically necessary outcomes of human self-seeking, expressions of subjective taste, or another of many answers proposed by those who have failed to notice the demise of that problem. Humans *are* knowing, valuing animals; human communities *are* knowing, valuing communities. Pragmatists, following Dewey, see and appreciate the life, history, and death of the defining intellectual problem of Enlightenment culture, and they understand that they may now turn intellectual effort in another direction.

Value is as much embedded in experience and culture as is fact. Value and fact are so much intertwined in life and experience that neither has conceptual or cognitive priority over the other. We may talk about either on specific occasions of interest where the other is an unquestioned item of background context, but neither has any absolute priority over the other; values are as ordinary and legitimate a part of human life as are facts. To the extent that we take for granted a problematic distinction between value and fact, we mistake an intellectual artifact of the seventeenth century for a permanent fixture of all intellectual culture. When we appreciate Dewey's genealogy of that artifact of Western intellectual culture, we may preserve it historically and cherish it as a treasured part of our past; but we need no longer take seriously in our own intellectual context that particular artifact. No longer need we seek to legitimate values as though they were more problematic than facts.

A third definitive difference between pragmatism and classical empiricism is its unreserved, though circumspect, respect for science. Science is the best tool Western culture has provided for achieving human goals. Since Newton, science has been responsible for dramatic revisions not only in the ways we pursue knowledge but also in the ways we live our daily lives—our modes of transportation, of feeding ourselves, of health care, of communicating, of educating, and so on. Pragmatists believe that science, intelligently pursued, holds promise of myriad improvements in the quality of individual lives and in the quality of human communities and their natural environments. Science is also a model institution in that it is a self-correcting, community enterprise that embodies in its practices values that are ideally realized in all democratic political communities.[7]

Pragmatism's respect for science is circumspect in having no tinge of ideology; it sees science as a tool that does not provide answers to metaphysical questions or to epistemological questions. Science is a variety of practices that implement systematically the many characteristic activities of human knowing; it enables effective cognitive interaction in various natural settings. Science does not enable knowledge of the truth about human nature, about the source of values, or about God or religion. Considered as a tool, science enables cognitive interactions within human environments, cultural and natural, but it does not enable knowledge transcending those environments. In this respect, pragmatists typically embrace Kant's perspective that human cognition is limited to the natural environment, and that attempts to transcend that environment cognitively are not viable scientifically or philosophically. Humans are cognitively embedded in their natural environments. The many thinkers in the contemporary scientific and philosophical worlds who seek scientific confirmation of metaphysical views—creationists and materialists are equally good examples of this historically naive tendency of thought about science[8]—are committed to an Enlightenment ideology of science, one that is as much an artifact of history as is the issue of the place of value in a world of fact.

These three aspects of pragmatism—its de-centering of Enlightenment problems of epistemology and metaphysics, its embrace of genealogy as a method for making explicit the cultural and natural settings of all human enterprises, and its respect for science as a tool though not an ideology—are central in works and thinkers of the pragmatist tradition.

I emphasize these three aspects of pragmatism for two reasons. First, American pragmatism is much associated in popular thought with strategies and values of American business and politics. Pragmatism, in accord with this frequent caricature, appears self-interested, egocentric, and concerned solely with "the bottom line," the profit dimension, or "the cash value" of all actions or enterprises. (Remember John McDermott's comment, mentioned at the outset of this chapter, about Richard Nixon.) But trying to think of humanity's deepest and most enduring values in accord with this caricature of pragmatism is profitless, because it yields no viable way of thinking about values. When pragmatism appears in this caricature, then instead of being radically alternative to philosophical theories about value, it appears to represent one particular, and indeed especially unattractive, perspective about value. Bertrand Russell's critique of James and Dewey relies on this sort of caricature and, though it is misguided, it nevertheless hangs on in popular thought about pragmatism.[9]

A second reason for emphasizing these three characteristics is that pragmatism, so understood, need offer no particular conceptual analyses of basic concepts, nor need it embrace any particular philosophical view about reality, truth, knowledge, or value. Philosophical analyses of these things, views about their nature and their source, rely on the Platonist perspective that sees theoretical understanding as somehow prior to wise practice, and they assume that something like a transcultural perspective is attainable by those who are talented and willing to work hard. The understanding of pragmatism whose center is the three aspects mentioned above refrains from philosophical analyses of knowledge, truth, and value. Philosophical views about these ideas suppose there is a transcultural way to get these things right. Pragmatists embrace their own finitude and their own culture, and their embrace disables anything historically recognizable as philosophical method. Pragmatists will not attempt philosophical theories of ethics, value, knowledge, or reality; they will be content with the tools and strategies of science. The tools and strategies of science, including the strategies of genealogy, accept human finitude and the authority of human communities in all issues of value, knowledge, and reality. Pragmatists believe that nobody in any human culture has access to the content or the source of values that is not granted by that culture itself. The problems of value, and their solutions, have their locus fully within the natural environments within which humans are born, grow to maturity, and then die.[10]

How does one get to this perspective that systematically embeds human life in communities of practice that make possible the many modes, including the intellectual, of human activity? Although many answers might be given to this question, I here trace a path through Charles Sanders Peirce's account of beliefs as habits of action.

TAKING PEIRCE SERIOUSLY

Charles Peirce's 1879 essay, "How to Make Our Ideas Clear," expresses an understanding of belief that departs radically from traditional ways of thinking about it.[11] Peirce's understanding of belief resonates naturally with the idea that humans are parts of the natural world whose activities are rooted in nature and culture. A Darwinian perspective about human intellectual skill harmonizes naturally with Peirce's understanding of belief.

Beliefs, according to Peirce, are habits of action. Thought of in this way beliefs are embedded in human organisms as expressions of their ways of being in the world. Beliefs become organic dimensions of character and personality; they become as fully expressive of one's individuality as are one's height and weight. Beliefs are organically part of every individual in every community. My beliefs are my habits of action; more subtly, they are the myriad tendencies, dispositions, and habits—many of which cohere, compete, and overlap—that yield my behavior. There is no algorithmic or precise way of determining what my beliefs are; my beliefs are as vague and indistinct, and as little so, as are the myriad tendencies, dispositions, and habits that yield my specific actions. Furthermore, just as my physical features change across time, in just the same way my beliefs, since they too are organic expressions of my individuality, likewise change across time. I return to this point in the later chapters on deliberation and education.

Why might one resist thinking of beliefs in this Peircean way? A prominent, and typically philosophical, reason begins with the fact that I may share beliefs with others of different communities and languages; I may share with Chinese, Russian, and African speakers the beliefs, for example, that there are quarks, that democracy is superior to monarchy, that Kantian moral theory is a pale shadow of Christian morality, or that God exists. These affirmations appear to indicate firm, content-specific commitments that I may share with many other people. In traditional philosophy they express propositions that can be held in common with others, that are true or false, and for which I may have good or bad evidence. In affirming them I signal my own commitment to the same belief, the same intentional content, the same proposition as is likewise affirmed by those others who speak different languages. How might I think that my affirmation that God exists is idiomatic and that others' similar affirmations are equally idiomatic? This question is natural, and it typically engenders a more traditional philosophical understanding of belief.

The most prominent traditional understanding of belief is that it is an individual psychological relation to a proposition, to an intentional content, and that the proposition affirmed may be true or false in the sense of corresponding or not to the way the world is. Although nobody has successfully explained this relationship of correspondence between one's intended content, the proposition one affirms, and the world itself when one believes truly, the idea nevertheless continues to underlie most philosophical thought about belief and truth.[12] This traditional understanding of belief makes of each belief a specific object, a proposition that may be shared by different people who have the same belief; this understanding then inquires about these propositions, shared objects of belief, what makes them true or false. Propositional content is central to traditional understandings of belief, and it comes packaged with myriad difficult philosophical problems: How does belief, as a psychological state of relatedness to an intentional content, differ from other states such as fear or hope? What constitutes one person's belief the same belief as that of another? What are the criteria of identity for beliefs or for propositions? These problems, and others, are serious intellectual responsibilities for philosophers who understand belief as a psychological relation to an intentional content.[13]

What makes a Peircean, pragmatist understanding of belief compelling is partly its evasion of these typical philosophical problems about belief. But beyond evading these typical philosophical problems about belief, the pragmatist understanding of belief coheres with natural, scientific understandings of persons. Every person has individuality; every person has commonality with others. These aspects of individuality and commonality with others find expression differently in different individuals. Individuals are psychologically unique in a variety of ways, and they also have in common distinctive tendencies, skills, and abilities. Both its evasion of philosophical problems about belief and its coherence with scientific understandings of humanity empower the Peircean, pragmatist understanding of belief as habit of action.[14] One's beliefs, in this pragmatist view, are as embedded in who one is individually and culturally as are one's manners of work and play. This compatibility of the Peircean understanding of belief with natural and scientific understandings of humans gives that understanding positive impetus; no longer need belief be a philosophical problem engendering epistemological and ontological controversy; instead it becomes a natural part of life.

However, philosophers inevitably raise questions of justification; they want to know who is right, or who has the correct understanding, and they will ask this question about the two accounts of belief. Is the Peircean understanding of belief preferable to, more justifiable than, the traditional account of belief as psychological relation to an intentional content or proposition? This particular question I address later in the chapter on deliberation, but a large version of this issue, the tension between the ideas of justification on one hand, and genealogy or explanation on the other, needs immediate attention.

JUSTIFICATION AND EXPLANATION

Peirce's account of belief as habit of action establishes an explanatory context for beliefs. All beliefs may be understood in terms of conditions that make possible their genesis, their continuation, and sometimes their demise. When individuals come to believe that there is only one God and that Mohammed is His only prophet, they do so largely in virtue of cultural conditions that give rise to that belief, that sustain it, and that occasionally change so as to undermine it. Peirce's account of belief makes all beliefs, in principle at least, transparent to strategies of explanation; it enables explanations of beliefs in terms of sources and sustaining conditions. Genealogies of beliefs of all kinds, from the most mundane to the most sacred, become possible when one accepts Peirce's account of belief. Beliefs become complex empirical functions of one's native constitution and one's cultural environment, and they become so in a way that exposes all beliefs about what Western philosophy has sorted out as "fact" and as "value" to empirical explanation, to genealogical accounts that expose them as malleable features of human cultural environments.[15]

Philosophers in the Anglo-European tradition, however, have usually been interested in another feature of beliefs—whether or not they are justified. Whether or not a belief is justified appears to be an irreducibly normative issue about the belief and one's reasons for holding it. If one has justifying evidence for one's beliefs, then those beliefs are normatively required for those who have that evidence. One's belief that God exists, for example, is justified or not relative to the quality of evidence one has for it. If one is unable to defeat through some accepted evidential strategy the apparent incompatibility of God's existence and the fact of evil, then one is not justified in believing that God exists. In this case, one must give up the belief that God exists, since it is not justified. This apparent normative dimension of all belief has motivated philosophical activity designed to defend God's existence or the absolute objectivity of morals or the idea that scientific method reveals ontological fact or other ideas that have emerged from the large cultural inertia of modern philosophy.

The serious issue that arises from these two different understandings of belief is their apparent incompatibility. The pragmatist understanding of belief makes explanatory context primary in thought about it; the traditional understanding of belief as relatedness to propositional content makes justification of belief primary in thought about it. Which of these understandings of belief is better? Why should one prefer one to the other? This question generalizes to the questions, which mode of intellectual activity is more basic and which reveals the more important perspective about the human condition? The quick answer to these questions is that they have no answer.

One cannot seek to *justify* the view that one of these intellectual activities is more basic without begging the question in favor of the view that the context of justification is primary. Likewise, one cannot seek to *explain* a preference for the context of justification without assuming that the context of explanation is primary. If one seeks to justify a propositional content understanding of belief as the more basic, then one has already assumed that proper belief is justified affirmation of propositional content. Likewise, when one explains the preference for a propositional content understanding of belief in terms of native individual tendencies and cultural conditions—for example, an acute intellect and systematic training in techniques of analytic philosophy—then one likewise already assumes that contexts of explanation or genealogies of belief are more basic than are issues of justification. No intellectual strategy enables one to straddle these different intellectual contexts or to bring them under a single umbrella of technique that might mediate their conflict about belief.

The fact that no mediation or compromise is possible about which of these intellectual contexts is more basic means that neither perspective may pretend absolute superiority. Interested parties must make conscientious choices about which perspective to embrace apart from anything that might qualify as justification for such choices. Many reasons, however, tell in favor of the Peircean pragmatist understanding of belief and tell also in favor of the larger disposition to give general intellectual primacy to contexts of explanation and genealogy. The largest such reason is that thereby one enables and empowers more systematic focus on, as Dewey puts it, "the problems of men."[16]

The problems of humanity are cultural, political, economic, moral, religious, and scientific. Each of these problems comes with different cultural and historical contexts. To understand these contexts in ways that may enable amelioration of the various problem conditions of humanity is a worthwhile ambition, and surely as worthwhile as more traditional philosophical ambitions like justifying belief in God or justifying an absolutist moral perspective. Such, at any rate, is the commitment of pragmatists. And pragmatists may take comfort, I suggest, from the fact that the assumptions they make about belief and, more comprehensively, about value may not be defeated by philosophical argument. The contexts of explanation are as legitimate as contexts of justification, and they may not be rejected simply because they insist on seeing issues of justification fully within motivating cultural contexts.

Another way of putting the pragmatist point of the preceding paragraphs is to say that there is no "genetic fallacy" of the sort that appears in logic textbooks. Genealogies may be subtle and persuasive or they may be ham-fisted and implausible. The idea of a genetic fallacy *simpliciter* is conceived within the womb of the assumption, here rejected, that the context of justification is primary in thinking about belief.

Pragmatists' commitment to the priority of practice and experience emerges from such background as Peirce provides for thinking about beliefs as habits of action. To think of beliefs as habits of action is to think of them as organic dimensions of individual humans in their particular historical and cultural settings. Likewise, we may think of desires and of values as also organic dimensions of individual humans in their historical and cultural settings. To think in such particular, experiential, and practice-oriented ways about human phenomena exposes those phenomena to reflective strategies that may yield possibilities for amelioration. Amelioration of typical beliefs, desires, and values is possible only when those beliefs, desires, and values are understood as functions of individual psychology and cultural context; focusing in a more traditional way on issues about the justification of beliefs, desires, and values detracts from the kind of focus that empowers amelioration. Pragmatism, since it involves both the classical empiricist emphasis on experience and a full orientation toward practice, empowers ameliorative effort.

The three marks of pragmatism that emerge from the Peircean understanding of belief are, again, the de-centering of problems of epistemology and metaphysics, the empowering of explanatory, genealogical perspectives, and the deep though circumspect respect for science as an institutional locus of human knowing.

Those three characteristics of pragmatism are prominent among factors that motivate abandoning the Platonist presumption of the priority of theory to practice. Other ways of thinking about pragmatists' abandonment of this Platonist perspective are various, but three additional factors echo the reasons already given and deserve mention. *The first factor* is a historically engendered skepticism about the prospect that philosophers might achieve even a minimally useful result from their moral theorizing. Controversy about theoretical perspectives of morality does not abate over time but appears rather to intensify. Kantians, utilitarians, virtue theorists, contractarians, and more eclectic thinkers are as far from seeing beyond their disagreements as they were several centuries ago. What success might be in these theoretical controversies is unclear, and unclear in a way that does and should discourage even the best intentioned of participants. Theoretical controversies among physicists, chemists, and other scientists are characterized by wide agreement about what a successful resolution of controversy would look like. (The discovery of the structure of the DNA molecule, the double helix, is an example of how resolution of controversy in science is successfully attained.)[17]

Partly responsible for the fact that progress on these issues of moral theory is elusive is the fact that moral theorists, unlike their counterparts in science, cannot agree about basic data moral theories should take into account. Kantians and deontologists focus on data that support their commitment to moral primacy for the ideas of duty and responsibility. Consequentialists and utilitarians focus on data that cluster in support of favorable outcomes for action. Each of these theoretical perspectives takes on burdens of dealing with a specific set of counterexamples, "data" of morality that support competing theories. Kantians need to deal, usually much as does Kant himself, with the specter of morally required actions that have disastrous consequences.[18] Utilitarians need to deal with similar issues, the problem of moral saints, for example.[19] Different moral theories carry different theoretical burdens and none is exempt from its own characteristic set of problems. Problems of this sort are central in chapter 3. The root of these theoretical problems may be nothing more dramatic than the fact that theorists cannot agree about what to take as data for their moral theory. Scientists do not suffer from this source of disagreement.

The second factor in pragmatists' abandonment of typical philosophical approaches to moral value is that they are committed to a Darwinian perspective that sees humans as fully embedded in their natural environments, in their geographical, linguistic, religious, and moral settings. This Darwinian perspective does not yield an understanding of humans consistent with their having any ability rationally or religiously to transcend their natural, earthbound setting. The conceptual analysis that appears a pinnacle of achievement for human rational skill cannot, in this Darwinian perspective, enable a definitive result of the sort analytic philosophers seek—for example, a necessary truth about the nature of correct behavior—and it cannot do so any more than the most highly developed skill of any other animal might achieve an analogous definitive result. When birds build nests, for example, they do so in typical ways circumscribed by their species, their ecological niche, and the particular resources available at the time and place they are living. Similarly, philosophers' approaches to morality are circumscribed by cultural contexts and by intellectual tools available within those contexts. The fact that human behavior is similarly circumscribed means, on the positive side of the ledger, that scientists may seek to understand and explain human skills in the same way they seek to understand and explain the skills of each of the wide variety of animal species with which humans share their planet.[20] Every human phenomenon is open to the probing methods of the sciences.

The third factor, one intimately connected to the others, is that particulars themselves become primary to thought about morality. Particulars are not secondary to generalizations about action, generalizations that reason must isolate, justify, and apply to particulars. To suggest how particularity may be understood apart from its customary philosophical servitude to generality is a principal task of this book. Displacing the Platonist perspective that makes understanding and using abstractions a condition of good or appropriate living requires an explicit account of how particulars are primary in thought about action, belief, and value. A consequence of following the pragmatists in embracing the primacy of particulars in thought about morals is potentially greater respect for diversity of thought, culture, and value. The hope of the editors of the 1998 volumes of the proceedings of the World Congress of Philosophy for a

"more encompassing and . . . inclusive vision of philosophy" might come
to fruition through greater attention to American pragmatism.[21]

I have now given a basic account of what pragmatism is, emphasizing
the passionate idealism that motivated John Dewey and has also motivated other principal thinkers in the American tradition. I have empha-
sized also that pragmatists need not offer analyses of central concepts that
have motivated the work of other philosophers in the Anglo-European
tradition; they may be content with the methods and strategies of science.
Before turning to Dewey's account of the reflective life, I turn in chapter 3
to exposing the Achilles' heel in contemporary theories of morality in the
hope that a clear vision of that mortally exposed part may motivate a turn
toward the pragmatist alternative I elaborate in chapter 4.

NOTES

1. McDermott is a friend and a Distinguished Professor of Philosophy and Hu-
manities at Texas A&M University. One source for this remark is McDermott's
"Pragmatic Sensibility: The Morality of Experience," *New Directions in Ethics*, ed.
DeMarco and Fox (New York: Routledge & Kegan Paul, 1986), 114.

2. LW14:226.

3. See William James, *Essays in Radical Empiricism* (New York: Longmans, Green
& Co., 1912).

4. See, for example, Richard J. Bernstein, *Beyond Objectivism and Relativism*
(Philadelphia: University of Pennsylvania Press, 1983). The portion titled "The
Cartesian Anxiety" is especially relevant to the point I am making here.

5. For an account of Nietzsche's view, see *On the Genealogy of Morality* (Indianapolis, Ind.: Hackett Publishing Co., 1998).

6. The insight is not only Nietzsche's; Emerson and others in the American tradition made use of genealogical strategies of argument before those strategies
brought Nietzsche philosophical acclaim. See George Stack, *Nietzsche and Emerson:
An Elective Affinity* (Athens: Ohio University Press, 1992).

7. John Dewey makes this point repeatedly, but infrequently directly. For a
more direct account, see LW13. See especially chapter 6, "Science and Free Culture." An account of this issue appears in my later chapter on the reflective life, especially in the section on the source of moral value.

8. See, for example, William Dembski, *Intelligent Design: The Bridge between Science and Theology* (Downers Grove, Ill.: Intervarsity Press, 2007), and Edward Wilson, *Consilience* (New York: Vintage Books, 1999).

9. See Bertrand Russell, *A History of Western Philosophy* (New York: Simon and
Schuster, 1945). This caricature hangs on as well in the work of some scholars who
write about the pragmatist tradition. See, for example, Louis Menand, *The Metaphysical Club: A Story of Ideas in America* (New York: Farrar, Straus, and Giroux,
2001). Allen Guelzo, reviewing Menand's book, expresses his commitment to the
same unfortunate caricature; see his "American Philosophy's Uneasy Embrace of

God," *Harvard Divinity Bulletin* 30, no. 4:35–36. Bruce Kuklick, too, shares in this unfortunate representation and critique of the American pragmatists; see *A History of Philosophy in America, 1720–2000* (London: Oxford University Press, 2000). Another such work is John Patrick Diggins, *The Promise of Pragmatism* (Chicago: University of Chicago Press, 1994).

10. This perspective may seem strange to those educated within Western intellectual culture, but in most of the world's cultures this claim is unremarkable. To get a feel for its wide acceptability, readers may consult Barbara Kingsolver, *The Poisonwood Bible* (New York: HarperCollins, 1999), and the series of novels by Alexander McCall Smith set in Botswana and beginning with *The No. 1 Ladies Detective Agency* (New York: Anchor Books, 2001). Another useful source is David Hall and Roger Ames, *Democracy of the Dead* (Peru, Ill.: Open Court Publishing, 1999).

11. This essay is widely anthologized. See, for example, H. S. Thayer, *Pragmatism, the Classic Writings* (Indianapolis: Hackett Publishing Co., 1982), 79–100.

12. Discussions of these issues are ubiquitous in philosophy. An easily accessible discussion appears in Bertrand Russell, *The Problems of Philosophy* (London: Oxford University Press, 1912).

13. Addressing these issues has been a frequent project of those concerned with issues in philosophy of mind. Roderick Chisholm has sought to sort the various psychological relations to propositions that constitute the various "propositional attitudes" one might take toward propositions. Distinguishing among belief, fear, hope, love, and other intentional states in terms of the logical properties of those intentional states was, and remains for some, an important project of philosophy. See, for example, Roderick Chisholm, *On Metaphysics* (Minneapolis: University of Minnesota Press, 1989). W. V. Quine has been an important opponent of propositions as ontological objects; he sees propositions as not having logically acceptable conditions for identity and thus as spurious objects. See, for example, Willard Quine, "Three Grades of Modal Involvement," *The Ways of Paradox* (New York: Random House, 1966), 156–74.

14. Though my use of the word "evasion" is natural in this context, it nevertheless calls to mind the title of Cornel West's book, *The American Evasion of Philosophy* (Madison: University of Wisconsin Press, 1989); West sees and argues that, as I have expressed it here, evading philosophy is largely the point of the American tradition in philosophy.

15. For an elaborate and accessible account of Peirce's understanding of belief, see Douglas Anderson, *Strands of System: The Philosophy of Charles S. Peirce* (West Lafayette, Ind.: Purdue University Press, 1995).

16. John Dewey, "The Need for a Recovery of Philosophy," in MW10:3–48.

17. James Watson, *The Double Helix* (New York: Scribner, 1998). Many other examples in the history of science make clear how these controversies are resolved in science. See Thomas Kuhn, *The Structure of Scientific Revolutions* (Chicago: University of Chicago Press, 1962); see also Hans Reichenbach, *From Copernicus to Einstein* (New York: Philosophical Library, 1942).

18. See *Foundations of the Metaphysics of Morals* (Upper Saddle River, N.J.: Prentice-Hall, 1997).

19. See the essay by Susan Wolf, "Moral Saints," *The Journal of Philosophy* 79, no. 8 (August 1982): 419–39. Her essay gave rise to a series of essays defending utilitarian theories from the untoward result that they required sainthood of all morally reputable persons.

20. Human linguistic and rational skill are especially interesting to scientists, largely because these skills are widely thought to be unique to humans. See, for example, the interesting work by Steven Pinker, *The Language Instinct* (New York: HarperCollins, 1995). Edward Wilson's work on ants has encouraged Wilson to believe that humans and their skills are explicable using standard techniques of biology and sociobiology; see *Consilience*, referenced in note 8 above, and *On Human Nature* (Cambridge, Mass.: Harvard University Press, 1978). Others who share this roughly Darwinian perspective are Stephen Gould, Daniel Dennett, Steven Weinberg, and other prominent scientists. David Hume is the Enlightenment philosopher who significantly anticipated the work of the pragmatists and of these contemporary scientists. See "Of the Reason of Animals," *A Treatise of Human Nature*, ed. L. A. Selby-Bigge (London: Oxford University Press, 1888), 176–79.

21. Richard Rorty has sought in his work to turn philosophers from their pursuit of conceptual analysis and toward genealogy, or as he puts it, from issues of justification to issues of hermeneutics. See *Philosophy and the Mirror of Nature* (Princeton, N.J.: Princeton University Press, 1979).

3

—∿∿—

From Moral Theory to the Reflective Life

In this chapter, I examine some recent ethical theory in order to under-mine the prospect that ethical theory might succeed in achieving its tra-ditional goals. I also suggest that the reflective life, pragmatism's alterna-tive to philosophical theories of morality, evades the difficulties typical of ethical theory. The reflective life is a distinctive understanding of moral living rooted in the philosophy of John Dewey; it is a pragmatist alterna-tive to conventional theories of morality that makes possible the respect for global perspectives on moral living that has eluded Anglo-European philosophers.

UNSETTLING DEVELOPMENTS IN MORAL THEORY

In his presidential address to the Central Division of the American Philo-sophical Association, May 2, 1986, Marcus Singer says, "The concept of morality is systematically ambiguous. It may mean either positive moral-ity, or personal morality, or true or rational morality."[1] Singer continues to argue that true or rational morality, the result of rigorous moral theory, ul-timately has priority over other dimensions of the concept of morality. Positive (conventional) morality and personal morality, on Singer's view, must defer to rational morality, the morality of rigorous theory. Singer's conclusion about rational morality is consonant with normal assumptions about the point of moral philosophy. Simple illustrations of his claim ap-pear in the case of a homosexual man—call him Barney—who lives in a homophobic society.[2] Barney's personal morality is inconsistent with his positive morality that judges gay behavior morally wrong. Consequently, Barney lives in an incoherent situation of conflict between his personal morality and his positive morality. According to Singer, Barney's hope lies in seeking resolution of his morally incoherent situation by appeal to principles of true or rational morality. Moral philosophy, in Singer's view, may provide the guidance Barney needs to resolve his moral questions. Singer believes along with most moral philosophers that serious, theoretical work on central concepts of morality may yield life shaping and action guiding principles that all should follow regardless of the divergent content of their personal and positive morality. Barney's hope, according to Singer, is the hope of philosophical success at making rational moral theory yield the guidance Barney and others need.

Setting aside the fact of its utopian intellectual ambition, Singer's view falls prey to its own description of the human moral situation. In his claim that "the concept of morality is systematically ambiguous," Singer undermines the possibility of resolving Barney's situation of moral incoherence in any way at all. To see this point, consider any situation in which some concept is, as Singer puts it, "systematically ambiguous." The concept of the parallel will do for illustration. Two lines are "parallel" just in case (in Euclidean space) they never meet. Two philosophy colleagues in separate rooms may make parallel points about Kant's stodgy lifestyle in their lectures about his moral theory. In this illustration, the concept of the parallel is systematically ambiguous. The fact of systematic ambiguity in the concept of the parallel in these examples of parallel items may not be overcome by any development of the theory of parallels, no matter how rigorous, serious, and dispassionate that theory may be. Systematic ambiguity is incompatible with resolution into a unified understanding of whatever is systematically ambiguous. So it is with the concept of morality. If Singer has not simply put another point unhappily in talking about systematic ambiguity, then he has in effect admitted, whatever he might hope, that there is no prospect for overcoming the discord among personal, positive, and rational morality. The unhappy result of Singer's distinction among concepts of morality, and his admission that the concept is systematically ambiguous, is that rational morality has no claim to superiority over, or even of commensurability with, personal or positive morality.

Thomas Nagel, in "The Fragmentation of Value,"[3] frankly embraces this unhappy result. According to Nagel, moral thought is fragmented across five dimensions of value; these dimensions of value are, in Singer's words, systematically ambiguous. Nagel is explicit that incommensurability among the five sources of value he mentions means that no unitary theoretical resolution for ordinary normative questions is possible. A homosexual Barney in a homophobic society must cope, according to Nagel, with (1) obligations to other people or institutions, (2) general rights everyone has, (3) utility, (4) intrinsic ends or value, and (5) goals of self-realization. In Barney's case, this means (1) that he must respect his parents, their contributions to his well-being, and their hopes for his life, etc.; (2) that he must respect the stereotypical "little old lady" who lives next door and refrain from wholesale assaults on her moral sensibility, and so on; (3) that he must consider questions about the consequences of his preferred lifestyle on others and on his various communities and on his society as a whole; (4) that he must consider the intrinsic value or the artistic worth of his sexual liaisons and what they yield; and (5) that he must consider the role of his sexual activities and desires in his own larger values and hopes for a productive or artistically lived life. Even mentioning these few specific ways Barney must deliberate about his sexual behavior suggests a need for even greater complexity and subtlety of thought about his, or about any, specific moral decision. In any case, moral theory's effort to attain generality of rule or law to guide human behavior founders on the diversity and incommensurability of considerations relevant to moral decisions. Those decisions, however, are not according to Nagel arbitrary or inevitably left to Barney's whim. The alternative Nagel finds lying between the traditional goal of theoretically resolving such decisions and regarding them as arbitrary is recourse to the idea of "*judgment*— essentially the faculty Aristotle described as practical wisdom, which reveals itself over time in individual decisions rather than in the enunciation of general principles."[4]

Annette Baier may be even more discouraging about the prospects for moral theory than is Nagel. She suggests unequivocally that moral theory is not only unproductive in encouraging moral behavior but is counterproductive in encouraging moral skepticism.[5] She further suggests that moral behavior, and the moralities that make for it, are products of sentiment rather than of rational thought or of moral theorizing. Parents, and other "sentiment guardians," are much more shapers of moral thought and behavior than are moral theorists. As she sees it, "pulpits and [parents'] knees" are more effective purveyors of morality than "we philosophers [who] are very squeamish about pulpits and knees."[6] The moral theorists who principally serve as Baier's targets are "Kantian philosophers," among whom she includes Alan Donagan, Alan Gewirth, Richard Brandt, and all who seek "a system of laws or precepts binding upon rational creatures as such."[7] She cautions, however, that one may equally go astray in seeking to replace such theoretical systems of moral law by virtue theory, for one may also seek too systematic, too theoretical, an understanding of the virtues. After discussing Aristotle's account of gentleness in a way that elicits the theoretical difficulties that interfere with a systematic account of precisely what it is as a virtue, she notes, "Norms in the form of virtues may be very difficult to formulate, while being not so difficult to recognize and encourage."[8] Baier's point in all of these essays is that recognition of particular examples of moral qualities or virtues is independent of moral theory; such recognition is as available to Barney, to his parents, to his "little old lady" neighbor, to his plumber, to his preacher, and to others as it is to moral theorists.[9]

Baier and Nagel agree that, in spite of the shortcomings they see in moral theory, persons are able to recognize particular examples of moral qualities and virtues, to exercise judgment, and to learn from example, and they are able to do this in spite of their usual ignorance of moral theory. If they are right, a pressing question for moral theorists is the question of the point of moral theory. The title of one of Baier's essays, indeed, is "Doing without Moral Theory." In their reluctance to embrace moral theorizing in its dominant contemporary style, Nagel and Baier are in effect accepting Singer's suggestion that moral concepts are systematically ambiguous, and accepting also the implication of his suggestion that moral theorists are ivory tower residents mostly beyond and above, if not aloof from, the ordinary problems of moral living that require moral virtues and moral reflection.

The agreement of these three philosophers finds reinforcement in the work of Martha Nussbaum. Nussbaum sees in Aristotle's work on ethics an acknowledgment that reflective, morally astute living properly focuses on particulars and wise judgment about them rather than on laws, rules, or principles to apply to those particulars. She explicates Aristotle's view as follows:

> He says that the standard of excellence is determined with reference to the decisions of the person of practical wisdom: what is appropriate in each case is what such a judge would select. And he says that the "judgment" or "discrimination" in ethical matters rests with, or is "in," something which he calls perception (aesthesis), a faculty of discrimination that is concerned with the apprehending of concrete particulars, rather than universals. . . . Principles, then, fail to capture the fine detail of the concrete particular, which is the subject matter of ethical choice. This must be seized in a confrontation with the situation itself, by a faculty that is suited to confront it as a complex whole. . . . "Perception" can respond to nuance and fine shading, adapting its judgment to the matter at hand in a way that principles set up in advance have a hard time doing.[10]

Nussbaum agrees with Nagel, Baier, and Singer—and Aristotle is the authority who confirms her thought about this issue—at least to the extent of believing that recourse to law, principle, or rule is inadequate to, and probably inappropriate for, the reflective needs of moral living.

These four philosophers—Singer, Nagel, Baier, and Nussbaum—do not agree in their understandings about moral theory, about how it should proceed or about how it might be useful; nevertheless, the general tendency of their views about its inadequacies resonates consensus, the consensus that Enlightenment and post-Enlightenment moral theorizing is largely an ivory tower exercise. In Baier's way of seeing it, such theorizing is blinded by "Kantian prejudices, whose self-evidence does not survive self-consciousness."[11] Baier's judgment may seem harsh, but it does reinforce the judgment of the editors of the 1998 World Congress *Proceedings* volumes of a need for a "more encompassing and inclusive vision of philosophy."[12] Two reactions to the near consensus of these four about Enlightenment moral theory remain to be considered before moving to the American tradition's focus on particularity and its promise of a more encompassing, inclusive vision of philosophy.

DEFENSIVE REACTIONS TO THE UNSETTLING DEVELOPMENTS

The first of these two reactions seeks to defend the Kantian tradition, in Baier's large understanding of that tradition. The second seeks to turn moral theorizing away from its "Kantian prejudices" toward an Aristotelian or a Thomistic way of thinking about morality, toward virtue theory.

DEFENDING THE ENLIGHTENMENT TRADITION

Thomas Scanlon and Allan Gibbard offer separate and adjacent defenses of the large Kantian tradition of moral theory.[13] Each of these efforts at defending the Kantian tradition is at best inadequate and each is probably best considered an awkward admission that the large critique hits its mark.

Section 3 of Scanlon's essay is titled "Fragmentation of the Moral." In this section of his essay, Scanlon takes note of Nagel's above-mentioned essay and admits that his account of "the nature of morality" captures at best one particular part of "the moral," the part concerned with "what we owe to each other." For our homosexual Barney, according to Scanlon, morality mostly concerns his responsibilities to the stereotypical little old lady who lives next door, or his responsibilities to his parents, or to others. The other dimensions of Barney's decision making that Nagel mentions Scanlon admits "have not received the attention they deserve" but suggests that he "cannot pursue them here."[14] Barney's life, however, is a tapestry of concern woven not only around responsibilities to others, but around issues of love, meaning, productivity, and growth as these emerge from everyday situations he confronts. Moral philosophy, as Scanlon conceives it, is not useful for Barney's efforts to live a meaningful life. Scanlon concludes that moral philosophy probably is not useful for finding resolutions of controversial issues, issues like homosexuality on which "secular liberals like me" and "conservative Christians" disagree.[15] Nonetheless, he believes that "more accurate and informed" understanding of disagreement is an important form of progress. Moral theory, in Scanlon's view, does not enable moral living, but it does enable understanding of disagreement among contending parties, the disagreement for example between secular liberals and conservative Christians about homosexual behavior. Unfortunately, Barney, his parents, and the little old lady next door likely have so ample an understanding of that particular disagreement that moral philosophy is unlikely to augment it meaningfully. Scanlon's defense—if indeed a defense it is—of moral theory is transparently feeble. Nagel, Baier, Nussbaum, and Singer (insofar as his view also implies that "rational morality" is ineffectual) will not be deterred in their skepticism or implicit skepticism about moral theory by Scanlon's defense.

Allan Gibbard's effort is no more effective. Gibbard claims that commonsense inquiry into how to live is committed to "there being methods of inquiry" that may lead to "a body of general principles, at a level of abstraction removed from common-sense, from which—given enough knowledge and reasoning power—moral conclusions about particular cases could be derived."[16] This commitment of commonsense inquiry, Gibbard points out, means one should admit "at least the possibility of moral expertise." Gibbard's suggestion is typical of foundational philosophical work. The central idea is that careful, analytical, rigorous, methodologically sophisticated inquiry—Gibbard calls it "the hard slog"—must illuminate the concept on which it is exercised, and must do so in such a way that one becomes able to wield the concept in everyday life more adequately and fruitfully than one would otherwise wield it. One might even say that Gibbard here openly confesses his contentment to being a "footnote to Plato" in this respect;[17] intellectual clarity, he believes, precedes progress in moral judgment and action.

The suggestion that moral theory might, even in principle, yield expertise in moral judgment and action, should raise eyebrows of incredulity. Claims to expertise motivated by knowledge of theory have, throughout recent history, produced myriad cultural disasters. Moral experts during the nineteenth century in America proclaimed the wisdom of such various strategies for implementing social and political policies as phrenology, Caucasian genetic superiority, slavery, and manifest destiny for America, among others. The twentieth century saw even greater diversity of abuse in the name of expertise.[18] Robert Coles, a professor of psychiatry and medical humanities at Harvard, reports in *Academe* an interview with a student from a working-class family who was attending Harvard.[19] Coles begins his essay with a quote from one of Emerson's lectures at Harvard: "Character is higher than intellect." He continues by reporting the student's experiences and a conversation with the student who was deeply troubled by the failure of connection between intellect and character. Of particular concern to this student was a fellow student who had excelled in the two moral reasoning courses they took together. The fellow student—the one with As in his two moral reasoning courses—repeatedly behaved crudely and inappropriately toward her, so much so that she was considering dropping out of Harvard. She also pointed out to Coles the irony in the intellects and the lives of such brilliant philosophers and thinkers as Martin Heidegger, Carl Jung, Paul de Man, and Ezra Pound, all of whom "nonetheless had linked themselves with the hate that was Nazism and Fascism during the 1930s." Little was more evident to Coles's student, and to Coles himself, than the truth of Emerson's assertion that character is higher than intellect. Beyond the Emerson quote and more generally, however, one can say with much evidence that character is utterly independent of intellect. Students who take moral philosophy, as well as students who become professional moral philosophers, have parents and relatives who have not studied moral philosophy at all and yet are frequently persons of better character and behavior than are their more knowledgeable offspring. The challenge this commonsense fact puts before moral theorists like Gibbard is more than daunting. Moral theory yields few useful results, and moral expertise is a theoretical fiction. The point of moral theory as Gibbard conceives it is equally fictitious since, as Baier points out, it is more likely to produce moral skeptics than moral experts or good people. Perhaps an alternative approach to moral theory can be more helpful? Many believe that virtue theory offers a viable alternative to the "Kantian" proclivities of Scanlon and Gibbard. Does it?

VIRTUE THEORY AS AN ALTERNATIVE DEFENSE

Some contemporary representatives of the Aristotelian virtue tradition of moral thought are Martha Nussbaum and Alasdair MacIntyre. This tradition, in their representation of it, is more plausible as an account of moral life and thought than is the Kantian (in Baier's large sense of "Kantian") style of thinking about morality. The Aristotelian tradition does largely overcome the Achilles'-heel need of the Kantian theories to appeal to persons simply as rational agents. Aristotelians recognize the central place of character development, of individuals' journey to maturity, in moral living and thinking. Unlike Kantians, they recognize the complex communal, familial, and interpersonal roots of morality. For Aristotelians, exemplars of virtue and desirable character play central roles in every person's journey to moral maturity. Gentleness, to recur to Baier's example, is known in gentle people and is appropriated by individuals' desires to model those who are gentle. Like other virtues, gentleness evades efforts to capture it in rules or principles, but it is nonetheless palpable in its appeal to individual psyches, as are the other virtues. Maturity is having an understanding of gentleness and finding ways to appropriate it in one's own character. Maturity is also appreciating the relationship between gentleness and other virtues, as well as knowing how to negotiate tensions among the virtues' diverse claims on one's behavior. The youth of a community are naturally less reliable in moral action and thought than the more mature. Youth need guidance that is more than rational; such guidance must be compelling at least affectively and it may need even to be coercive. The rational faculties of the young are not adequate to the task of making good moral decisions, and they need wider resources than reason to aid in guiding them toward maturity. MacIntyre puts this point as follows:

> Aquinas follows Aristotle in holding that one reason why the young are incapable of adequate reflective moral theorizing is that they have not as yet that experience of actions which would enable them to frame adequate moral and political arguments. . . . Only a life whose actions have been directed by and whose passions have been disciplined and transformed by the practice of the moral and intellectual virtues and the social relationships involved in and defined by such practice will provide the kind of experience from which and about which reliable practical inferences and sound theoretical arguments about practice can be derived.[20]

A great advantage of virtue theory is that it accords with common sense in admitting character and character development to be central to productive thought about morality. In Baier's idiom, "pulpits" and "parents' knees" are vital dimensions of morality itself. MacIntyre, in representing the virtue tradition, captures well this dimension of its intellectual commitments.

This significant advantage of virtue theory is accompanied, at least in MacIntyre's account of it, by an equally significant disadvantage, one no doubt plausible to Catholic theologians and philosophers but implausible to others, especially to those whose pulpits and parents' knees brought them to maturity on Enlightenment values, including the value of individual competence in matters moral and religious. This disadvantage is the central role of coercive authority not only over the beliefs and actions of the young who lack moral maturity but also over the beliefs and actions of all who lack the intellectual skill to make proper judgments about the content of such basic moral ideas as "the good life for humans." According to MacIntyre, only the most acute and determined of thinkers can surmount the structures of theory that lie between them and proper understanding of the good life for humans; only acute and determined theorists can appreciate the wisdom of those structures of authority that control the lives of those who do not measure up to their own level of rigorous intellectual skill. In MacIntyre's view, the structures of moral authority, the rules for the proper conduct of behavior and policy, remain firmly in the hands of the intellectually gifted.[21]

In this aspect of his thought, MacIntyre's virtue theory shares in the unfortunate commitment of Allan Gibbard's "hedged consequentialism" to moral expertise. The difference between MacIntyre and Gibbard on this issue is little more than a difference over who may serve as proper sources of moral guidance and authority. The analytic moral philosophers Gibbard has in mind are no doubt very different from the Aristotelian or Thomistic intellectuals MacIntyre has in mind.[22] Unfortunately, neither of these alternatives is palatable to ordinary men and women, steeped as they likely are in the values of Enlightenment individualism, or to ordinary moral thinkers of less than heroic intellectual ability, including beyond philosophers such thinkers as psychologists, sociologists, historians, and ministers. Of course, MacIntyre will not find, no more than will Gibbard, the distastefulness of his view to these theoretically unsophisticated individuals a proper obstacle. MacIntyre will agree on this issue with Scanlon, who says, "[O]ur confidence in the defensibility, even the objectivity, of our position depends on our assessment of its substantive grounds, not our ability to convince others."[23] Still, its distastefulness, along with its general inaccessibility to ordinary individuals, as well as its commitment to raw moral authority, may undermine Aristotelian/Thomistic virtue theory at least to the extent that it motivates the search for an alternative way of thinking about morality.

Along with this motivation to search for an alternative, one might add as a reputable argument against MacIntyre's view the difficulty of discerning the proper content of such foundational ideas as "the good life for humans." This idea is elusive, even for those Aristotelians and Thomists who work to embrace it. What is the truly human good? One sees a vast diversity of human lives spread over vast diversities of culture. One sees a vast diversity of apparently satisfying, happy, or good lives equally spread over those diversities of culture. For MacIntyre, following Aquinas, these diversities do not undermine the reasonableness of seeking, and seeking to formulate, a single human *telos*, a single end, the seeking of which constitutes the good life for humans. MacIntyre's formulation of this end in *After Virtue* is, as he says, "provisional," and reads as follows:

> [T]he good life for man is the life spent in seeking for the good life for man, and the virtues necessary for the seeking are those which will enable us to understand what more and what else the good life for man is.[24]

This account of the good life for man is, of course, vague and obscure, but perhaps this sort of defect is inevitable, given the need to arrive at some general account that accommodates considerable diversity in the way humans pursue their lives. To those who seek clarity and precision of conceptual expression, however, these defects will seem to render the account at best useless.

MacIntyre, to be sure, is not unaware of the foibles of his *After Virtue* account of the good life. In his 1990 *Aquinas Lecture*, he readily admits—now following Aquinas rather than Aristotle—that precise accounts of essences are unattainable. As he puts the point there, "Aquinas, like Aristotle, asserted that enquiry moves towards a knowledge of essences, but unlike Aristotle he denies that we ever know essences except through their effects." MacIntyre continues his explication of Aquinas by confessing that general accounts of essence, such as he had attempted in *After Virtue*, are unavailable.

> The proper object of human knowledge is not the essence itself, but the quidditas of the existent particular through which we come to understand, so far as we can, the essence of whatever it is. . . . So our knowledge is of what is, as informed by essence, but this knowledge is what it is only because of the nature of the causal relationship of the existent particular and its quiddity to the intellect.[25]

Essences, such as that of the good life for man, MacIntyre admits are not proper objects of knowledge for humans. This capitulation on his part to the critics of Aristotelian essentialism MacIntyre believes need not undermine intellectual commitments to Thomism. Our knowledge remains, as MacIntyre puts it, "informed by essence," but it remains so informed in a way that is opaque to our intellects; hence, we should not expect to be able to provide accurate accounts of essences such as that of the good life for man. Given this admission that precise accounts of essences are rationally unavailable, what might motivate accepting Thomism?[26]

Noting that philosophers are, in Aquinas's view, "lovers of stories," MacIntyre espouses genealogical histories as ways of subverting contemporary alternatives to Thomism. A subversive history, written on behalf of Thomism, will suggest that

[T]he predicaments of contemporary philosophy, whether analytic or deconstructive, are best understood as arising as a long-term consequence of the rejection of Aristotelian and Thomistic teleology at the threshold of the modern world.[27]

Thinkers who are not already Thomists may feel themselves in something of an intellectual "Catch-22" at this juncture. They have been told that the Thomist teleology, including the essence of the good life for man, is not rationally accessible; they have also been told that their rationale for accepting Thomism probably includes a genealogy showing that contemporary conundrums of philosophy are consequences of the Enlightenment and early modern rejection of natural essences. How should thinkers who are not Thomists react to these claims?

A long story needs telling in response to this question, one likely different from the one MacIntyre imagines subverting the early modern distancing from Aristotelianism and Thomism. John Dewey, as I mentioned earlier, tells a story quite different from MacIntyre's in his 1929 Gifford Lectures, *The Quest for Certainty*.[28] Suffice it to say here that Aristotelian/Thomistic essentialist perspectives do look weak as an alternative to the Kantianism Annette Baier targets.[29] In MacIntyre's defense of Thomism, the implicit authoritarianism and paternalism of Allan Gibbard's defense of contemporary analytic moral theory finds roots in a more traditional intellectual context. Is virtue theory no more adequate or useful than the many varieties of Kantianism available on the contemporary philosophical scene?

Virtue theory is no more adequate *as theory* than is any version of Kantianism. The need for judgment, the need for respect for the particulars of morally fraught situations, and the need for autonomy of choice about their lives and actions on the part of individuals, all these elements of morality require honest acknowledgment by all serious thinkers that *theory* cannot serve individuals who are pursuing the good in their lives. MacIntyre's honest confession, in his interpretation of Aquinas's virtue theory that the *telos* of humans remains beyond intellectual reach, is admirable. MacIntyre faces up to the central challenge of virtue theory and confronts it directly, finally acknowledging that the challenge cannot be met. Other interpreters of virtue theory have not measured up to MacIntyre's level of honesty about these clay feet of virtue theory.[30]

Martha Nussbaum, mentioned earlier as a critic of Kantianism and who is also an insightful advocate of Aristotelian thought about morality, seems either not so candid as MacIntyre or not so systematic in her pursuit of understanding about Aristotle's moral theory as is MacIntyre. Nussbaum's interpretation of Aristotle emphasizes the way Aristotle appreciates the role of particulars in forming character and judgment and in arriving at decisions about morally difficult situations, but she fails to confront directly the Achilles' heel of virtue theory in the way MacIntyre does. Rules in morality, according to Nussbaum, can be at best "rules of thumb," or "guidelines in moral development, for people not yet possessed of practical wisdom and insight need to follow rules that summarize the wise judgments of others."[31] Rules in this sense, of course, do not require moral theory, and they are fully adequate for purposes of moral education and character formation; they live socially in proclamations from "pulpits and parents' knees," a prime cultural locus, according to Baier, of moral education. The difficulty in this conception of moral rules, as Nussbaum acknowledges, is that the rules may bear no direct relation to the "proper *telos*" of human life, to the "single best human way of life."[32] This lack of connection between moral considerations relevant to choosing and living and the ideal *telos* of human life ought to be disturbing to theorists. If, as Aristotle believes, there is a single best human way of life, rules for achieving it should be designed specifically for achieving that best way of life. The rules of morality in that case must be more than "rules of thumb" derived from "a long experience of life"; they must be rules properly chosen because of their reliable tendency to produce that best human life, and they must have that reliable tendency because of their relationship to the proper human *telos*—they are rules that conduce to that proper human *telos*. For such properly conducive-to-the-good-life rules, their failure to produce will be due to contingencies of character or circumstance they cannot anticipate. Such "reliabilistic" rules are more than the summary style "rules of thumb" Nussbaum sees in Aristotle's understanding of rules, and they are less than the Kantian-style universal rules she rejects. This reliabilistic conception of rules is likely the one MacIntyre, given his Thomistic/Catholic commitments and his evident respect for moral and religious authority, accepts. Nussbaum, however, does not attend to the issue of the proper content of the idea of the single best human way of life and embraces the rule-of-thumb, experience-based understanding of moral rules. Nussbaum seems much less interested in Aristotle's understanding of the content of the single best human way of life, and much more interested in his appreciation of the role of particulars in the human activities of growing, living, and choosing; it is Aristotle's appreciation of these particulars, after all, that empowers Nussbaum's appropriation of Aristotle for her goal of making literature central to moral, social, and political thought.[33]

Virtue theory, however, requires theoretical attention to the issue of the human *telos*. Without such theoretical attention, virtue theory becomes little more than an admonition to Kantians that they should attend more to the details and particularities of everyday life. In this admonition dimension of her work, Nussbaum excels. In the idea that she may be a moral theorist, a virtue theorist, there is the anomaly that she fails to give systematic conceptual attention to the content of that central idea of virtue theory. MacIntyre, by contrast, is a virtue theorist and confronts this issue directly, unsuccessfully to be sure, but nonetheless directly. Nussbaum's powerful and fruitful work, while rooted in and admiring of Aristotle's wisdom about morality, fails as a contribution to moral theory, save in its critique of such theory for its lack of sufficient respect for the particularity of life. In this respect, Nussbaum is fully in harmony with the views of Annette Baier. Their heroes of particularity are different thinkers, even though both Nussbaum and Baier use their different heroes in very similar ways—to engender proper respect for the inadequacy of moral theory in the face of the particularities of living and acting.[34]

PARTICULARS AS PRIOR IN THOUGHT ABOUT MORALITY

The conclusion of this stage of the argument is that particularity, judgment, and practice must come fully to the fore in our understanding of morality. Moral practice and judgment must respect and sustain individuals in their diverse circumstances and must likewise respect the particulars of unique situations about which moral judgments must be made. Yet the very ideas of judgment and practice require more than individuality and particularity; they require as well principles, goals, ideals, visions of what might be beyond what is, as well as communities that sustain and perpetuate them. The central problem motivating moral thought is the need to give viable accounts of these principles, goals, ideals, and visions beyond what is. Moral theorists construe this need for a viable account, whether in the Kantian form Baier identifies or in the virtue theory form MacIntyre defends, as need for a rational, theoretical account of those principles, goals, ideals, and visions. These rational, theoretical accounts fail, as is suggested by the preceding discussion. The need, however, for some viable account of these goals, ideals, and visions beyond what is remains. The hope of the editors of the World Congress *Proceedings* for "a more inclusive vision" requires transcending the dominant footnote-to-Plato model of thought about morality. Such transcending of the Platonist model requires thinking about morality in ways Baier and Nussbaum should approve, because it sets aside thinking as theory, as the effort to specify or bring into focus the content of a ruling principle or ideal in words and with rational justification that might somehow empower it in individual psyches and in culture. The story of moral philosophy is the story of the failure of moral thought as moral theory. What alternatives are available beyond those failed theoretical accounts?

THE AMERICAN TRADITION

An answer to this question appears in the context of the American tradition of thought, a tradition that spans the temporal distance between John Winthrop and Richard Rorty, between the seventeenth century and the twenty-first century. The reasons for looking to this American tradition in search of an answer are many; those of most immediate interest, however, are that tradition's respect for particularity and its early and continuing refusal to allow thought to narrow into theory, into the Platonist mold that has been dominant for other efforts to think about morality. In these respects, the American tradition shares the deep regard of Annette Baier and Martha Nussbaum respectively for Hume and Aristotle. This sharing of deep regard is limited in the American tradition, however, by the fact that Hume and Aristotle are thoroughly embedded in their own intellectual cultures, a fact most obviously evident in their most common philosophical appropriations—Hume on behalf of skepticism and Aristotle on behalf of Catholicism.

Hume is an Enlightenment thinker, and one of the best; he is the one who best reveals the Achilles' heel of Enlightenment thought. In revealing the Achilles' heel of the Enlightenment—its boundless respect of reason—Hume remains the intellectual hero who shows what reason cannot do; he remains the premier skeptic in the history of thought. Hume remains the one who turned humanity away from its Enlightenment, rational fantasy and back toward more "earthy" roots in life, in family, and in society. He enables our now increased, but still limited, respect for the inertia of social, cultural, and moral tradition. Hume is the thinker who most ably encourages us to turn away from the heaven of reason and to turn instead toward our humanity, toward our families, our friends, our histories, and our traditions. We must respect Hume for his undermining of human rational fantasy, but because of this service Hume remains in our intellectual lives largely the best internal critic of the Enlightenment. He does not inspire the constructive thought about morals that Baier, and only few others, see as a consequence of his large critique of reason. Finding inspiration for the project of thinking through particularity toward morality can come through a turn toward the American tradition.

Parallel remarks apply to Aristotle. Aristotle serves well to defeat the largest Platonist ambitions of reason; he shows that reason or dialectic cannot supplant the earthier tools of character development—family, discipline, and "the village"—in producing good or happy people. Aristotle continues to believe, however, that there is, in Nussbaum's terms, a "single best human way of life," a kind of life available mainly to Athenian aristocrats. This single best human way of life is, in Aristotle's culture and in his way of thinking, unavailable to women, slaves, or barbarians. For the

American tradition, this culturally local and undesirable commitment of Aristotle's thought about morality, along with its need to supply a rational, theoretical account of the *telos* of human life, undermines its usefulness in finding a way to think about morality through the particularities involved in choosing, acting, and living. Aristotle, like Hume, is embedded in his own intellectual culture in a way that undermines our ability to appropriate his thought to address contemporary needs for thoughtfulness about morality, even though in Nussbaum's capable hands Aristotle becomes a valuable corrective to many current tendencies in moral theory.

William James and John Dewey are American thinkers who capture in their thought and embody in their lives the prominent values and intellectual commitments of our contemporary democratic, and democracy-aspiring, world. The strands of thought one finds in these thinkers are focal points for many diverse tendencies that express themselves in personalities, in politics, and in institutions of American culture. The commitments to equality, to individuality, to community, and to the hope for a better future for all humans are strong and vital throughout their written work. Also prominent throughout their work is a deep respect for the particulars through which moral thinking unfolds. James and Dewey also avoid the skeptical and the socially conservative attitudes that undermine Hume's usefulness, and they avoid the elitist and socially conservative attitudes that undermine Aristotle's usefulness.

Dewey's critique of Western philosophy, including moral philosophy, as much as predicts the kinds of difficulties here found to infect prominent contemporary accounts of morality. In his 1929 Gifford Lectures, *The Quest for Certainty*, Dewey provides an historical argument that accounts for the most serious conundrums of Western intellectual and philosophical culture. As he explains it there, Western intellectual culture has not been able to recover from the divided allegiance engendered by the advent of modern science. In Dewey's account, individuals live in a world dominated by science and its technological productions, and a world dominated as well by the apparently scientific individualism of economic capitalism in Western societies. Individuals are committed to a fully scientific understanding of themselves while they also cling to a belief that they have moral and religious value in a way they themselves believe is not fully coherent with a scientific understanding of themselves. Modern philosophy, in Dewey's understanding of it, is the enterprise of reconciling the two sides of this divided allegiance.[35] This task of reconciliation falls most heavily on theoretical thought about morality and religion, since they are the side of that divided allegiance we typically believe is most seriously threatened by science. Fear of losing our moral and religious value is, according to Dewey, humanity's strongest motive for the theoretical work of philosophy. "This effect of modern science has, it is notorious, set the main problems for modern philosophy. How is science to be accepted and yet the realm of values to be conserved?"[36]

Dewey's critique of Western philosophy in these Gifford Lectures is similar to the critique, familiar to many philosophers, Alasdair MacIntyre offers in *After Virtue*. Dewey's critique is broader in concept than MacIntyre's, intending to cover not only moral philosophy but also the epistemology that became dominant in the philosophy of the seventeenth and eighteenth centuries. In MacIntyre's *After Virtue* account, abandoning the teleology of Aristotelian and Thomist moral thought eviscerated modern and contemporary efforts to think rationally and systematically about morality. Likewise, in Dewey's account, abandoning the teleology pervasive in Aristotelian thought produced a divided allegiance that led to the abortive efforts of modern philosophers to recover an understanding of human significance that, in the Aristotelian scheme, was unproblematic. Dewey and MacIntyre offer different responses to the threat of this incoherence or divided allegiance, responses instructive because they reveal very different characters intellectually, morally, and religiously; the two thinkers serve almost as stereotypes for the American democrat and the Catholic Thomist, and their thought clashes at precisely the proper places to capture prominent tensions between these stereotypes.[37] Having seen already the Achilles' heel in MacIntyre's virtue theory, our task now is to find the intellectual path beyond moral theory fully prepared by Dewey's work in philosophy.[38]

THE IDEAL OF THE REFLECTIVE LIFE

The ideal of reflective living as a full-scale alternative to moral theory in its traditional guises appears in much of Dewey's work on ethics, and especially in part 2 of his 1932 *Ethics* where it contrasts with the habit of living in accord with custom.[39] Reflective morality is largely the idea of intelligence at work in the conduct of life and contrasts primarily with customary morality, the conduct of life in accord with the expectations, traditions, and customs of one's community. This contrast between reflective intelligent choice about what to do and habitual following of community traditions is fundamental to all thought about morality, whether one finds that thought in Plato, Mill, and Kant, or in James and Dewey. Dewey, however, deliberately sustains this contrast between reflective living and living in accord with custom while refusing to allow moral thought, so vital to the idea of reflective living, to become a variety of traditional moral theorizing.

Central to Dewey's success at sustaining this contrast between reflective morality and customary morality short of traditional moral theory is his determined attentiveness to the phenomenology of moral living. Moral thought, in his understanding of it, must attend scrupulously to detail; it must be sensitive to the real problems real people face in their efforts to negotiate the pitfalls of life, the vicissitudes of fate and fortune, and the occasional ill will or animosity of friends and enemies. Real problems emerge with predictable regularity each day in every life, and each individual must choose many times each day the good or the bad, the right or the wrong, the better or the worse. Each individual also makes retrospective judgments about each of these occasions of choice, "second-guessing" choices already made and hoping to do better on the next occasion of choice or perhaps even being pleased with the wisdom of a choice already made. These familiar facts of moral phenomenology, common coin in our psychological lives, are the foundation of Dewey's thought about morality and in general of pragmatist thought about morality. In this characteristically moral dimension of our lives, we humans can always do better. We can be more thoughtful, more intelligent; we can be better informed in many ways; and we can be more sensitive to the many kinds of nuance typical of troublesome situations. Think back to our hypothetical homosexual, Barney. Every day of his life, Barney faces choices, each of which has moral significance for him, each of which requires reflection and decision, and each of which may be matter for retrospective judgment. Each of these choices can go well or badly for Barney; can contribute to his well-being or not; can set a constructive tone for the next week of his life or not; can offend a parent or another especially dear to him or not; can encourage destructive habits of behavior in himself or others or not; and so on indefinitely. Barney's life is a veritable minefield of choices and possibilities, each of which is significant for Barney's efforts to live a successful life. Moral thought, as well as our idea of moral thought, *ought*, in the pragmatist understanding of morality, to take account of these facts of moral living. Reflective morality starts with thinking about morality.

Since it starts with these facts of moral phenomenology, reflective morality is rooted in the particularities of moral living. Reflective morality respects the particularities of choice and action, and it seeks to bring intelligence and experience to the task of securing better choices and actions in every situation—think of Barney's life and his choices—where one continues to hope that choice and action might be more successful. As is evident from earlier sections of this chapter, this respect for particularities of choice and action precludes the intellectual unification—into a singular rule, principle, set of rules, or a *telos* or *teloi*—demanded by moral theories of the Kantian or Aristotelian variety. Since it respects the particularities of moral living, however, one legitimately wonders how moral thought might "work" in an environment that requires before all else respect for those particularities. Theory, as characteristically pursued, is too mono-dimensional, too committed to achieving an abstraction or a generality that can be defended against intellectual challenges, to enable constructive intellectual address of the particularities that genuinely motivate moral thought. Freeing moral thought from moral theory, however, is no mean task. What might moral thinking be apart from moral theorizing?

Dewey's explicit answer to this question is reflective morality. Reflective morality is deliberate, intentional thought aimed at improving customary habits and expectations, at improving personal habits of response to situations of consequence, and at improving strategies of education and character formation to enable our fellows and our youth to respond more appropriately in situations of significance to themselves and others. One prominent way Dewey expresses his commitment to reflective morality in this sense is by talking about the need to bring to bear "the experimental method" when engaging issues of human morality, society, and politics. This talk about bringing "the experimental method" to bear on issues of morality and society may be unfortunately misleading, and apart from careful reading of Dewey himself may lead to serious misconceptions of his views about morality. Dewey is not a materialist or a reductionist, one who might share with B. F. Skinner or E. O. Wilson or Steven Weinberg or Richard Dawkins or Daniel Dennett a desire to reduce human values solely to terms of human biology and physiology. When Dewey talks about the importance of "the experimental method" in addressing issues of human significance, he means simply that deliberate, intentional thought can improve our understanding of ourselves, our societies, and our traditions and customs in ways everyone might appreciate, and appreciate for specific reasons:

> What is needed is intelligent examination of the consequences that are actually effected by inherited institutions and customs, in order that there may be intelligent consideration of the ways in which they are to be intentionally modified in behalf of generation of different consequences. (LW4:218)

What Dewey additionally intends by "the experimental method" is a commitment to reflective strategies that displace subjectivism, egoism, and relativism in thought about morals, and that further embrace the idea that principles, rules, and standards are hypotheses, hypotheses that are more or less well grounded and more or less revisable in the light of further experience.[40]

All of this vagueness, unfortunately frequent in discussions of Dewey's views, can be largely dispelled by thinking concretely about particular cases. Consider again the situation of Barney. What makes Barney's situation so difficult, both socially and psychologically, is the conflict between entrenched tradition, custom, and expectation, on one hand, and Barney's personal hopes for a good and generally satisfying life on the other. This conflict is completely typical of individual moral situations. In Barney's case this conflict is not only typical; it is also personal. Barney's parents, Barney's church, Barney's neighbors, and Barney's employer have legitimate expectations of Barney, expectations Barney feels in all of his interactions with these people and institutions. These expectations, in all of their dimensions, are embedded in intimate details of Barney's life; they are part of the landscape of his life in as concrete a way as are the buildings he works in, worships in, and plays in. Furthermore, beyond these "external" expectations that are the concrete landscape of his life, Barney also has his own desires and hopes for a satisfying life that operate "internally" in Barney's psyche independently of the interwoven textures of customary expectation that make up the concrete landscape of his life. Barney's moral problem is the problem of negotiating this complex web of "internal" hopes and desires and "external" customs, traditions, and expectations. Barney's problem is to find his way through this complex web to as satisfying a personal life as he is able to negotiate for himself. Barney's problem, in this respect, is no different from the moral problems of others. The details of Barney's particular problem are different from the details of the problems of others, but the structure of his problem is the same as the problems of others.

All good literature, no matter the setting in time and place, brings this structural problem to a focus in its central characters. Dostoyevsky's Raskolnikov in *Crime and Punishment*; Thomas Hardy's Gabriel in *Far from the Madding Crowd*; Dickens's Pip in *Great Expectations*; Faulkner's Addie in *As I Lay Dying*; and indefinite numbers of others too numerous to mention bring focus to this structural problem of life. According to Dewey, this problem is the central problem of human life, the central problem of morality itself. And this problem moral theory does not address. Significant moral thought, however, should address this problem, and reflective morality, as Dewey understands it, and as it is more widely understood in the large tradition of pragmatism, does address this problem. What is reflective morality?

NOTES

1. Marcus G. Singer, "The Ideal of a Rational Morality," *Proceedings and Addresses of the American Philosophical Association* 60, no. 1 (September 1986): 16.

2. My use of this name is controversial. I chose it because of Massachusetts congressman, Barney Frank, who is openly homosexual. My colleagues have suggested I should use another name because of the well-known children's TV character

named Barney. I considered "Bob," since Bob is a name in common use and might offend no particular person; however, my colleague Bob Baird and my other colleague Bob Roberts came to mind as deterrents to that name choice; I also considered "Mike," but that one failed on the same score as did Bob. In the end I chose to stick with Barney as the name for this hypothetical homosexual man.

3. Thomas Nagel, *Mortal Questions* (Cambridge: Cambridge University Press, 1979), 128–41.

4. Nagel, *Mortal Questions*, 135.

5. See, for example, Annette Baier, "Doing without Moral Theory," *Postures of the Mind* (Minneapolis: University of Minnesota Press, 1985), 234. (See also "Theory and Reflective Practices," 209.)

6. Baier, "Doing without Moral Theory," 234.

7. Baier, "Doing without Moral Theory," 235.

8. Annette Baier, "Theory and Reflective Practices," in *Postures of the Mind*, 220.

9. Baier recounts Arthur Caplan's story of his contribution to hospital practice: his suggestion that physicians respect patients' privacy by no longer intruding on their use of the bedpan. "This is a fine contribution, but as Caplan has noted, a Ph.D. in philosophy scarcely seems a necessary condition of making it" (Baier, *Postures of the Mind*, 244).

10. Martha Nussbaum, "Non-scientific Deliberation," *The Fragility of Goodness* (Cambridge: Cambridge University Press, 1986), 301.

11. Baier, "Doing without Moral Theory," 235.

12. See the introduction to this volume for an account of the editors' introduction to this World Congress *Proceedings* volume.

13. Their back-to-back essays appear in *Philosophy and Phenomenological Research* 55, no. 2 (1995). Allan Gibbard, "Why Theorize How to Live with Each Other?" 323–42, and T. M. Scanlon, "Moral Theory: Understanding and Disagreement," 343–56. These essays are revisions of presentations each made in a symposium of the American Philosophical Association's Eastern Division meeting in December 1993. The other participant in the symposium, serving as commentator, was Alasdair MacIntyre.

14. Scanlon, "Moral Theory," 348–49.

15. Scanlon, "Moral Theory," 352.

16. Gibbard, "Why Theorize How to Live with Each Other?" 330.

17. The allusion here is to Alfred North Whitehead's famous remark that all of Western philosophy is a series of footnotes to Plato. Nagel, Baier, and Nussbaum, referenced in this essay, along with others, including Nietzsche, James, Dewey, and Rorty, assert their refusal to be such footnotes.

18. Alasdair MacIntyre's *After Virtue* (South Bend, Ind.: University of Notre Dame Press, 1981) is especially hard on those in American culture who claim to be experts.

19. "The Disparity between Intellect and Character," *The Chronicle of Higher Education*, September 22, 1995, A68.

20. Alasdair MacIntyre, *First Principles, Final Ends, and Contemporary Philosophical Issues* (Milwaukee: Marquette University Press, 1990), 15.

21. For discussions illuminating this dimension of MacIntyre's virtue theory, one he intends to capture the moral thought of St. Thomas, see the previously

cited work and also *Whose Justice, Which Rationality?* (South Bend, Ind.: University of Notre Dame Press, 1988), 176–81.

22. One might be tempted to quip that MacIntyre's counterparts to Gibbard's analytic moral philosophers are Catholic priests, or perhaps better, Catholic bishops, or perhaps better still, the pope himself. However one settles this issue about who is a proper source of moral guidance and authority, Gibbard and MacIntyre remain equally committed to the proper role of de jure intellectual authority, authority established by attainment of appropriate intellectual credentials that warrant legitimate authority in matters of moral significance.

23. Scanlon, "Moral Theory," 355.

24. MacIntyre, *After Virtue*, 204.

25. MacIntyre, *First Principles*, 47.

26. MacIntyre's view about this issue is a mirror image of a similar view of Robert Cumming Neville. Neville too holds there may be a causal relationship between what we may intend in referring, though all other symbolic relationships between the object we intend and our conceptions of it are inappropriate or inadequate. Neville's source for this view is Charles Sanders Peirce rather than St. Thomas. See Neville's "A Peircean Theory of Religious Interpretation," *Pragmatism and Religion*, ed. Stuart Rosenbaum (Urbana: University of Illinois Press, 2003).

27. MacIntyre, *First Principles*, 58. MacIntyre discusses this issue at 52–68.

28. LW4.

29. For part of this long story, see my "MacIntyre or Dewey," *The American Journal of Theology and Philosophy* 19, no. 1 (January 1998): 35–59.

30. MacIntyre's more recent *Dependent Rational Animals* (Chicago: Open Court, 1999) affirms Aquinas's virtue theory. He also targets for critique Richard Rorty's liberal irony, another form in which appears a Baier-like respect for particulars and judgment conceived without those metaphysical ideas that pose as foundations for Aristotelian and Thomistic respect for particulars and judgment. For a developmental perspective on MacIntyre's views, as well as an accompanying critique coherent with the one I offer here, see Jeffrey Stout, *Democracy and Tradition* (Princeton, N.J.: Princeton University Press, 2004), 124–35.

31. Nussbaum, "Non-scientific Deliberation," 304. See also Martha Nussbaum, "An Aristotelian Conception of Rationality," *Love's Knowledge* (Oxford: Oxford University Press, 1990), 54–105, especially 68.

32. Nussbaum, "Non-scientific Deliberation," 305.

33. See again Nussbaum, "An Aristotelian Conception of Rationality," especially section 2, "Priority of the Particular," 66–75, especially 74. Nussbaum appears to approach this "reliability" conception of rules instead of her explicitly avowed rules-of-thumb conception in her effort to address the charge that she embraces "an empty situation morality." See her section 6, "An Empty Situation Morality?" 93–96.

34. Nussbaum retains her affection, officially, for moral theory in its virtue form. See her "Perceptive Equilibrium: Literary Theory and Ethical Theory," *Love's Knowledge* (Oxford: Oxford University Press, 1992), 168–94, especially 190–93.

35. For Dewey's account of several prominent figures of modern philosophy in terms of their efforts to overcome this divided allegiance, see his chapter 3, "Conflict of Authorities," LW4:40–59.

36. LW4:33.

37. Some dimensions of this difference between Dewey and MacIntyre I explore in "MacIntyre or Dewey," 35–59. Again I mention the previously cited book by Jeffrey Stout as further exploration of similar tensions between MacIntyre and Dewey.

38. William James in 1904 published a brief enthusiastic note on what he saw to be the promise in what he called "Dewey's Chicago School" of thought. His summary of his understanding of Dewey's work appreciates Dewey's grasp of the significance of particulars in the intellectual life, and he evinces an understanding of how Dewey, even then, was striking off in a new direction relative to customary philosophical tendencies of the late nineteenth and early twentieth centuries. William James, "The Chicago School," *Psychological Bulletin* 1:1–5.

39. LW7. See especially the opening section of chapter 10, "Reflective Morality and Ethical Theory," 162–66.

40. See LW4:219–22.

4

—⁓⁓—

The Reflective Life

The reflective life is an ideal of moral living that John Dewey seeks to capture in his writing about morality.[1] Giving account of the reflective life as Dewey understands it leads naturally to the idea of reflective morality as a general way of referring to his ideas about the moral life, the good life or the full life. Understood in this way, reflective morality is a fully formed pragmatist alternative to more traditional Western theories of morality. Accordingly, reflective morality is not a theory of morality that might compete with classical theories of morality; it does not compete with any version of consequentialist, deontological, or virtue theory, although it appreciates those theories as each emphasizing distinctive elements of morally significant situations.[2] Reflective morality offers instead a way of thinking about morality that is independent of issues of epistemology and metaphysics that have traditionally motivated those classical theories of morality.

How may one think constructively about morality apart from epistemological and metaphysical strategies that seek above all else cognitive legitimacy for morality? How might one achieve what Dewey calls "a *working* theory of morals" (emphasis added)?[3] The account of reflective morality offered here seeks to express a working theory of morality coherent with Dewey's own understanding of morals as rooted in human traditions and communities. What Dewey intends by the expression "a working theory of morals" is a way of thinking about institutions of morality in as systematic a way as one can short of raising the epistemological and metaphysical issues that typically motivate Western moral philosophy. I interpret Dewey as suggesting a turn toward a scientific way of thinking about morality, much in the way William James suggests a turn toward science of religion in preference to the philosophical thought about religion that has dominated Western culture. This scientific thought about morals is attuned, as is Dewey, to individuals, to their hopes and needs, and to the human communities that nurture and sustain them. Many commentators on Dewey's ethical thought believe there is no theory to be found in his writing on ethics, to say nothing of a working theory of morals.[4] In what follows, I give account of Dewey's working theory.

REFLECTIVE MORALITY AND CUSTOMARY MORALITY

For a dominant strand of pragmatism expressed in Dewey's work, morality is as much a part of everyday life as are politics, religion, and science; nothing uniquely problematic appears in knowing or thinking about morality; and more generally nothing uniquely problematic appears in knowing or thinking about value as opposed to knowing or thinking about fact. Cultural institutions embody morality as much as they embody politics, religion, and science. The normative dimensions of life, as much as the factual dimensions of life, find expression in all institutions of human culture. Western philosophical tendencies to accord greater respect to some institutions of culture—from the seventeenth century through most of the twentieth century the most prominent such institution was science—in preference to other such institutions results from a dominant Anglo-European intellectual culture. Nonetheless, in the context of American pragmatism each institution of culture has its own legitimacy as an expression of human needs and interests; no such institution need take a defensive, or apologetic, posture so long as it adequately serves the needs and interests that are its source. To think that knowledge of fact is more fundamental than is knowledge of value results from giving preference to the claims of one set of needs and interests over those of other sets.

Reflective morality turns away from the philosophical culture that finds values to be problematic so as to require justification or defense. Values need no philosophical intervention and are no more philosophically problematic than are facts. To believe there are fundamental philosophical problems about values, problems that do not infect facts, is to be committed to a particular culture of philosophy that has roots in the Anglo-European context in which science developed. Seeing and appreciating the roots of that intellectual culture enables transcendence of that large, but still local, intellectual context.[5]

When one moves beyond these philosophical ideologies that find values uniquely problematic, one finds significant issues of value and morality that continue to need careful thought. In John Dewey's *Ethics*, for example, the contrast between demands of custom or tradition, on one side, and demands of careful and deliberate thought on the other remains significant. To understand the complex dynamics of these simple dimensions of morality remains a philosophical task of large human significance.

The significant contrast for pragmatist thought about morality is between customary morality and reflective morality, between expectations of conformity to traditional standards of behavior and behavior formed as a result of reflective thought. What does an appropriate understanding of this contrast require in terms of how we think about individuals, their communities, their own and their communities' goals and ideals, and their own and their communities' places in the larger world? What of philosophical interest might one say about these issues?

In what follows, I provide an account of the idea of reflective morality as that idea informs the thought of John Dewey. This account maintains the tension with other theories of morality that is characteristic of Dewey and of pragmatist thought generally, a tension that results largely from their evading the issues of epistemology and metaphysics that remain central to most philosophical interest in morality.[6] What is reflective morality as this idea appears in primary sources of pragmatism?

REFLECTIVE MORALITY

The reflective life has three large dimensions. Living reflectively is living autonomously, self-consciously, and independently of environing custom and tradition. Furthermore, reflective living is living in harmony with, and in creative tension with, a nurturing community; it is seeking one's own integrity as well as seeking to preserve the integrity of one's community. Finally, living reflectively is seeking to realize ideal values that define both individual and communal aspirations for a better future. Each of these three dimensions of reflective living is evident in Dewey's thought about the moral life. For ease of reference, these dimensions of the reflective life may go under the labels *autonomy*, *community*, and *ideality*. Briefly put, to live reflectively is to live autonomously while being committed to the well-being of one or more communities and being committed also to realizing specific ideals both personal and communal.

The three dimensions of the reflective life—autonomy, community, and ideality—require individual attention to explain more precisely what each of them amounts to on its own and to exhibit the roots of each in John Dewey's thought.[7]

AUTONOMY

Dewey's insistence on autonomy is perhaps the strongest part of his commitment to the ideal of life characteristic of Enlightenment thinkers. Dewey's respect for individuals and their prospects for development are decisive in his thought; consequently, he approves of social structures that nurture individuals toward full realization of their potential. Dewey's valuing of democracy as moral ideal results directly from democracy's maximal empowerment of individuals to realize their own goals and hopes. In *Freedom and Culture*, Dewey notes that "democracy has always been allied with humanism, with faith in the potentialities of human nature" and that "belief in the 'common man' has no significance save as an expression of belief in the intimate and vital connection of democracy and human nature." This "humanistic view of democracy . . . tells us that we need to examine every one of the phases of human activity to ascertain what effects it has in release, maturing and fruition of the potentialities of human nature."[8] Dewey's respect for democracy as a social and political, indeed as a *moral*, ideal derives explicitly from its maximal nurturing of individual self-realization, and individual growth is the goal of morality:

> The only distinction . . . that can be drawn without reducing morals to conventionality, self-righteous complacency, or a hopeless and harsh struggle for the unattainable, is that between the attained static, and the moving, dynamic self. . . . If we state the moral law as the injunction to each self on every possible occasion to identify the self with a new growth that is possible, then obedience to law is one with moral freedom.[9]

Dewey's respect for individuals and their potential for growth, hence his great respect for individual autonomy, is not distinct from his respect for democracy. Dewey's insistence that individual growth is a moral imperative, and his belief that democracy maximizes that growth, insure his commitment to individual autonomy. These commitments are characteristic of pragmatist moral thought, and they are inseparable in their opposition to custom and convention, for simply following custom and convention is abdicating reflective autonomy and losing opportunity for growth. The health, and thus the autonomy, of individuals is the center of Dewey's idea of the reflective life. The following passage captures his emphasis:

> The growing, enlarging, liberated self . . . goes forth to meet new demands and occasions, and readapts and remakes itself in the process. It welcomes

untried situations. The necessity for the choice between the interests of the old and of the forming, moving, self is recurrent. It is found at every stage of civilization and every period of life. . . . For everywhere there is an opportunity and a need to go beyond what one has been. . . . Indeed, we may say that the good person is precisely the one who is most conscious of the alternative, and is the most concerned to find openings for the newly forming or growing self; since no matter how "good" he has been, he becomes "bad" . . . as soon as he fails to respond to the demand for growth. Any other basis for judging the moral status of the self is conventional.[10]

The autonomy that is reflective independence from conventional morality is inseparable from living well.

COMMUNITY

The emphasis on autonomy as essential to reflective living may appear to commit pragmatists to "liberal individualism," the commitment communitarians criticize as an untoward and disastrous result of "the Enlightenment project."[11] The individual autonomy Dewey defends, however, is very different from the individual autonomy communitarians caricature because in Dewey's account it coheres fully with community integrity. In Dewey's thought, even the fullest realization of individual autonomy is not incompatible with integrity of community, but is rather inseparable from genuine community. In Dewey's understanding of them, individual goods, including the good of reflective autonomy, are not only inseparable from but are also supportive of community goods. Individual goods and community goods, in Dewey's thought, cohere in symbiotic harmony. The coherence of these two kinds of goods is the theme of section 4, "The Inclusive Nature of Social Interest," of the last chapter of *Ethics*.[12] Here is an explicit statement:

> When selfhood is taken for what it is, something existing in relationships to others and not in unreal isolation, independence of judgment, personal insight, integrity and initiative, become indispensable excellences from the social point of view.[13]

The community that nurtures individuals to maturity, Dewey sees, needs their independence as much as it needs their faithfulness; the idea of incompatibility between their independence and their faithfulness is foreign to his thought.[14] The relationship between individuals and their communities should be characterized by creative tension—the tension produced by individuals' pursuits of their own vision of what is good and the natural inertia of their communities' stable vision of what is good.

Even in ideally healthy communities, and certainly in actual communities, this tension is a fact of daily life. Pathological individuals who care not at all for the integrity of their nurturing communities are rare, and they are as problematic for pragmatist thinkers as they are for conservative communitarian thinkers. Strategies for dealing with such individuals and the cultures that produce them differ, however, between pragmatists and communitarians.[15]

This tension between individuals' pursuits of their own goods and the inertia of community traditions concerning the good is prominent in literature, and probably is so because of its prominence in daily life. In Thomas Hardy's *Far from the Madding Crowd*, for example, this tension is a defining feature of Gabriel Oak's life from the time he first meets Bathsheba Everdeen. Gabriel's desire to court and marry Bathsheba is frustrated by the fact that they live in different social and economic classes. She lives a life of aristocratic privilege, while Gabriel works in her employment as a common laborer. The inertia of social convention keeps them apart and conflicts with Gabriel's long-suppressed hope of bringing them together. This tension between personal desire and social custom that consumes Gabriel and Bathsheba is not untypical. The various themes wrought by this ubiquitous tension in individual lives are significantly responsible for the color and texture of great literature.

This tension between personal goals and the more stable goods protected by custom and convention suggests a bifurcation in the concept of the moral within ordinary life.[16] Personal goals and goods are different from social goals and goods. From the standpoint of the personal, one ought to do a thing—as Gabriel ought to declare to Bathsheba his undying ardor; from the standpoint of the conventional, one ought not to do the same thing—as Gabriel not only ought not to declare his love for Bathsheba but ought even to repress it and seek a mate among his own class. Dewey is aware of this division in the idea of the moral between customary expectation and personal growth, and he sees that individuals must regularly make choices in virtue of it. He says about customary morality, for example, that it is

[a] morality of praise and blame based on the code of valuations which happens to be current at a particular time in a particular social group. Whatever conforms, at least outwardly, to current practices, especially those of an institutional sort, receives commendation or at least passes without censure; whatever deviates exposes one to censure. The practical effect is a negative morality; virtue is identified with "respectability," and respectability means such conduct as is exempt from overt reproach and censure rather than what is inherently *worthy* of respect.[17]

Insofar as one does not violate expectations of convention, one avoids censure. When one pursues personal goals against customary expectation, one invites censure in doing what one ought not to do. Nevertheless, from the standpoint of personal goals, perhaps one ought to invite censure. In building a life one must entertain acting, and sometimes one must choose to act, against customary expectations; sometimes one ought personally to do what one ought not conventionally to do. Such is Gabriel's lot.

The social pressure of customary expectation tends to perpetuate consistent patterns of behavior, and their prudence for the most part keeps most people from straying too far from conventional expectation. On the other hand, people not infrequently decide they must, for the sake of their own goals or happiness, go beyond conventional expectations. In the late 1980s, *Ms.* magazine printed an article titled "I Left My Husband for the Woman I Love." Jane Doe (a pseudonym) reports that she left her husband of twenty-five years and her two children for a female lover. In Jane Doe's case, the intensity of her love produced a personal goal that compelled her, for her own sake, to break out. She projected her life into two different scenarios, one with her lover and without her family, the other with her family and without her lover.[18] She then chose in favor of the scenario with her lover and without her family, and she did so even though the choice violated customary expectation. Dewey's explicit account of deliberation fits Jane Doe's choice:

> Deliberation is actually an imaginative rehearsal of various courses of conduct. We give way, in our mind, to some impulse; we try, in our mind, some plan. Following its career through various steps, we find ourselves in imagination in the presence of the consequences that would follow; and as we then like and approve, or dislike and disapprove, these consequences, we find the original impulse or plan good or bad. Deliberation is dramatic and active, not mathematical and impersonal.[19]

Dewey embraces the tension between prudence as a force for maintaining community values and imagination as prodding toward individual goods beyond those community values. His realization that these goods, in the various ways they pervade human life, are vital, inevitable, and frequently incommensurable encourages his vision of the reflective life as accommodating the autonomy of individuals as well as the symbiotic harmony between individual goods and social goods. Reflective individuals are those who respect in their actions the healthy tension between their own goods and larger social goods. Gabriel Oak, in Hardy's novel, was such an individual, and so too was Jane Doe, even though she left her family for her female lover.[20]

THE IDEAL

Reflective morality also involves commitment to ideal values that guide one's choices and enable one to move coherently toward future goals. For individuals, this commitment to an ideal value, a vision of who they might become, guides their striving for personal growth. For communities, this commitment to an ideal expresses the vision of a healthy, properly functioning community, a community in which, like Plato's *Republic*, the parts work coherently toward the mutual good of all citizens.

The primary expression in Dewey's work of this ideal value component of reflective morality is his own enduring commitment to democracy. Democracy is a community ideal precisely because it not only respects but it nourishes individual integrity, the sort of integrity that must be part of all individuals' efforts to realize their own goals. In *Freedom and Culture*, Dewey expresses his commitment to democracy:

> [T]he source of the American democratic tradition is moral—not technical, abstract, narrowly political nor materially utilitarian. It is moral because based on faith in the ability of human nature to achieve freedom for individuals accompanied with respect and regard for other persons and with social stability built on cohesion instead of coercion.[21]

The creative tension between individual goals and social goals takes its most dramatic form in the historical context of the American democratic experiment. The challenge for this experiment is whether or not it is able to realize its promise of full individual freedom and integrity along with "social stability built on cohesion instead of coercion," and the task of addressing that challenge is the premier social problem of the contemporary world.

> The struggle for democracy has to be maintained on as many fronts as culture has aspects: political, economic, international, educational, scientific and artistic, religious. The fact that we now have to accomplish of set purpose what in an earlier period was more or less a gift of grace renders the problem a moral one to be worked out on moral grounds. . . . An American democracy can serve the world only as it demonstrates in the conduct of its own life the efficacy of plural, partial, and experimental methods in securing and maintaining an ever-increasing release of the powers of human nature, in service of a freedom which is cooperative and a cooperation which is voluntary.[22]

Dewey's understanding of democracy as a community ideal includes individual ideals insofar as those individual ideals are not idiomatic; it includes an ideal of individual character to the extent that a certain individual character is requisite to the success of democracy. Democracy requires individuals having the virtues of courage, temperance, justice, and wisdom, the characteristic virtues of an Aristotelian aristocrat. These Aristotelian virtues are the virtues of democracy in the sense that democracy both requires and nourishes them.[23] Benjamin Barber has implicitly acknowledged this connection between democracy and the Aristotelian virtues in characterizing democracy as "an aristocracy of everyone."[24] Dewey's commitment to democracy as a moral ideal is his simultaneous commitment both to individual fulfillment and to community integrity, and also to the qualities of character, or virtues, requisite to the ongoing success of democracy as an institution of human culture.

THE QUESTION OF THE SOURCE

An important question for pragmatists is the question of the source of the virtues that are requisite to the success of democracy.[25] Unlike Aristotelians, pragmatists may not have recourse to a human *telos* that might underwrite their commitment to a set of virtues. Where do these qualities of character come from? How might those who are pragmatists and not Aristotelians legitimate qualities of character as genuine virtues? If democracy is an aristocracy of everyone, where in a democracy might one find the virtues that constitute an aristocratic character? And how might those aristocratic virtues involve commitment to democracy? Dewey acknowledges in the quotation just cited from *Freedom and Culture* that American democracy, along with the virtues required to sustain it, were once a "gift of grace," and he acknowledges also that we have now to maintain through deliberate effort what in an earlier time was fortuitous. Where in our Western, American, democratic, liberal culture do we find resources to sustain an aristocracy of everyone?

John Dewey's answer to this question is that we find these resources in the institution of science.[26] Science as it is realized in Western culture is an integral part of the gift of grace Dewey acknowledges; it is integral to democracy, and morally speaking science is inseparable from democracy.

Science and democracy are linked in Dewey partly because of their approximately simultaneous and parallel development, but principally because the values of science, the habits of intellect and character that make it successful, are those values required for the success of democracy. This value connection between science and democracy was prominent in Dewey's thought early in his professional life. Robert Westbrook's account of this connection shows it to have been fundamental in Dewey's thought as early as the 1908 *Ethics*.[27] Dewey is confident that science uniquely embodies, enforces, and exemplifies moral values crucial to the success of democracy. Dewey sees these values as (using

Alasdair MacIntyre's terminology) "internal to" the practice of science. In *Freedom and Culture* Dewey expresses in a memorable way the depth of this commitment:

> Some of its obvious elements are willingness to hold belief in suspense; ability to doubt until evidence is obtained; willingness to go where evidence points instead of putting first a personally preferred conclusion; ability to hold ideas in solution and use them as hypotheses to be tested instead of as dogmas to be asserted; and (possibly the most distinctive of all) enjoyment of new fields for inquiry and of new problems.
>
> Every one of these traits goes contrary to some human impulse that is naturally strong. Uncertainty is disagreeable to most persons; suspense is so hard to endure that assured expectation of an unfortunate outcome is usually preferred to a long-continued state of doubt. "Wishful thinking" is a comparatively modern phrase; but men upon the whole have usually believed what they wanted to believe, except as very convincing evidence made it impossible. Apart from a scientific attitude, guesses, with persons left to themselves, tend to become opinions and opinions dogmas. To hold theories and principles in solution, awaiting confirmation, goes contrary to the grain. . . . Fear of the unknown, fear of change and novelty, tended, at all times before the rise of scientific attitude, to drive men into rigidity of beliefs and habits; . . .
>
> The chief reason for calling attention to [these considerations] is the proof they furnish that in some persons and to some degree science has already created a new morale—which is equivalent to the creation of new desires and new ends. The existence of the scientific attitude and spirit, even upon a limited scale, is proof that science is capable of developing a distinctive type of disposition and purpose: a type that goes far beyond provision of more effective means for realizing desires which exist independently of any effect of science.[28]

Since these values are internal to the practice of science, they become standing qualities of character and intellect of participants in the practice. The values are those of

> fair-mindedness, intellectual integrity, of will to subordinate personal preference to ascertained facts and to share with others what is found out, instead of using it for personal gain.[29]

Such values must be realized as fully as possible in each individual in order that democracy may become a way of life and not just a political system. Democracy, so conceived, is a way of life in which individuals realize themselves as they choose, and in which they respect and aid other individuals' efforts to realize themselves. As an ideal, democracy is an aristocracy of everyone. Science is the established cultural institution embodying the values and qualities of character that make moral democracy possible.[30]

What makes democracy a moral value for Dewey, rather than just a political system, is precisely this connection with scientific character. Not that study of any particular scientific subject matter is desirable, or even that study of any science at all is desirable; what is important is the moral and intellectual character that is internal to the practice of science. What is needed is not the study of any particular subject matter one might identify as scientific, but acquisition of the moral and intellectual character apart from which science is institutionally impossible.

> While it would be absurd to believe it desirable or possible for every one to become a scientist when science is defined from the side of subject matter, the future of democracy is allied with the spread of the scientific attitude. It is the sole guarantee against wholesale misleading by propaganda. More important still, it is the only assurance of the possibility of a public opinion intelligent enough to meet present social problems.[31]

Again:

> From one point of view everything which has been said is a laboring of the commonplace that democratic government is a function of public opinion and public sentiment. But identification of its formation in the democratic direction with democratic extension of the scientific morale till it is part of the ordinary equipment of the ordinary individual indicates the issue is a moral one. It is individual persons who need to have this attitude substituted for pride and prejudice, for class and personal interest, for beliefs made dear by custom and early emotional associations.[32]

While Dewey believes that only scientific character makes possible the realization of democracy as a moral ideal, he certainly does not think that everyone should aim at being a professional or even an amateur scientist. What Dewey values is the customary moral and intellectual character of scientists. This scientific character results from participation in virtually any enterprise requiring the same moral and intellectual commitments as science. Historians, for example, though not conventionally regarded as scientists, participate in an enterprise requiring the same virtues and the same levels of moral and intellectual integrity. Musicians engage in a similarly demanding enterprise, as do many others. All art, of intellect or of other skill, embodies opportunity for acquisition of the morale of science, the moral and intellectual character requisite for democracy. Though Dewey himself does not explicitly draw this conclusion in *Freedom and Culture*, nevertheless his conception of the relation between art and science, where science is a particular mode of artistic activity, requires it.[33]

Dewey's commitment to science is better understood as a commitment to artful practices that require the integrity of a participating community, an integrity that needs both the faithfulness of individuals and their individuality. Only such communities enable fullness of individuality as well as fullness of integrity. Only in such communities is the democratic life as Dewey conceives it possible. The moral ideal of democracy requires pervasive commitment to realizing in all citizens the morale of those artful community practices that include the more specialized practice of the sciences. The virtues of science are the virtues of democracy.

How to bring about conditions under which the ideal of democracy may be realized is *the* practical problem of democracy. That it is the primary practical problem of democracy is the reason for Dewey's involvement in education. His concern for education was, like his commitments to science and democracy, a lifelong concern. Westbrook notes Dewey's claim in *Democracy and Education* that "without initiation into the scientific spirit one is not in possession of the best tools which humanity has so far devised for effectively directed reflection."[34] And for education into that spirit,

> [b]ecause scientific thinking was essentially social, the schools should organize themselves as, in part, little scientific communities—"laboratories of knowledge-making." Children should be engaged in ongoing experimentation, communication, and self-criticism, constituting themselves as a youthful commonwealth of cooperative inquiry.[35]

Dewey's conception of moral democracy and its connection with science informs all of his thought about morality and society. As an ideal it motivates his understanding of individuals' goods as inseparable from the goods of their communities. Westbrook expresses this commitment nicely:

> Democracy was the social ideal not only because it nurtured individual growth but because it envisioned a growing community that would itself be a complex, organic work of art, harmonizing "the development of each individual with the maintenance of a social state in which the activities of one will contribute to the good of all the others."[36]

Westbrook's account of Dewey's moral democracy coheres with the idea of the reflective life as the unitary ideal underlying all of Dewey's moral and social thought.

Hilary Putnam offers an alternative way of seeing Dewey that unfortunately bifurcates his moral and social thinking between his commitments on one hand to instrumental rationality and on the other to consummatory experiences of an aesthetic character:

For Dewey there are fundamentally two, and only two, dominant dimensions to human life: the social dimension, which for Dewey meant the struggle for a better world, for a better society, and for the release of human potential; and the aesthetic dimension. To the criticism that he fundamentally saw all of life as social action, Dewey could and did always reply that, on the contrary, in the last analysis he saw all "consummatory experience" as aesthetic. The trouble with this answer is that a bifurcation of goods into social goods which are attained through the use of instrumental rationality and consummatory experiences which are ultimately aesthetic is too close to the positivist or empiricist division of life into the prediction and control of experiences and the enjoyment of experiences to be adequate.[37]

Putnam's account of Dewey forces a wedge between his social thought and his larger perspective about value, including his moral thought, the former served by instrumental rationality and the latter served by consummatory experience. Putnam does not see moral democracy as a unitary ideal pervading all of Dewey's thought. The account of the reflective life I offer here avoids Putnam's quasi-positivistic bifurcation of Dewey. But Putnam need not, and perhaps in accord with the principle of charity should not, see a gulf between Dewey's commitment to instrumental rationality and his commitment to consummatory experience. Certainly the idea of instrumental rationality, insofar as it is a symptom of Dewey's commitment to scientific method, is not distinct in Dewey from the consummatory and aesthetic dimensions of experience. Dewey insists on this point again and again throughout *Art as Experience*: The province of scientific thought is just one domain in the larger country of art.[38] The protest Putnam imagines Dewey making to the alleged bifurcation is genuine, and Putnam is wrong to insist against his protest. The present account of Dewey's moral and social thought, one shared by Westbrook, as unified by the ideal of moral democracy avoids this untoward imposition of positivistic tendencies on Dewey.

Even Richard Bernstein, another sympathetic commentator who understands Dewey's commitment to democracy as a moral ideal, has Putnam-like doubts:

We may also feel that even after a sympathetic reading of Dewey's understanding of "scientific method," he does not sufficiently help us to understand the crucial differences between scientific and democratic communities, or how instrumental rationality and scientism can deform the deliberation and judgment required for the practice of democracy.[39]

A response to Bernstein is that Dewey does not think there are any differences in principle between scientific and democratic communities. The differences there are in fact between such communities are functions of the particular historical communities they are. Scientific communities as well as democratic communities inevitably, because they are made up by different individuals, vary from the ideal. But Dewey's point remains that practicing scientific communities are no different in their value structure from practicing democratic communities. Democracy as a moral ideal infuses both, but it also infuses actual scientific and democratic communities and keeps them moving toward a better future. A further response is that instrumental rationality and scientism certainly can deform the deliberation and judgment required for the practice of democracy, but the sort of instrumental rationality and scientism that can have that untoward effect are not the sort Dewey endorses; on the contrary, he is always concerned to portray unfavorably the narrow instrumental rationality and scientism that does deform the deliberation and judgment required for the practice of democracy. Dewey's scientific spirit, the spirit embedded in science and democracy as an ideal of moral and intellectual character, is incompatible with scientism, as it is also incompatible with any narrowly conceived instrumental rationality. Neither Putnam nor Bernstein takes seriously enough Dewey's determination to avoid the kinds of dichotomies that can engender invidious struggles for priority.[40]

DEMOCRACY AS MORALITY

His understanding democracy as a moral ideal needs explication from the side of Dewey's explicit account of morality. How is there unity between Dewey's pervasive view about democracy as a moral ideal and his explicit writings about morality? How does democracy as a unitary ideal enable Dewey's moral ideals as well as his social ideals?

Near the end of part 2 of his 1932 *Ethics*, Dewey writes of the conception of virtue in reflective morality.[41] He expresses there his commitment to the unity of the virtues. Indeed, he is so much concerned with their unity that he seems only reluctantly willing to accept the occasional appearance of their individuation from one another.

> The mere idea of a catalogue of different virtues commits us to the notion that virtues may be kept apart, pigeonholed in water-tight compartments. In fact virtuous traits interpenetrate one another; this unity is involved in the very idea of integrity of character. At one time persistence and endurance in the face of obstacles is the most prominent feature; then the attitude is the excellence called courage. At another time, the trait of impartiality and equity is uppermost, and we call it justice. At other times, the necessity for subordinating immediate satisfaction of a strong appetite or desire to a comprehensive good is the conspicuous feature. Then the disposition is denominated temperance, self-control. When the prominent phase is the need for thought-

fulness, for consecutive and persistent attention, in order that these other qualities may function, the interest receives the name of moral wisdom, insight, conscientiousness. In each case the difference is one of emphasis only.[42]

The Aristotelian tenor of this passage is inescapable. The virtues Dewey finds embedded in reflective morality are the classical Aristotelian virtues of wisdom, courage, temperance, and justice. Most important about Dewey's commitment to these virtues is that he sees them to be identical with the virtues he sees arising out of the practice of science and as inseparable from the moral ideal of democracy. The description of the scientific spirit in *Freedom and Culture* is a mirror image of his account of the Aristotelian virtues of reflective morality:

a morale of fair-mindedness, intellectual integrity, of will to subordinate personal preference to ascertained facts and to share with others what is found out, instead of using it for personal gain.[43]

This description, along with others he provides, shows that Dewey regards the different descriptions as different expressions of the same moral ideal. Fair-mindedness includes justice; intellectual integrity includes wisdom; the will to subordinate personal preference to ascertained facts includes temperance; sharing with others what is found out, instead of using it for personal gain includes courage. The virtues specified in *Freedom and Culture* as virtues of democracy are the same virtues specified in *Ethics* as the classical Aristotelian virtues. Virtue is one. Furthermore, it is rooted in scientific communities where these are broadly understood as communities constituted around any kind of artful practice. The virtue of reflective morality, also of the "scientific morale," and also of the democratic way of life, is that same virtue. That one virtue manifests in different ways as circumstances differ, but in addition Dewey's descriptions of it differ as his concerns provide different opportunities. In *Freedom and Culture*, his concerns are primarily social, while in *Ethics*, his concerns are primarily moral. Nevertheless, the single ideal, moral democracy, rooted in scientific communities, underlies these different descriptions.

Dewey is a visionary in his hope that we may be able to realize more adequately our own ideals, that we may see more clearly what they require of us, and that we may act, personally and corporately, more consistently with them. His challenge to us both personally and communally is that we become who we are. Embedded in these encompassing ideals are the only normative solutions available for our various cultural maladies. Those possible solutions require imagination, determination, and resolve, but most of all loyalty to our own ideals, the ideals deeply rooted in our own Western and American cultural traditions.

IDIOMATIC INDIVIDUAL IDEALS

Beyond this commitment to democracy, a commitment both to individual character and to community integrity whose ground is the institution of science broadly conceived, Dewey acknowledges the more idiomatic ideals that animate individuals along their various courses of life. Each individual has an individual task of development, an individual task of growth and fulfillment that involves a more specific ideal of achievement not shared by others. Gabriel Oak, for example, sought a life of connubial bliss with Bathsheba, and Jane Doe sought a life of contented passion with her lover. Others seek to realize ideals other than that of contentment in personal relationships. Entrepreneurs, musicians, politicians, scholars, actors, managers, and others aim at concrete, usually vaguely conceived, futures of achievement and self-realization. Their idiomatic personal goals represent a wide range of possibilities for individual fulfillment, all of which are not only compatible with, but are best achieved in context of, the individual and social ideals of democracy. Dewey sees these individual personal goals as manifestations of indefinite variety among individual creative impulses. The pervasive and creative tendency in each individual confronts the world and seeks to make it conform to an individual vision of order. In *Individualism, Old and New*, Dewey puts this idea as follows:

> Individuality is at first spontaneous and unshaped; it is a potentiality, a capacity for development. Even so, it is a unique manner of acting in and with a world of objects and persons. It is not something complete in itself, like a closet in a house or a secret drawer in a desk, filled with treasures that are waiting to be bestowed on the world. Since individuality is a distinctive way of feeling the impacts of the world and of showing a preferential bias in response to these impacts, it develops into shape and form only through interaction with actual conditions; it is not more complete in itself than is a painter's tube of paint without relation to a canvas. The work of art is the truly individual thing; and it is the result of the interaction of paint and canvas through the medium of the artist's distinctive vision and power. In its determination, the potential individuality of the artist takes on visible and enduring form.[44]

The idiomatic ideals that guide individual action take concrete form only in the achievements of individuals. Thus the creativity of a Mozart, a Matisse, a Leibniz, a Henry Ford, a Harrison Ford, or a Yo-Yo Ma yields a life of distinctive achievement not different in its raw creativity from the life of Gabriel Oak or Jane Doe. Each of these lives is in the same sense a creation that originates in confrontation with an environing medium of possibilities. Dewey affirms this individual creativity in the suggestive last paragraph of *Individualism, Old and New*.

To gain an integrated individuality, each of us needs to cultivate his own garden. But there is no fence about this garden: it is no sharply marked-off enclosure. Our garden is the world, in the angle at which it touches our own manner of being . . . we, who are also parts of the moving present, create ourselves as we create an unknown future.[45]

The reflective life is the life of creativity informed on one side by ideals pervasive, democratic, and scientific, and informed on the other side by idiomatic, individual ideals that define possibilities for personal growth. Both sorts of ideal enable the potential, in the moving present of human lives, for the creation of a future both personally satisfying and consistent with community integrity.[46]

SUCCESS IN REFLECTIVE LIVING

The reflective life may of course be more or less successful along any of its three dimensions. One may be more or less successful at realizing individual autonomy; one may be more or less successful at respecting community integrity; and one may be more or less successful at sustaining and pursuing democratic or idiomatic ideals. For example, autonomy with respect to environing conditions is more successfully realized by some individuals than by others. A crude example of failure of autonomy is found in a stereotypical adolescent who listens only to hard rock or rap or country western music, and who sneers not only at Dvorak and Shostakovich but also at Mozart and Beethoven. This failure to develop the skill of appreciating various modes of musical expression signals lack of independence from a dominant culture, and a resultant lack of autonomy. This example of an adolescent failure of musical autonomy represents only one of many possible ways to fail of autonomy. One may fail of autonomy with respect to political opinion, through echoing the opinions of the party chairperson, of the local newspaper, or of one's employer. One may also fail of autonomy with respect to religion, literature, economics, science, and in many other ways. Some of these failures are more significant than others for different individuals, depending upon individuals' own expectations as well as on expectations attached to their particular positions in their communities. Scientists, qua scientists, usually need not have political autonomy; politicians, qua politicians, usually need not have literary or scientific autonomy. The ideal of absolute autonomy—autonomy with respect to every possible mode of opinion or action—is likely never realized. Even those we think of as "renaissance men" usually have Achilles' heels of opinion or action where they simply follow custom for no better reason than that it is custom. In addition, just as failures of autonomy may undermine efforts to live a reflective life, so likewise failures of respect for community values and failures of respect for appropriate ideal ends may also undermine efforts to live a reflective life. Failure in some respect and to some degree is likely inevitable and also, at least on the occasion of the failure, likely invisible to the one who fails, and consequently the reflective life is inevitably a matter of degree, a matter of more or less success.[47]

Although it is vague, the idea of the reflective life does have significant content; one can see through it how pragmatists conceive a good life. A reflective life is a life of significant autonomy, a life that respects the integrity of tradition, and a life lived toward significant ideal values both personal and communal. An advantage of the reflective life is that it can be lived by virtually anyone, whether or not they have the intellectual inclinations required for the life of the mind, or for moral theory. Mozart, Matisse, or Hemingway are candidate individuals who might have achieved the reflective life, or the good life according to pragmatists, as much as are Spinoza, Kant, or Mill and as much as are Gabriel Oak and Jane Doe. Furthermore, although it is vague, pragmatism's understanding of the reflective life is incompatible with alternative, more traditional accounts of how one should live.

The reflective life is not an absolute ideal that one might strive to realize in one's own life; it is a vague and always highly individualized expression of some particular balance among the dimensions of autonomy, community, and ideality that are here identified as elements of reflective living. For pragmatists, finding a successful, individual combination of these three elements in one's life is the moral task of every life during every day. There is nothing like an ideal balance of these parts that properly makes for something like the good life as conceived by Aristotelians. Recognizing these three dimensions of what is for all of us inherently worthy of respect does enable a different approach to thinking about moral living. Kantian theory, in Annette Baier's large understanding of Kantian,[48] and virtue theory in all of its traditional guises must be transcended in thought about morals, and in philosophical thought about ethics, by the practice-oriented alternative of the reflective life, by John Dewey's *working* theory of morals.

Talk about superseding traditional alternatives of moral theory by recourse to the idea of the reflective life requires a more detailed account of the ideals that are part of the reflective life. Ideals in Western philosophy are inevitably abstract and ontologically problematic; they typically induce "ontology of the gaps" thinking. Ideals are, almost in their very concept, not "real" or at least they are radically different from the normal stuff of experience that is not intellectually problematic. Ideals, in short, appear not the stuff of experience. How may pragmatists like Dewey embrace ideals as though they are empirically unproblematic and as though there are no special epistemological issues infecting claims about ideals?

NOTES

1. LW7. See especially part 2 of this work, *Theory of the Moral Life,* and for the idea of reflective morality in particular, see section 1.

2. Again, see the section of LW7 referred to in the previous note. For a good secondary account of Dewey's thinking about these traditional theories, see James Gouinlock, *John Dewey's Philosophy of Value* (New York: Humanities Press, 1972); chapter 4 of this book, "The Method of Experience in Moral Philosophy," sets Dewey's thought about morality into the context of its reaction to traditional theories of ethics.

3. "[T]he present time is one which is in peculiar need of reflective morals and of a working theory of morals" (LW7:176).

4. See, for example, Gregory Pappas, "New Directions and Uses in the Reconstruction of Dewey's Ethics," *In Dewey's Wake: Unfinished Work of Pragmatic Reconstruction,* ed. William J. Gavin (Albany: SUNY Press, 2003), 41–61. Pappas says, "For those of us willing to resurrect (reconstruct) moral theory and put it to some 'use,' Dewey's texts on ethics are of very little help" and further "[T]here is no explicit, systematic, or detailed explanation of what form a reconstructed ethical theory might take in order for it to be useful" (41). See also Pappas's comment in footnote 4 (58). Pappas elsewhere characterizes Dewey as a situation ethicist; see "Dewey's Ethics: Morality as Experience," in *Reading Dewey: Interpretations for a Postmodern Generation,* ed. Larry Hickman (Bloomington: Indiana University Press, 1998). An additional useful source, especially about Dewey's scientific style of thinking about morality, is Jennifer Welchman, *Dewey's Ethical Thought* (Ithaca, N.Y.: Cornell University Press, 1995), chapters 6 and 7.

5. Dewey's works typically include systematic efforts to disclose the historical and cultural roots of the ideology in question, an ideology loosely identifiable as scientism. *Experience and Nature* is one prominent locus of Dewey's typical effort, as is *The Quest for Certainty;* my own preference is for *The Quest for Certainty,* Dewey's Gifford Lectures, largely because I think that volume offers less opportunity for misunderstanding. Beyond philosophers, many contemporary thinkers remain committed to this scientific, or from a pragmatist perspective "scientistic," ideology; for a warning against interpreting Dewey in a scientistic way, see Stephen Toulmin's introduction to *The Quest for Certainty* LW4:vii–xxii; for an explicit cautionary remark, see ix. I offer more comment about this issue in the section, "The Question of the Source."

6. For the genesis of this use of the idea of evasion, see Cornel West, *The American Evasion of Philosophy* (Madison: University of Wisconsin Press, 1989).

7. Other sources within the classical tradition of pragmatism point to these dimensions of reflective morality, but Dewey is the most systematic of the pragmatists when it comes to addressing classical problems in distinctively philosophical ways.

8. LW13:151–52.

9. LW7:307–8.

10. LW7:307.

11. See MacIntyre's *After Virtue* (South Bend, Ind.: University of Notre Dame Press, 1981); *Whose Justice, Which Rationality* (South Bend, Ind.: University of Notre Dame Press, 1988); and *Three Rival Versions of Moral Enquiry* (South Bend, Ind.: University of Notre Dame Press, 1990). For a secondary account of this reaction against the autonomy that is naturally part of liberal individualism, see also Jeffrey Stout, *Democracy and Tradition* (Princeton, N.J.: Princeton University Press, 2004). Stout's part 2: *Religious Voices in a Secular Society* captures typical objections to liberal individualism and the autonomy that accompanies it; Stout's sympathy with pragmatism is evident but does not adversely affect his accounts of communitarian voices.

12. LW7:298–303.

13. LW7:300.

14. This symbiosis of individuality and community is well recognized among Dewey scholars. See, for example, Jennifer Welchman's account in *Dewey's Ethical Thought*, 165–66. Again, see Gouinlock, *John Dewey's Philosophy of Value*, 259–66.

15. Although this topic is large, I offer the sketchy observation that the strategies of education Dewey finds critical to the health of democratic cultures are more useful in dealing with such pathological individuals than are the authoritarian or paternalistic methods typical of religious, communitarian thinkers. (For an alternative, see the works of Alasdair MacIntyre, already cited, but especially *Whose Justice, Which Rationality*, 177–80; and also again, Stout's *Democracy and Tradition*, part 2.)

16. Marcus Singer's Presidential Address to the Central Division of the American Philosophical Association expresses views about morality that accord with this Deweyan observation about morality. See "The Ideal of a Rational Morality," *Proceedings and Addresses of the American Philosophical Association* 60, no. 1 (September 1986).

17. LW7:253.

18. This essay is reprinted in Robert M. Baird and Stuart Rosenbaum, *Same Sex Marriage* (Buffalo, N.Y.: Prometheus Press, 1997), 37–41.

19. LW7:275.

20. One can hardly overestimate the significance of social setting and social traditions in understanding and evaluating, as an observer, decisions such as these. The setting for Hardy's novel, nineteenth-century England, is vastly different from the 1980s American setting for Jane Doe's choice to leave her husband for the woman she loved. (I note also that Gabriel Oak chose to respect in a way that Jane Doe did not the constraints of social custom; he and Bathsheba found their way into a permanent relationship only because of Hardy's creative twists of plot that worked to their advantage.) For a similar account of difference in social setting and how it might affect human choices, see Richard Rorty's "Religion as a Conversation Stopper," *Philosophy and Social Hope* (New York: Penguin Books, 1999), 168–74. Rorty mentions Tennyson's love for his friend, Hallam, and observes that two who loved each other as did Tennyson and Hallam would be likely these days to go to bed together. See page 168.

21. LW13:178.

22. LW13:186–87.

23. The connection between democracy as a social ideal and the Aristotelian virtues is not often explicit in Dewey's work. For an account of the connection, see LW7:257–60. Perhaps because this connection is not frequently explicit in Dewey's work, many scholars overlook the virtue dimension of his moral thought as well as the similarity of his moral thinking to that of Aristotle. The methodical, experimentalist way of understanding Dewey's moral thought is prevalent among secondary accounts as it is, for example, in Welchman's account cited in note 4. Gouinlock also emphasizes this experimentalist dimension of Dewey's moral thought, but concedes that habit is also central to an adequate understanding; see Gouinlock, cited in note 2, 354–56. Although Gouinlock notes that habit is indeed central to understanding Dewey's moral thought, his account of Dewey's philosophy of value places greater emphasis on method and experiment than on character and virtue. My suggestion here that Dewey's moral thought is strongly Aristotelian accords with a suggestion by Ralph Sleeper; see "Dewey's Aristotelian Turn," *The Necessity of Pragmatism* (Champaign: University of Illinois Press, 2001); see especially 100.

24. Benjamin Barber, "America Skips School: Why We Talk So Much about Education and Do So Little," *Harper's*, November 1993, 44.

25. The question of the source of morality is one moral theories typically address. Most strategies locate the source of morality in the commands of God, in reason, or in human nature. Todd Lekan's *Making Morality* (Nashville, Tenn.: Vanderbilt University Press, 2003) seeks to offer a pragmatist account of morality, but Lekan admits that he does not address the question of pragmatism's account of the source of morality; see his 85. Perhaps (one might speculate) this issue of the source that for typical theories of morality invokes metaphysical views that pragmatists typically shun inclines most scholarly commentators on Dewey's moral views to stress the experimentalist, methodist approach that is unquestionably prominent in much of Dewey's thought.

26. William Caspary provides an enlightening discussion of Dewey's understanding of the methods of ethics and science as parallel; see his "'One and the Same Method': John Dewey's Thesis of Unity of Method in Ethics and Science," *Transactions of the Charles S. Peirce Society* 39, no. 3 (Summer 2003): 445–68. Caspary's discussion does not acknowledge, however, that science, as my discussion here suggests, is the institutional source of moral value; for all his profitable discussion of parallels in method between ethics and science, Caspary treats the issue of the source in an indirect and consequently unsatisfying way. See especially 460–61. Jennifer Welchman, in the already cited *Dewey's Ethical Thought*, provides another interesting account of the relationship between morality and science in Dewey, especially in relation to the 1908 *Ethics* (MW5); see her chapter 6 and especially 172–81. Welchman, in my view, overly emphasizes the more traditional, dialectical, and rationally striving understanding of Dewey's account of moral deliberation; more directly, I think she overly "scientizes" Dewey's account of moral deliberation.

27. Robert Westbrook, *John Dewey and American Democracy* (Ithaca, N.Y.: Cornell University Press, 1991); see especially 164–71.

28. LW13:167. This entire chapter from *Freedom and Culture* is richly suggestive of the virtue dimension of Dewey's moral thought that I emphasize in this book.

29. LW13:168.

30. For a compelling account of the internality of values to practices, see MacIntyre's already cited *After Virtue*. MacIntyre's *After Virtue* account of the locus of values in practices accords well with the idea Dewey intends throughout his work on morality. The institutions of a culture are, generally speaking, the locus and source of value for pragmatists, and Dewey surely holds this view. MacIntyre, in later work, retreats from the fullness of this idea of the internality of values to practices. For an account of his retreat, see again my "MacIntyre or Dewey."

31. LW13:168.

32. LW13:170.

33. See *Art as Experience* (LW10), chapter 4, especially 80 and 340–43. See also Thomas M. Alexander, *John Dewey's Theory of Art, Experience, and Nature: The Horizons of Feeling* (Albany: State University of New York Press, 1987).

34. See MW9:197, quoted in Westbrook, *John Dewey and American Democracy*, 169.

35. See Westbrook, *John Dewey and American Democracy*, 170. I note that Westbrook does not acknowledge the virtue dimension of Dewey's thought about the relation between science and morality that I here emphasize; Westbrook, like most commentators, sees moral education as equipping children to be good experimentalists. Again, I emphasize in contrast the analogy between Dewey's view about morality and Aristotle's virtue theory.

36. See Westbrook, *John Dewey and American Democracy*, 416. Westbrook's quote is from LW7:350.

37. Hilary Putnam, *Renewing Philosophy* (Cambridge, Mass.: Harvard University Press, 1992), 196.

38. LW10. See especially chapters 4 and 14 and more particularly 80 and 339–47. Putnam seems even more extensively ungenerous with Dewey in another part of his chapter titled "A Reconsideration of Deweyan Democracy." He supposes, for example, that Dewey would urge consequentialism and the scientific method on Sartre's Pierre who, in *Existentialism and Humanism*, must choose between joining the resistance and staying to care for his aging mother. Dewey would urge neither of these alternatives on Pierre. One of the strengths of Dewey's view about such situations is that it acknowledges that who one is is always to be created anew and that such critical situations as Pierre's are the heart of the moral life, for in such situations one is always choosing who one is to become.

39. Richard Bernstein, *Philosophical Profiles* (Philadelphia: University of Pennsylvania Press, 1986), 271.

40. James Gouinlock shares the unitary understanding of Dewey's moral and social thought in opposition to both Putnam and Bernstein. See "What Is the Legacy of Instrumentalism? Rorty's Interpretation of Dewey," *Journal of the History of Philosophy* 28, no. 2 (April 1990): 251–69, especially 267. Westbrook reinforces this response to Putnam and Bernstein in discussing other charges of scientism against Dewey; see 185–88.

41. LW7:255–61.

42. LW7:258.

43. LW13:168.

44. LW5:121–22.

45. LW5:123.

46. For further elaboration of this theme, see *Art as Experience* (LW10), especially chapters 3 and 4.

47. Dewey's view about success and failure in these dimensions follows that of Aristotle. Whether or not a life has been successful, for Aristotle, is discernible only at its end (see *Nichomachean Ethics*, book 1); likewise for Dewey, frequently only in retrospect does one discern one's successes and failures along these three dimensions of the reflective life.

48. See, for example, Annette Baier's "Doing without Moral Theory," *Postures of the Mind* (Minneapolis: University of Minnesota Press, 1985), 234. See also her "Theory and Reflective Practices," 209.

5

—ʌʌ—

Ideals

Thinking about ideals in the spirit of pragmatism requires giving them substance in our psyches and enabling them to guide our actions while not enabling them to appear transcendent of the natural world. Pragmatists do not require any special epistemological access to get to moral values, and they also do not accept ontological gaps between the world of ordinary life and the world of moral ideals. The pragmatist understanding we seek should show also that the ideals we respect, we respect not only individually or idiomatically, but also in cohesive groups and communities. Our ideals must be concrete, not abstract; they must be psychologically available to ordinary individuals, not an achievement of reason or theory.

PRAGMATISM'S CONCRETE IDEALS: SAINTS

Such a concrete understanding of ideals is at least implicit in the pragmatist canon. Three sources are (1) lectures 11–15, titled "Saintliness" and "The Value of Saintliness," in William James's *The Varieties of Religious Experience*; (2) chapter 14, "Moral Judgment and Knowledge," from John Dewey's *Ethics*, especially the section titled "Conscience and Deliberation"; and (3) lecture 2 of Dewey's *A Common Faith*.[1]

James's remarks about the value of saintliness suggest a concrete understanding of moral ideals as antecedent in situations of deliberation. In James's account ideals are saints. Again, ideals *are* saints. Though James is not fully explicit about this understanding of ideals, he comes close to expressing it directly. Here is one passage:

> According to the empirical philosophy, however, all ideals are matters of relation. It would be absurd, for example, to ask for a definition of "the ideal horse," so long as dragging drays and running races, bearing children, and jogging about with tradesmen's packages all remain as indispensable differentiations of equine function. You may take what you call a general all-round animal as a compromise, but he will be inferior to any horse of a more specialized type, in some one particular direction.[2]

The idea that all ideals are matters of relation, as well as James's use of scare quotes around "the ideal horse," is evidence of a turn away from the understanding of ideals as ontologically transcendent, a turn away from problems of ontology. Ideals are concrete, as concrete as humans are, and in relationship to humans they beckon toward real possibilities for human life; they are saints. About this understanding of saints as ideals, James is again almost explicit:

> The saints, with their extravagance of human tenderness, are the great torchbearers of this belief, the tip of the wedge, the clearers of the darkness. . . . The world is not yet with them, so they often seem in the midst of the world's affairs to be preposterous. Yet they are the impregnators of the world, vivifiers and animaters of potentialities of goodness which but for them would lie forever dormant. It is not possible to be quite as mean as we naturally are, when they have passed before us.[3]

The conclusion about ideals in pragmatism is that they are concrete and experiential. Saints are moral ideals. Moral ideals are saints. The "are" of these identity sentences may seem to generate what philosophers once called "howlers," sentences that strike one's conceptual ear as somehow incongruous or semantically inappropriate. Nonetheless, pragmatists require such an explicitly concrete account of ideals. Putting aside the appearance of semantic incongruity—it is after all just an appearance (and no more inappropriate than "Valley Girl talk," a mode of speech filled with incongruity!)—consider some advantages of this pragmatist way of conceiving ideals.

A distinct advantage is the very concreteness that seems incongruous to philosophical ears. This concreteness means that ideals are, as James puts it, "like pictures with an atmosphere and background";[4] they are substantial enough to be part of every individual's phenomenal world. These ideals can be experienced; they need not be excogitated or approached through sophisticated argumentation. The fact that these ideals are experienced means that they *can* affect human lives, and that they *do* affect human lives. When one becomes aware of the saints as they are portrayed in James's subtle descriptions, one does almost "see" them "like pictures with an atmosphere and background"; they enter concretely into our imaginations in ways that produce distinct affective responses. We likely find repulsive such saints as St. Louis of Gonzaga, whose search for purity was indistinguishable from a pathological femophobia, and Mary Margaret Alacoque, whose spirit of adoration for God became a swooning incompetence; and we likely find attractive St. Francis, St. Paul, George Fox, and Walt Whitman.[5]

This picture-like quality of our ideals/saints gives them power in our psyches as ideals. Consider, for example, the idea of justice; when understood as ontologically transcendent, and approachable only through strategies of dialectic, it has little power in human psyches. If the ideal of justice is properly understood only through strategies of theory and dialectic, then most individuals have limited access to it. If, however, justice is like a picture with an atmosphere and a background, then only those who are "blind" can fail to "see" it; almost everyone will have as much access to it as even the most sophisticated philosophers. The biblical story of King Solomon's effort to deal justly with two mothers who claimed the same infant is a better picture of justice than is Plato's *Republic*, though the latter is discursively and theoretically more satisfying.[6] In addition, one observes that almost all individuals believe they have as firm a grasp on the idea of justice as even the most sophisticated philosophers. This fact that justice is a power in almost every psyche speaks in favor of pragmatism's concrete understanding of ideals; it underscores the greater power of the King Solomon story as a picture of justice than *The Republic*. In human life, ideals are not transcendent; they are particular concrete realities with which one interacts, frequently daily or even hourly.

In addition to empowering ideals in our psyches, an understanding of ideals as flesh and blood saints gives us a model for thinking about moral deliberation that closely approximates the real thing. How humans think, reflect, and deliberate as we come to morally significant decisions is a product not of our discursive, analytical skill, but rather of our imaginative abilities not only to "see" what we will or might produce in a particular situation, but also to "see" what St. Paul or St. Francis or Mother Teresa or Gandhi might do or think or say about it. Our imaginative abilities are our primary deliberative resource in every morally significant situation we encounter. Bringing our saints to the center of attention when we think about ideals shows how moral deliberation is primarily imaginative rather than discursive.

John Dewey's explicit account of moral deliberation recognizes the power of ideals as concrete presences in individual lives:

> Deliberation is actually an imaginative rehearsal of various courses of conduct. We give way, in our mind, to some impulse; we try, in our mind, some plan. Following its career through various steps, we find ourselves in imagination in the presence of the consequences that would follow; and as we then like and approve, or dislike and disapprove, these consequences, we find the original impulse or plan good or bad. Deliberation is dramatic and active, not mathematical and impersonal; and hence it has the intuitive, the direct factor in it.[7]

When one is in a situation requiring decision, one must choose the good or the better in light of the deliberative resources at one's disposal. In Dewey's thought, these resources are two. The prospective resource is one's ability to "see" alternatives and prospects for oneself and for others. The retrospective resources are one's "saints," the ideals that serve as background for one's choices and also as stabilizers of one's tendencies of choice. Dewey's account of moral deliberation, unlike discursive accounts typically expressed or assumed in moral philosophy, captures precisely these resources that are available to every person who faces a choice.[8]

Although this passage emphasizes consequences projected in imagination, it also conceives deliberation as "dramatic and active" and thus suggests imaginative engagement. Such engagement means different things to people in different situations. For George H. W. Bush, for example, it might mean that his deliberations preceding the 1990 Gulf War included imagined interactions with, perhaps rereading the works of, Dwight Eisenhower or Winston Churchill. These retrospective dimensions of deliberation are different for individuals in different situations, but such is the phenomenology of deliberation; pragmatists' account of deliberation is faithful to the facts of experience, especially in James's and Dewey's accounts of those facts.

Dewey embraces the understanding of ideals as products or outcomes of reflection, but also their character as antecedent to occasions of reflection and choice. Ideals have this dual character in pragmatism generally; they are not only products of reflection but also antecedents of reflection. The task of moral agents is Janus-like, one head facing forward, the other head facing backward. Imagination projects toward the future; and imagination respects toward the past. Dewey, like James, embraces this retrospective understanding of ideals. In *A Common Faith*, Dewey says,

> [T]he intellectual articles of a creed must be understood to be symbolic of moral and other ideal values, but that the facts taken to be historic and used

as concrete evidence of the intellectual articles are themselves symbolic. These articles of a creed present events and persons that have been made over by the idealizing imagination in the interest, at their best, of moral ideals. Historic personages in their divine attributes are materializations of the ends that enlist devotion and inspire endeavor.[9]

The idealizing imagination makes over past events and persons in the interest of moral ideals. The conferring of sainthood is an explicit making over of past persons; it makes past persons official as worthy of emulation and respect. Sainthood, in the relevant sense, is of course not always or even usually a matter of canonization by the Catholic Church or by any other organization with recognized powers; it is rather a matter of the place within the traditions of a culture of specific individuals, "saints" or heroes or prominent figures of various kinds.

Dewey here is less explicit than one might wish; he says that historic personages in their divine attributes are "materializations of the ends" that enlist devotion. One might read his statement as less than fully concrete, at least given the fully concrete understanding of ideals offered here. One might read Dewey as granting independent, ontological status to the ends while seeing historic personages as materializations *of* those ends. To read Dewey this way, however, is to remain reluctant to embrace the fullness of his pragmatism, and it may even be to insist that, no matter how fully empiricist one may be, one must yet acknowledge the reality of abstract ideals. Robert Roth does read Dewey in this "ontologically pregnant" way, as does Victor Kestenbaum.[10] I comment on their views later in this chapter.

The primary goal of this chapter, to express a way of conceiving ideals that is consistent with pragmatism and shuns recourse to ontological abstraction, is now accomplished.[11] The ideals of experience that need not be known by a special faculty of intuition and need not be conceived as ontologically different from humans and the cultural contexts of their worlds are the flesh and blood saints who are "made over by the idealizing imagination" and who become deeply embedded in the cultures and traditions of humanity. Again, our ideals are our saints.

Understanding moral ideals as saints yields an explicit understanding of moral ideals as already present in our deliberative situations. The Janus-like character of our ideals—their looking both forward and backward—is deeply embedded in the thought of the classical pragmatists about morality.

This Janus-like understanding of ideals, their being both prospective and retrospective, is the heart of pragmatism's understanding of ideals; it is fully empiricist and fully concrete. William James's radical empiricism is fully coherent with Dewey's account of ideals; it sees moral ideals as saints and has no need for abstract ideals remote from ordinary experience. Saints as ideals are as concrete and particular, as little general and abstract, as are the humans who live and love and have children and die. Our saints populate our imaginations variously, depending on who and where and when we are, and they help us in our deliberations about how we might wring the good, or the better, out of the morally difficult situations we encounter. We have no need of generals or abstractions or ideals as ontologically transcendent, and from which we must reason, in order to understand our moral lives.[12]

The idea that moral ideals are saints enables full recognition that the ideals of experience are already with us, are antecedent to our deliberation, on every occasion of choice and action. A problem that remains for pragmatist thought about morality is squaring its conception of ideals as saints with the fact that Western philosophy has concentrated on large, encompassing ideals that should be applicable to all of humanity in all cultural traditions. How may we think concretely about the large ideals of justice, courage, temperance, wisdom, and others? How may these large theory-motivating ideals be expressed in the pragmatic terminology that insists on thinking of ideals as saints, as concrete, flesh and blood parts of the natural world?

THE LARGE IDEALS OF MORAL THEORY

Why are these large ideals important in Western philosophy? How may they continue to be important in pragmatists' understanding of values and ideals? These questions become acutely important for an understanding of value that sees every human interest, as does apparently Dewey's initial account, as potentially a moral ideal. I make an effort later to show how Dewey makes his way toward the account of ideals I here attribute to him, but I begin with the question how this concrete, pragmatist understanding of ideals incorporates these large ideals that are so important in Western philosophy.

If one supposes that interests are the beginnings of values, then how might these large ideals that have dominated moral philosophy have come to seem important?[13] They are, after all, not interests on the part of some individuals. The answer to this question has two parts. The first part is that these large ideals are summaries of, or shorthand ways of talking about, experienced individuals or traditions of particular cultures. The second part is that these large ideals are projections of an imagined and concrete possible future, perhaps of every human community, but certainly of human communities that fall within the vague sphere of Western culture.

To say that these large ideals are summaries of, or shorthand ways of talking about, experienced and concrete traditions of particular cultures is to say that prominent sources within the traditions of these cultures are concrete and compelling models not only for individual behavior in everyday situations but also for what individuals and their communities might become. Both the retrospective and the prospective dimensions of pragmatism's account of ideals are fully present in this suggestion. Examples that illuminate this way of thinking about ideals are readily available; in fact, they are so completely ubiquitous that selecting any particular one for illustration seems arbitrary.

Begin with Charles Dickens's *Great Expectations*. The central character of the novel is Pip, who, despite modest beginnings in life, is tantalized again and again by the prospect that he might have the great expectation of becoming a gentleman. The novel is about the long-mysterious circumstances that indeed bring to pass his becoming a gentleman rather than the blacksmith that his apprenticeship to his brother-in-law, Joe Gargery, portends. Dickens's account of Pip's strained and painful transition from life as a commoner to life as a gentleman is psychologically plausible, even though the plot is laden with deus ex machina devices. Most prominent in the novel, despite an excess of contrivance in the plot, are the characters that stand out against the plot like, in James's words, "pictures with an atmosphere and a background." Joe Gargery is one of these characters.

Joe Gargery is a picture of loyalty. He loves and is loyal to his wife, and her untimely death devastates him. When Pip's struggles with his own identity bring him into conflicts between the loyalties of his past as a commoner and the imagined loyalties of his new life as a gentleman, Pip fails to be loyal to those who cared for and sustained him in his early life. Joe, however, not a gentleman and lacking all learning, always does what he can for Pip on every occasion when he can be helpful. Joe, again, is a picture of loyalty, and perhaps his contrast with Pip in relevant ways makes him an even more striking picture of loyalty; Joe Gargery is Dickens's saint, and if we read well, Joe is also our saint.

But words can mislead, and we must take care to sustain our own loyalty to the concreteness I have insisted is central to pragmatism's understanding of ideals. What is that thing of which Joe is a picture? Loyalty. And what then is loyalty? In just the natural way these questions arise arises also the temptation that, when we succumb to it, keeps us bound to our condition as "footnotes to Plato."[14]

Joe *is* loyalty. To speak about Joe's loyalty is to speak in a summary way about Joe himself; it is to speak in a way that enables us to think connections between Joe and ourselves, or between Joe and the more ideal selves we project in our futures. This thinking to connections is the heart of moral deliberation. As James says in an already cited remark, "all ideals are matters of relation," where these relations are those we think when we are deliberating morally. Pragmatism lets us see that the root and branch of loyalty is Joe himself. Talk about loyalty *as a characteristic* we might have or lack is no more than a summary, shorthand way of talking about Joe himself. Joe himself is the picture, and human efforts to talk usefully about Joe as a picture yields the awkward expressions that tempt us toward Platonism.

Joe, however, is no more than one loyalty. (Or as one might put this sentence in a Platonist tone of voice: Joe is no more than "one instance" of loyalty.) Joe is a saint and comes complete with an atmosphere and a background. Each of us has individual saints; they are those who come to mind when we think seriously about James's remark that all ideals are matters of relation. I might mention several flesh and blood individuals from my own history who occupy central positions in my psyche; they are my saints and ideals. To speak about those saints in the ways to which Western intellectuals are tempted, to speak about them as "instances" or as "exemplars," is to flatten, and perhaps undermine entirely, their significance. The transcendental ambition of our ordinary Platonist modes of speech deprives my saints and ideals of their particular substance in my psyche; it forces me to turn away from or to look beyond these definitive parts of my self. So it is also with others who have absorbed, as it were, "with their mother's milk," canonical Platonist modes of thought about ideals.

Joe Gargery, as I have discussed him, may appear to be only the single large ideal of loyalty. Although loyalty surely is one of the large ideals that have motivated Western moral theory, one wants perhaps more examples of individuals who are other large ideals, ideals such as justice, responsibility, beneficence, goodness, and so on. And I have said that examples of such individuals are ubiquitous. Who are the candidate individuals for these other large ideals? The answer to this question is not clear and precise, but it is, within the commitments of pragmatism, clear and diffuse.

King Solomon earlier appeared as a picture of justice. St. Francis and St. Benedict are also such pictures, as are Mother Teresa, Gandhi, and Martin Luther King Jr. Specifying precisely which ideals these individuals picture is difficult; they picture certain ideals not precisely, but diffusely. Much as Joe Gargery is loyalty, however, each of these individuals is also loyalty. These other individuals are also pictures of other ideals, and one might think some of them picture better other ideals than the ideal of loyalty. Mother Teresa one might think better pictures beneficence than loyalty; Gandhi one might think better pictures generosity or asceticism; Martin Luther King Jr. one might think better pictures justice; and so on for other morally significant individuals.

However one might think about particular individuals, one must acknowledge that the pictures they offer are, as I noted, clear and diffuse. There are no clear and precise pictures of individual ideals. To think there might be such clear and precise pictures is to err in the direction of philosophical theory about ideals; it is to think that if one cannot achieve a "clear and distinct" conceptual account of ideals, one can at least achieve a "clear and distinct" picture of ideals. Pragmatists realize, on the contrary, that ideals are, though clear, nevertheless diffuse. Hence, to cite Joe Gargery as loyalty or Martin Luther King Jr. as justice, and so on, is to focus the diffuse picture in one specific way among other possible ways. Joe Gargery thus is no more a picture of loyalty—although he is a clear picture of loyalty—than he is of justice; and Martin Luther King Jr. is no more a picture of justice—although he is a clear picture of justice—than he is of beneficence or loyalty. The same point holds for the other pictures of large ideals we might mention either from "real life" or from among the many characters of fiction that populate Western psyches.

Fortunately this clarity and diffuseness of picture that one finds in this pragmatist account of ideals does not become an intellectual problem for the understanding of ideals as saints. Pictures are multifaceted and many dimensional. The many textures and representations that appear in a whole life are capable of uniting, in the concrete, many ideals that appear different to conceptual thought, as do the textures and representations that appear in the lives of Joe Gargery, Martin Luther King Jr., and others. In classical thought about the virtues, this unitary dimension of the myriad textures and representations of a whole life appears as the idea of the unity of the virtues. John Dewey explicitly recognizes this fact about ideals and virtues in his embrace of the idea of the unity of the virtues, and his attitude in this respect is characteristic of pragmatist thought about ideals and virtues:

> The mere idea of a catalogue of different virtues commits us to the notion that virtues may be kept apart, pigeonholed in water-tight compartments. In fact virtuous traits interpenetrate one another; this unity is involved in the very idea of integrity of character. At one time persistence and endurance in the face of obstacles is the most prominent feature; then the attitude is the excellence called courage. At another time, the trait of impartiality and equity is uppermost, and we call it justice. At other times, the necessity for subordinating immediate satisfaction of a strong appetite or desire to a comprehensive good is the conspicuous feature. Then the disposition is denominated temperance, self-control. When the prominent phase is the need for thoughtfulness, for consecutive and persistent attention, in order that these other qualities may function, the interest receives the name of moral wisdom, insight, conscientiousness. In each case the difference is one of emphasis only.[15]

The clarity and diffuseness of ideals that is characteristic of pragmatist thought about ideals accords well with the Aristotelian view that the virtues are in fact united in their concrete realizations. Pragmatism accords with this traditional view, but it resists seeing the ideals or virtues as "realizations" or "exemplifications." Joe Gargery is loyalty, but he is also courage, justice, and wisdom; the same is true of the other saints who are ideals.

To speak about the large ideals that are typical concerns of Western moral theory is, for pragmatists, to speak about those individuals, saints, or heroes who express in themselves what we fellow humans might be. That these individuals, saints, or heroes are different and are differently revered in different communities is no more than a sociological fact or an anthropological fact obvious to all who are well enough informed to see beyond their own situation. When thinking about justice, responsibility, duty, courage, faithfulness, loyalty, or other large ideals of concern to moral theorists, one finds at the root of such thought the flesh and blood, concrete individuals who are those ideals—our saints. To theorize about those ideals toward abstractions or principles that might "capture" them in order to enable their "application" has the effect of diminishing the significance of the ideals themselves. Insofar as it diminishes them, intentionally or not, moral theory demeans our ideals.

In 1997, as I have noted in another context,[16] the world mourned within the space of a single week the death of two magnificent women, Mother Teresa and Princess Diana. Many individuals worldwide were psychologically devastated by the deaths of these two women, and a simultaneous outpouring of emotion in many nations testified to the centrality of these women in the psyches of many people in different cultures. What might account for this almost universal grief at the deaths of two women who were personally unknown to the majority of those who grieved? Pragmatists' answer to this question is straightforward: these women are among our saints; they are among our ideals; they are pictures of moral possibility. To say that they are "instances of" or "exemplars of" some value property—charity, purity, gentleness, or perseverance—makes them serve something abstract, remote, and distant. But their power in our psyches gives the lie to that Platonist conception of their significance.[17] They are with us in the same concretely significant way as are our mentors, our parents, our siblings, our friends, our therapists, and our ministers.

Again, these large ideals that have motivated Western moral theory are summary or shorthand expressions of the fact that certain individuals, our saints, have definitive significance for our understandings of who we are and who we might become.

Some cultures, those not subject to the Platonist temptation of Western philosophy, naturally recognize this phenomenological fact. James

Stephenson's account of his experiences among the Hadzabe tribe of Tanzania is a descriptively compelling example of how this fact finds its way into the language and culture of the Hadzabe.[18] Stephenson lived among the Hadzabe for many months and found their lives to be in every way fully a matter of relations, concrete relations to friends, neighbors, animals, trees, and also to ancestors. In the context of Stephenson's description of Hadzabe life, Western Platonism may begin to appear (even to sophisticated Western intellectuals) what I suggest pragmatism claims it is: a highly intellectualized surrogate for these concrete relationships, and for the Hadzabe in particular, for their relationships to the ancestors. (Remember James's remark: All ideals are matters of relation.) Other cultures explicitly practice ancestor worship as do the Shinto of Japan. Such institutionalized respect for ancestors, and even religious worship of ancestors, testifies to the diversity of ways to recognize the power in our psyches of what philosophers demean as "instances" or "exemplars." Pragmatism offers a way of thinking about ideals and saints and heroes that is friendly to these alternative ways of thinking about the power of the ideal in individual lives, a way that undermines the Platonist, philosophical way of thinking about ideals that is ubiquitous in Western culture.

A "RED HERRING" IN DEWEY'S WORDS ABOUT IDEALS

I have attributed the account of ideals as saints to Dewey as well as to James. Dewey is not as explicit about his embrace of this concrete account of ideals as James appears to be. Finding a way from Dewey's explicit remarks about ideals to the account I have offered above requires some sleuthing through his work. Some things Dewey says about ideals are misleading, and they have misled some scholars in their thought about pragmatism. Consider an explicit remark he makes in an effort to distinguish ideal values from material values.

> The distinction is one between goods which, when they present themselves to imagination, are approved by reflection after wide examination of their relations, and the goods which are such only because their wider connections are not looked into.[19]

Following this remark, one might conclude that ideals are just those values, goods, or interests that one continues to find worthy after serious reflection on their interconnections or "wider relations." Should I own a new, large SUV? According to this account, assuming I want a new, large SUV, I decide by looking into the wider connections of that possibility. If

I respect the environment, presumably I will become aware through investigating its wider connections that my owning an SUV would be environmentally irresponsible. Other examples—I leave these to readers—make clear the complexity of most interests or goods. On this initial account, goods or interests are ideals just in case they pass the wider connections test.

In the absence of elaboration, however, this account is misleading. Turning interests into ideals simply by certifying them in terms of wider connections appears to generate too varied a landscape of ideals; it also appears to look only to the future to find ideals. The problem is that any interests might by this account become ideals, given appropriate gerrymandering of the field of wider connections. Examples: Some Muslim activists want to destroy American capitalism; is their interest an ideal? Some gay activists want legal marriage for homosexuals; is their interest an ideal? Some Baptists and Catholics want their youth educated in the techniques of Christian apologetics; does their interest express a proper educational ideal? The wider connections account of ideals is unsatisfying partly because it generates diverse and controversial sets of ideals and partly because it does not respect values or ideals already present in human communities.

One easily gets the impression that ideals are just those interests, however idiomatic they may be, that survive the reflective consideration brought to bear to elicit their wider connections. This way of thinking about ideals makes them completely future projections out of the present. Individuals presumably have interests, and they carry out an operation of reflection about the wider connections of those interests to discover whether or not they are worthy ideals. But ideals are, and we feel then as, antecedent to experiences of interest and desire, and antecedent to reflection of any kind.[20]

John Patrick Diggins focuses on this perceived defect in pragmatism's account of value in *The Promise of Pragmatism*, and he takes this defect to justify a definitively negative judgment about pragmatism.

> With pragmatism in particular, the use of experience only prepares us for further experience, without experience itself being immediately self-illuminating or self-rewarding. The assumption that truth and value are produced in future action rather than revealed in present reflection holds out the promise of success, and as such pragmatism becomes not so much a philosophy as a story of the upward movement of life, a hopeful vision that appeals to America's romantic imagination. . . . Always looking ahead, pragmatism counsels adjustment and adaptation on the assumption that ideals, or at least something of meaning and value, are expected to emerge from experience and hence need not be regarded as external to it. Pragmatism reorients the meaning of history from retrospective reflection to prospective confrontation.[21]

Diggins captures the reaction many intellectuals probably have upon looking into pragmatism's thought about value. The human scene, in whatever richness and depth it offers, but nothing beyond the human scene, must suffice for all human purposes, moral, religious, and scientific. His harsh judgment about pragmatism Diggins delivers when he says, "Dewey taught Americans how to swim on the surface and how to conceive nature for the purpose of using it."[22] Diggins's dismissive remark misses the way pragmatism fully enables the antecedent character of moral ideals, the way moral ideals are already funded (if not foundationally given or ontologically fixed) prior to, or in Diggins's words "external to," the interests that need reflective thought to certify their worthiness as ideals.

Dewey's wider connections words are also misleading in the way they appear to overlook the larger ideals—justice, goodness, responsibility, duty, equality, and so on—that have motivated characteristic developments in moral theory. These large ideals, as well as their transcendence of idiomatic or culturally local interests, have motivated philosophical theories of morality. Where do these larger ideals appear in a pragmatist account of morality? How might one get from Dewey's wider connections account of ideals to these larger ideals?

These three problems of the wider connections account of ideals need explicit treatment to enable pragmatism's account of ideals. Simply stopping with Dewey's misleading wider connections account yields no adequate way of thinking about values or ideals. Thinkers who stop with that account too hastily conclude that pragmatism cannot offer a richer, more satisfying account.[23] These three problems of the wider connections account are quite tractable within the understanding of ideals as saints.

The three problems again are these: (1) the diverse and controversial interests or goods that seem equally candidates to be moral ideals; (2) the apparent overemphasis on the consequential, or product-of-reflection, character of ideals and its accompanying lack of regard for the way ideals are antecedent to experience, and sometimes even to awareness; and (3) the way the wider connections account apparently diminishes the large moral ideals—justice, fraternity, goodness, duty, responsibility, and so on—that have largely motivated Western moral philosophy. These three problems may be largely responsible for the lack of serious philosophical interest in the moral thought of pragmatism.[24]

The key to solving all of these problems is the conception of ideals as saints. This conception of moral ideals is sufficiently concrete to be consistent with pragmatism and also to enable thought about ideals as (1) diverse, but potentially unified, (2) antecedent to experience as well as consequent upon a survey of wider connections, and (3) large in the way moral ideals in Western moral philosophy have been large so as to motivate dominant varieties of moral theory. Consider first the wide variety and diversity of ideals among human communities.

Dewey's wider connections account does appear to diminish the privileged position of the large ideals that have dominated moral philosophy, and it does let into the mix of possible ideals such items as a worldwide communist society (Karl Marx), a large-scale Christian political culture (Jonathan Edwards), or racial segregation by geopolitical boundaries (The World Church of the Creator). For typical moral philosophers, these interests appear too ethnocentric, egocentric, or ideological to count as proper ideals. They are "thicker" than the philosophically common "thin" ideals of justice, wisdom, temperance, courage, and others, and they seem to undermine the effort of philosophical ethics to achieve conceptual universality.[25]

Nevertheless, a large part of the point of pragmatism is to begin with human experience in all of its diversity. And such experiential beginnings must seem from sophisticated perspectives of philosophy unwise, irrational, ill-informed, benighted, or plainly immoral. Dewey's wider connections account does not preclude such judgments of badness, but it does make such judgments depend on the results of deliberating about wider connections. Complicating those deliberations is the fact of wide diversity in starting points for deliberation, including assumptions that seem reasonable to some and absurd to others. Try to imagine, for example, deliberations among Karl Marx, Jonathan Edwards, and advocates of the World Church of the Creator! Those imagined deliberations become even more difficult if one includes in the mix such thinkers as W. E. B. Du Bois, Tich Nat Han, Gandhi, Thomas Hobbes, or Mother Teresa. In the face of such messy deliberative possibilities, moral philosophers will continue to find relief in the dispassionate, objective, abstract world of conceptual analysis; and they will stick with the tried and true "thin" concepts of moral philosophy.

The point of pragmatism, however, is to bring philosophy down to earth. This effort includes recognition of the complex and diffuse variety of intellectual effort to discriminate genuine ideals from mere interests. Dewey's realism about the human situation is at the heart of pragmatism. Humans must start from where they are, in all the diversity and variety of their interests and traditions; and they must seek a better future shaped by the saints/ideals of their traditions as well as by their best efforts to envision what is better. The vast differences among communities that frequently yield conflict cannot be finessed by philosophical technique.

The pragmatist conclusion about the diversity of interests and potential ideals is that this diversity is a genuine and inescapable dimension of morals and of thought about them. The task of moral philosophers is to seek to understand these differences and to guide them toward more inclusive understandings of what is ideal. Ideally, from many ideals/saints that guide different communities, we may be able to achieve commonality of respect for an agreed-upon set of such ideals/saints. Such is the task of moral philosophy; such is the task, using Dewey's language, of "a working theory of morals."

The understanding of ideals as saints is not misleading in the way Dewey's wider connections remark is.[26] Furthermore, that understanding is deeply coherent with the pragmatism Dewey shares with James, and it does not yield to any facile, dismissive technique like that of Diggins.

One more issue needs to be addressed in this context. Both Robert Roth and Victor Kestenbaum have argued that pragmatism, and Dewey in particular, needs and even invites an understanding of ideals as transcendent.[27] The thought, however, that ideals are transcendent invites ontological controversy about them, and the main point of understanding ideals as saints is to bring them down to earth, to make life and conversation possible among them, and avoid ontological controversy about them. Where have Roth and Kestenbaum gone wrong? Or have they?

WHY NOT ABSTRACT IDEALS?

The problem both Roth and Kestenbaum detect in Dewey, and generally in the classical pragmatists, is their lack of an adequate account of ideals as resident in the natural world, as, in my earlier way of putting the point, "earthbound." Both Roth and Kestenbaum, however, believe they detect in Dewey at least ambivalence toward the idea that ideals are earthbound. I direct my critical remarks at this point toward the interpretative effort of Roth.[28]

Roth pushes the pragmatists toward an intuition of the self-evidence of ideals that is available, he believes, only from an even more radical attentiveness to the content of experience than he thinks pragmatists embrace. Roth pushes pragmatists to admit that an intense focus on the content and context of experience—a genuinely radical pragmatism, as he puts it— must reveal ideals that are immanently transcendent in that experience itself. Roth puts his point as follows:

> I am now arguing that the pragmatic description of experience as applied to moral theory should be more radical. What it touches upon cautiously and almost covertly should be made more explicit. The ideal that guides moral inquiry is, like any hypothesis, a general and goes beyond specific sense qualities. It can apply without change to any particular set of individual instances, against which these instances can be judged and which is itself a guide and criterion for future instances.[29]

Roth believes that ideals are "abstract generals" and that they are known by intuition. Experience alone Roth believes cannot yield knowledge or intuition of such ideals. Roth believes further that Dewey flirts with recognizing the legitimacy of such intuitions, especially in *Art as Experience.* He quotes this passage: "We are, as it were, introduced into a world beyond this world which is nevertheless the deeper reality of the world in which we live in our ordinary experience."[30] Does this passage, and perhaps others Roth might cite, implicitly recognize that experience, when radically conceived, points beyond or through itself toward an ontological transcendence that must somehow be present in experience? And might Dewey be uncomfortably aware, because of his attunement to the aesthetic dimensions of experience, that his pragmatism might undermine his rejection of ontological transcendence?

Roth sees clearly the alternatives. One must show how the ideals present in experience are available empirically for pragmatist accounts of moral ideals. Or, as Roth insists more generally, that the "generals" present in all experience, regardless of any particular intellectual focus, are likewise available to pragmatists.[31] If one is to avoid endowing humans with unique intellectual faculties—as Roth must intend by recourse to intuition or to the idea of a soul—then one must have an account of ideals as available in experience in such a way as not to require recourse to any special intellectual faculty of intuition.

Again, however, the goal of this chapter is to make explicit a way of conceiving ideals that is consistent with pragmatism as an earthbound, scientific way of thinking that shuns recourse to special intellectual faculties and recourse to abstract, ontologically unique "generals" or ideals.[32] The ideals of experience, the relevant "generals," are the flesh and blood saints who are made over by the idealizing imagination and who become deeply embedded in the cultures and traditions of humanity. Our ideals are our saints.

CONCLUSION

Pragmatism's understanding of ideals enables an account of how our ideals affect us, of how we live with them, negotiate with them, and mediate among them so as to become the persons we are and will be; it offers an account that is descriptively accurate or at least as accurate as any yet suggested. That understanding of ideals is also philosophically innocent in enabling those who have ideals, and who seek to follow and realize those ideals, to avoid philosophical controversy about them. The epistemology and ontology that have stalked Western philosophers at every turn in their thought about value need no longer shadow those individuals in every station and condition of life who hold dear their own values, who live steadfastly by them, and who seek to realize and to propagate them.

Although it avoids classical controversies about how knowledge of ideals is possible and about the ontological status of ideals, pragmatism's account of ideals as fully concrete and fully particular invites further discussion about the issue of moral deliberation. How do our ideals, conceived in the radically particular way suggested here, figure in human deliberation? How do we reason as we make our way to a resolution of morally difficult situations and how do our ideals function in our choice and action? If we think of human ideals in the fully concrete and fully particular ways encouraged by the account of them in this chapter, how do they inform our actions? Do we reason our way to decisions and actions? And if we do reason our way to them, what is the role of our ideals in our reasoning? What, in short, is the relationship between our ideals and our actions, and what cognitive processes exhibit that relationship?

NOTES

This chapter was originally published as "Pragmatism's Ideals," *Contemporary Pragmatism* 6, no. 1 (2009). Used by permission of the publisher.

1. William James, *The Varieties of Religious Experience* (New York: Penguin Books, 1985), 259–378; LW7:262–84.

2. James, *Varieties*, 374.

3. James, *Varieties*, 358.

4. James, *Varieties*, 376.

5. These are some of the characters who appear in James's lectures, many in the lectures on saintliness.

6. One might suggest plausibly that Plato's *Republic* does offer a picture of justice rather than a discursive analysis of the concept of justice. In a way, this point is correct. However, one does have the sense that Plato's work generally seeks discursive and theoretical precision about concepts rather than "pictures" of them.

7. LW7:275.

8. For Dewey's account of what makes a situation of choice a situation of *moral* choice, see LW7:274.

9. John Dewey, *A Common Faith* (New Haven, Conn.: Yale University Press, 1934), 41.

10. Robert J. Roth, *Radical Pragmatism: An Alternative* (New York: Fordham University Press, 1998); Victor Kestenbaum, *The Grace and the Severity of the Ideal* (Chicago: University of Chicago Press, 2003).

11. Douglas Anderson's essay, "Peirce: Ethics and the Conduct of Life," in *Classical American Pragmatism: Its Contemporary Vitality*, ed. Sandra Rosenthal, Carl R. Hausman, and Douglas R. Anderson (Urbana: University of Illinois Press, 1999),

137–45, sees Peirce to sympathize at least with Roth's insistence on the ubiquity of "generals" in thought and also in ethical inquiry; see especially 144.

12. Robert Roth's perspective about what I have called the "ontological pregnancy" of pragmatism, and especially of Dewey, he shares with Victor Kestenbaum. For views that reinforce Roth's perspective and conflict with my own, see *Grace and Severity*, 118–20.

13. Dewey makes this suggestion in *Ethics* (LW7:212).

14. Plato's *Euthyphro* is a perfect classical source for the apparent naturalness of these kinds of questions in philosophy.

15. LW7:258.

16. See Stuart Rosenbaum, "Morality and Religion: Why Not Pragmatism," *Pragmatism and Religion: Classical Sources and Contemporary Essays*, ed. Stuart Rosenbaum (Urbana: University of Illinois Press, 2003).

17. See the editorial by Philip Lawlor, "A Life of Purity," *Wall Street Journal*, September 8, 1997. Lawlor's explanation of the emotional response to Mother Teresa—that she "exemplified purity"—is completely characteristic of the usual Platonist tendency of thought about value.

18. James Stephenson, *The Language of the Land: Living among a Stone-Age People in Africa* (New York: St. Martin's Press, 2000). I would attempt a detailed account of how the Hadzabe culture recognizes its saints and heroes in ways not typically Western, but I think reading Stephenson's account while having in mind a pragmatist understanding of ideals as I have presented it here has power I cannot hope to capture in a secondary account. I commend the book, especially to Western philosophers.

19. LW7:212.

20. Gregory Pappas is aware that a proper understanding of Dewey's moral views must take account of this "already present" character of ideals in situations requiring moral deliberation, and that ideals do not arrive in our worlds as a function solely of future projection. Pappas, however, says little about how those ideals are already present in situations of moral deliberation. He says, "To be sure, principles, ideals, and habits are instrumentalities that are available to a moral agent in such a situation. In order to transform a morally problematic situation into one that is determinative, however, these tools become a part of the concrete qualitative complexity of the situation." See Gregory Pappas, "Dewey's Ethics: Morality as Experience," *Reading Dewey: Interpretations for a Postmodern Generation*, ed. Larry Hickman (Bloomington: Indiana University Press, 1998), 114. Recognizing the already present character of ideals in morally significant situations, as Pappas does, does not help understand how ideals are already present in those situations.

21. John Patrick Diggins, *The Promise of Pragmatism* (Chicago: University of Chicago Press, 1994), 20.

22. Diggins, *Promise of Pragmatism*, 21.

23. See, for example, Louis Menand's *The Metaphysical Club: A Story of Ideas in America* (New York: Farrar, Straus & Giroux, 2001). See also Allen Guelzo's review of Menand's book in *Harvard Divinity Bulletin* 30, no. 4 (Spring 2002): 35–36; Guelzo quotes approvingly Menand's caustic and unperceptive remark, "Pragmatism explains everything about ideas except why a person would be willing to die for one."

24. I leave aside here what I think of as intellectually irresponsible assessments of pragmatism that see it simply as American business practice gone intellectual. Bertrand Russell's assessment of pragmatism typifies the harshest of this kind of response, but others that respond more negatively than careful consideration should warrant include John Patrick Diggins, *The Promise of Pragmatism*; Louis Menand, *The Metaphysical Club*; and Bruce Kuklick, *A History of Philosophy in America* (Oxford: Clarendon Press, 2001).

25. This use of "thick" and "thin" should be intuitively obvious. For a comparable usage, see Kwame Anthony Appiah, *Cosmopolitanism: Ethics in a World of Strangers* (New York: W. W. Norton, 2006), 46–47.

26. Probably I should say somewhere explicitly, though I believe I made it clear earlier in this chapter, that the relevant sense of "saint" does not require any official canonization by any particular institutional body, the Catholic Church for example; saints are those individuals who are revered within particular communities, whether or not they have any "official status" in their communities. John Wayne might serve as an example for many Americans; Martin Luther King Jr. would also serve.

27. See note 10 for these sources.

28. Kestenbaum's reading of Dewey is more subtle and richer than any other scholarly treatment of Dewey's thought about value I have seen, and Kestenbaum fully appreciates Dewey's respect for experience. I cannot deal with Kestenbaum's subtle treatment of Dewey here. What I can say apart from the elaborate effort that would be required to deal adequately with Kestenbaum's treatment of transcendence in Dewey is that I do not believe he has worked through the suggestions I make here that ideals are saints, and that as saints they are able to do all the worldly work that ideals need to do. Since I do not believe I can deal adequately here with the richness of Kestenbaum's treatment of Dewey, I leave that task for another occasion. I do believe, however, that thinking of ideals as saints brings James and Dewey, as well as other pragmatists, together in a happily concrete way that is fully coherent with their intellectual ambitions as earthbound idealists.

29. Roth, *Radical Pragmatism*, 45.

30. LW10:199.

31. Roth, *Radical Pragmatism*, 46.

32. Roth, *Radical Pragmatism*, 47.

6

—w—

Deliberation

We deliberate when we do not know what to do. Our impulses are at odds with one another or our habits are in conflict and we do not see a clear way into our future. We want that chocolate ice cream cone, but we know we are going to step onto the weight scale in the morning; we want that red sports car, but we know we have to balance our income and our expenses; we oppose abortion, but our thirteen-year-old daughter has been raped and is pregnant; we hate politics, but we have the responsibility of a citizen to vote; and so on indefinitely. These are occasions of deliberation. Every such occasion requires that we exert intelligence more strenuously than when we do not face such conflicts. The means by which we get through these situations into our future is deliberation. When we do something that closes off other possibilities we make a choice; the process that leads to our choice is deliberation.

One problem of philosophical writing about deliberation is that it tends to focus on a narrow range of contexts in which deliberation occurs. The commitment to the priority of the particular that characterizes pragmatism, much evident in the previous chapter, offers little hope for significant conceptual generality about deliberation. In fact, widening one's focus to include a sufficient variety of contexts for deliberation undermines the effort to achieve any full theory of deliberation. In what follows, I argue for this point by examining modest contexts requiring deliberation and then consider a different range of contexts in which more subtle deliberation appears. This subtle deliberation may have consequences for large understandings of what is significant for human communities, but it eludes philosophical theory aimed at conceptual generalizations.

CONTEXTS FOR BEING DELIBERATE

The first thing to say about deliberation is that it is *being deliberate*; it is the process by which one decides what to do in a problem situation. Consider a modest problem context that disables normal patterns of activity. If I am accustomed to stumbling into my kitchen at four in the morning to make coffee, I am helped through my bleariness by habits of behavior that normally see me to alert functioning. Any number of things might interrupt my normal habits. The electricity might be out because of a recent thunderstorm; the carafe might break into many pieces as I fill it in the kitchen sink; a strange cat, having found its way through the cat door, might be curled up on the kitchen rug; or a copperhead might have found its way through the cat door. Such unusual events are rare as I hope they continue to be. Nevertheless, these or similar unexpected events find their way into everyday life and require deliberation.[1]

These unusual situations are occasions requiring that one *be deliberate* about one's action; they are occasions for deliberation, situations in which one does not rely on habitual responses. One must choose among an indefinite number of possibilities in order to effect a desirable outcome, and one's choice depends on resources at one's disposal as well as on one's resourcefulness. If one is accustomed to dealing with animals, for example, then one has resources for facing the cat or the copperhead that are unavailable to those who have no experience with animals; if one is a zookeeper by trade, then one has an increased array of resources and heightened resourcefulness for facing those animals; if one is allergic to cat hair or if one has a phobia of snakes, then one has diminished resourcefulness. Any individual in a situation requiring deliberation brings a specific set of resources, as well as specific resourcefulness, to that situation. This particularity of available resources and individual resourcefulness characterizes every situation requiring deliberation.

Pragmatism acknowledges and embraces this particularity in situations requiring deliberation. When philosophers seek to understand practical reasoning theoretically, they diminish the possibility of recognizing the particularity of such occasions. Insofar as philosophers do not acknowledge this particularity they do not acknowledge the phenomenology of deliberation.[2] Pragmatism acknowledges the specific and individual dimensions of deliberation situations.

Even Todd Lekan, committed as he is to a pragmatist understanding of deliberation, does not fully embrace the particularity of deliberation situations. Lekan seeks to "schematize the process of practical deliberation" to capture in full generality what happens on occasions of deliberation. Lekan's account of the general schema for deliberation is adequate to some situations requiring deliberation but to many such situations it is not. Furthermore, Lekan's account unintentionally distorts our understanding of deliberation by seeking more system than our considered understanding allows. The example that undergirds his account of his general schema is Jane Addams's deliberation that led to her founding of Hull House, a deliberative event that consumed two years of her life.[3] When one applies Lekan's account of the general model for deliberative events to the example of wandering blearily into the kitchen at four in the morning and finding a strange cat or a copperhead, his account seems to miss the specific urgency of the situation. What do I have *here*? What can I do *now*? *Who* might help me? Such questions frequently take on urgency when one is deliberating, urgency so specific that it eludes the schema Lekan finds in Jane Addams's decision. Another limitation of Lekan's schema for deliberative events is that it misses deliberations with a different kind of urgency from the urgency of potentially explosive situations involving cats or copperheads; it does not acknowledge the fact that urgency comes in many different varieties. An attorney may practice successfully as a well-respected member of the legal profession for twenty years, after which a nagging dissatisfaction may yield a sudden retirement and an application to a school of divinity; this kind of urgency is visible only to the attorney and is different from the urgency that motivated Addams's turn toward Hull House.[4]

Situations requiring deliberation are highly particular. Some such situations appear to fit Lekan's schema for deliberation and some do not. Pragmatists are committed to saying the useful things they can about deliberation, but they are committed primarily to respecting the phenomenology of deliberation. One general thing that is appropriate to say about deliberation, because it is phenomenologically accurate, is that deliberation happens when one's habitual patterns of activity are interrupted in some way, either by external events or by some internal conflict in an agent's own habitual patterns of activity. Beyond this general observation, however, one may find little of useful generality to assert about situations requiring deliberation.

I also said that Lekan's model unintentionally distorts our understanding of the phenomena of deliberation. Seeing how his model distorts our understanding of deliberation requires a quick look at the model itself.

There are six dimensions in Lekan's model of deliberative events:

1. There is an indeterminate situation, including a felt sense of trouble due to a failure of habits.
2. There is a preliminary interpretation of the problem, including a view of what important goods and evils are at issue.
3. Action plans are created that attempt to take account of the important goods and evils at issue.

4. These action plans are tested in imaginative trials.
5. The most promising plan is tested in actions bringing about change in the situation.
6. These steps can be repeated by others or used to explain to others what was learned.[5]

As I noted, this model for deliberative events seems a vague general fit for many occasions requiring deliberation. What it distorts, however, is the phenomenal situation of the individual doing the deliberating. To put the point in the way Dewey put a similar point in his early essay, "The Reflex Arc Concept in Psychology," the "response is not merely *to* the stimulus; it is *into* it." Likewise, one deliberates or responds *into* the situation requiring deliberation. To represent deliberation situations in the general schematic way Lekan does misses the "into" of the deliberation situation; it misses the fact that one is fully engaged in the development of a problematic situation in order to secure a favorable outcome. I think it is fair to say about Lekan's model for deliberative events approximately the same thing Dewey says in his 1896 essay about the reflex arc concept in psychology, that it fails to account for the "continual reconstitution" of the problem situation in virtue of one's engagement with it. Even in Jane Addams's case, the two-year "deliberative event" that eventuated in her founding of Hull House is not helpfully illuminated by mentioning, for example, dimension (3) of Lekan's model that says, "Action plans are created that attempt to take account of the important goods and evils at issue." Jane Addams is fully engaged in the process of constituting herself in response to pressures in her situation, pressures that are not only "external" in her environment but also "internal" to her. (This use of "external" and "internal" is in scare quotes because it gives too much away to a representation of Addams's deliberation situation that is coherent with Lekan's representation of it; the reality of the situation phenomenologically is that Addams is fully engaged, embedded, in her deliberation situation. She is deliberating *into* it, to use Dewey's way of putting it.) Lekan's general schema for what he calls deliberative events distorts this basic fact about deliberation situations.

What can one usefully say about how one deliberates?

DELIBERATION AS IMAGINATIVE REHEARSAL

A passage from Dewey's *Ethics* cited in the previous chapter serves well as a starting point for further discussion.

Deliberation is actually an imaginative rehearsal of various courses of conduct. We give way, in our mind, to some impulse; we try, in our mind, some plan. Following its career through various steps, we find ourselves in imagination in the presence of the consequences that would follow; and as we then like and approve, or dislike and disapprove, these consequences, we find the original impulse or plan good or bad. Deliberation is dramatic and active, not mathematical and impersonal; and hence it has the intuitive, the direct factor in it.[6]

As Dewey puts it, deliberation is imaginative rehearsal and is dramatic and active. Deliberation is seeing possibilities for problem situations and trying out possibilities before acting in accord with them. If a copperhead is on my kitchen floor at four in the morning, my dramatic rehearsal is sudden and urgent; it involves a quick survey of resources and a projection in imagination about how to employ those resources to achieve a successful outcome. My dramatic rehearsal under these circumstances also has, as Dewey puts it, "the intuitive, the direct factor in it"; my resourcefulness in seeing and employing available resources is beyond possibility of finding algorithm or even general system in it. My dramatic rehearsal is irreducibly idiomatic. (To exploit Dewey's way of speaking, I deliberate *into* situations, and it is *I* who so deliberates.) All dramatic rehearsal is irreducibly idiomatic.

The outcome I desire in all situations, and especially in such sudden and urgent situations, is a function of who I am in many different ways. Do I love animals? Do I have an irrational fear of snakes? Am I a biologist with intimate knowledge of snakes and their role in maintaining ecological balance? Am I a philosopher who has argued in favor of animal rights? Am I a farmer accustomed to dispatching all snakes as dangers to baby chicks? Who I am in all of my specific characters and habits is present in all of my deliberations, decisions, and actions, from the most urgent and pressing to the least so, from the copperhead in the kitchen situation to a situation of Addams-like dissatisfaction with current professional prospects.

To say that favorable outcomes are functions of the agents who inhabit the worlds in which deliberation situations occur is only roughly to agree with currently fashionable ways of speaking philosophically about such situations; it is to say that what one does is roughly a function of one's beliefs and desires, as well as a function of the course of life that has brought one to the specific beliefs and desires with which one confronts a deliberation situation. To agree even roughly with this way of speaking philosophically about such situations, however, is not to embrace the typical bifurcation of persons into rational parts and emotional parts, into reason and passion.

BELIEFS AND DESIRES

A prominent and widely accepted view among pragmatists, following Charles Peirce, is that beliefs are habits of action.[7] To think of beliefs as habits of action is to think of them as fully embedded in individual character and personality. One's beliefs are as fully individual as are one's habits; they are expressions of a particular individuality as distinctively as are one's physical features. Just as no two people have exactly the same physical features, so no two people have exactly the same beliefs when these are understood as habits of action. One's habits are as specific and individual as any other dimensions of character and personality. To be sure, people do share vaguely general tendencies of behavior. We say, for example, that some people are abstemious, and when we say this we are referencing a vague tendency toward self-depriving behavior that comes in as many varieties as do the many individuals who bear the "family resemblance" to one another that enables that vague generalization about their tendencies of behavior.[8] To think, when asserting that some people are abstemious, that we are referencing a *characteristic* of behavior, an *item* those particular people share in common and is missing from other people is to think in a misleading way about human behavior. To speak of someone being abstemious is to speak loosely and vaguely, but usefully, about that person's habits. So it is with other tendencies of character and personality. Being reliable, ostentatious, garrulous, just, shy, extroverted, and so on are indefinite tendencies of myriad and subtle nuance, tendencies only vaguely and imprecisely captured by the general terms that point vaguely in their directions.[9]

To think of beliefs as habits of action is to think of beliefs also as vague general tendencies that may exhibit an indefinite range of nuance in individuals' characters and personalities. This pragmatist way of thinking about belief is definitively different from traditional ways of thinking about belief as a psychological relation to an intentional content or a proposition. Just as abstemiousness is not a single character that is present in all who are abstemious, so believing, say, that God exists is also not a single state of relatedness to a single proposition or intentional content. As abstemiousness is a vaguely observational tendency of action, so believing that God exists is likewise a vaguely observational tendency of action, as is believing that Roosevelt is president, believing that there are quarks, believing in liberty and equality, and so on for the various attributions of belief we typically make.

Once one thinks of beliefs as habits of action, then one is relieved from typical philosophical problems about the nature of belief, the nature of justification, and the nature of the relatedness to intentional content that is belief as opposed to the different sort of relatedness to intentional content that is hope, and so on. Thinking of beliefs in this pragmatist way changes their philosophical significance. The epistemological and ontological worries that follow other conceptions of belief disappear in pragmatism.

The same is true also of desire or passion, the other side of the traditional bifurcation between reason and passion. For pragmatists, desires like beliefs are habits of action, and desires like beliefs come in highly specific and particular versions that have roots in individual character and personality. To want to live in the city, for example, is as various a want as the people who have it; it is a vaguely specifiable tendency of action as various as the characters and personalities who have it. Thinking of desires and beliefs as habits of action systematically undermines traditional philosophical theory about belief and desire.

For pragmatists, no longer is the problem of reconciling persons' rational beliefs with their recalcitrant passions a philosophical issue. That particular problem, along with others, is rooted in a particular historical understanding of believing and desiring. Once one sees that thinking of beliefs and desires as habits of action is more useful than thinking of them as attitudes toward propositions, then one sees that philosophical concern about beliefs and desires may also change. The concern to have properly rational, or justified, beliefs may yield to a concern to have and engender constructive beliefs; the concern to find a way to get desires to submit to rational belief may yield to the concern to have and engender constructive desires. Philosophical concern may focus on the personal, family, and community phenomena that typically produce constructive habits of desiring and believing.

Some philosophers are accustomed to seeking conceptually general accounts of practical reason and to relying as they do so on concepts of belief and desire as distinct kinds of psychological relation to propositions, and they may object to the Peircean understanding of belief and desire; they may ask, for example, "Which of these understandings of belief and desire is correct?" These philosophers may seek philosophical justification for the pragmatist suggestion that they should abandon the concept of belief as a psychological attitude toward a proposition. The main problem with joining their search for a philosophical justification of one understanding of belief in preference to the other is that joining their quest requires relying on their own understanding of belief. One cannot try to answer the question of which understanding of belief is correct without begging the question in favor of a preferred account.

What might such circular, ineffectual dialectic look like? Such dialectic might take many forms, but here is a possibility for how it might begin: "You say that a belief is a habit of action. If you say so, then you must have a reason, an argument, for thinking so. Since we care for truth as much as you do, we ask that you produce this argument so that we may understand and assess it. If your argument is successful, then we will admit what you urge, that beliefs are habits of action; if your argument is unsuccessful, then we will urge that you admit your mistake and give up your mistaken understanding about belief." Notice that this generous, apparently even deferential, offer to engage in neutral dialectic to adjudicate a disagreement cannot be taken up without granting the conclusion this side of the dispute defends, the conclusion that beliefs are a particular psychological attitude toward propositions. If pragmatists accept the invitation to present an argument in favor of their view that beliefs are habits of action, they may do so only by themselves assuming the *proposition* that beliefs are habits of action, a proposition toward which they must claim to take the appropriate psychological attitude. But pragmatists do not believe propositions are required to understand phenomena of belief, so they must refuse to argue in defense of their account of belief. Pragmatists must decline the invitation to engage in this circular dialectic that is supposed to show them the mistake in their thought about belief. Pragmatists can offer reasons why their understanding of belief is preferable to the propositional understanding of belief, but these reasons they must not attempt to formulate in an argumentative effort to justify their account.

What are pragmatists' reasons for accepting the idea that beliefs are habits of action? A key reason is pragmatists' embrace of the historicity of all human phenomena. Not only are political and social institutions and practices rooted in contingencies of history and culture, but so too are obvious principles of thought. The things that seem most obvious and patently true—even things thought of as a priori—seem so because of cultural conditions within which such truths achieve their unquestioned status. Nothing, not even the most patently obvious truth, escapes the web of contingency that is human history and culture.[10]

Another reason for accepting the idea that beliefs are habits of action is that idea's coherence with a Darwinian understanding of humans and their larger environments. Part of this Darwinian understanding is the commitment to showing how it is possible to see even the minutest details of human intellectual history in genealogical perspective. In his Gifford Lectures, *The Quest for Certainty*, Dewey shows in subtle detail how most of the history of intellectual concerns we think of as Western philosophy—concerns with justification, justice, goodness, rightness, and generally with "finding a place for value in a world of fact"—have explanatory roots in a larger cultural context. Contemporary thinkers such as Richard Rorty, John McDermott, Hilary Putnam, and others take for granted this pragmatist understanding that all human phenomena have explanations in human need and interest as these find expression in culture and history.

These broadly Darwinian perspectives are the most significant larger context in which pragmatists' commitment to understanding beliefs as habits of action becomes vital to their wider philosophical perspectives. The net effect of the Peircean understanding of beliefs, along with its associated philosophical perspectives, is to undermine the idea that belief and desire are appropriate tools for understanding choice and action. A conceptual turn toward the ideas of habit, resourcefulness, imagination, and creativity as underlying choice and action opens toward more constructive agendas that are more significant for building a better future, creating more cohesive understandings of the tasks of being human in an uncertain world, and creating a more coherent human community. Thinking about habits and about how we come to have them turns intellectual effort toward tasks different from the apologetic tasks characteristic of the Anglo-European philosophical tradition. In the context of pragmatism, concerns for how to achieve growth as individuals and as communities become central to our intellectual effort. How to become who we might more ideally be takes precedence over the traditional philosophical tasks of showing that humans *already are* unique loci of moral and religious value.

Habits, especially concern about how to acquire desirable habits and how to engender them in families and communities, must become a central focus of our intellectual lives. This change in the focus of our intellectual lives brings to the fore issues about where our habits come from, what social factors engender them, and how we may put in place practices that enable wider realization of more desirable habits. These issues are at the forefront of broadly scientific approaches to psychology and culture; they are issues for psychologists, sociologists, historians, and political scientists; but given the pragmatist understanding of beliefs and desires, they are issues also for philosophers. As already noted, contemporaries such as Richard Rorty, Hilary Putnam, and John McDermott have turned their efforts in this direction.

Intensifying this contrast between the reason-and-desire approach to action and choice and a pragmatist approach may be useful in clarifying the most significant differences between Anglo-European analytic philosophers and American pragmatists about deliberation.

BELIEF, DESIRE, AND REASON VERSUS HABIT, IMAGINATION, AND CREATIVITY

The opposition between reason and desire has traditionally been inseparable from moral philosophy. The opposition between Hume and Kant on the relation between reason and the passions typifies customary understandings of the tension between these parts of the psyche.[11] What likely produces this tension between reason and passion within human psyches is the idea of justification. The idea of *justifying* one's behavior and beliefs to anyone regardless of their inclinations or customs, or to an impartial observer, has appeared to require commitment to following reason in spite of inclination or in spite of customary expectation. Bernard Williams holds Socrates generally responsible for this rational, justification-seeking perspective, and captures its independence of passion and custom, its intended impartiality and universality, this way:

> For morality, the ethical constituency is always the same: the universal constituency. An allegiance to a smaller group, the loyalties to family or country, would have to be justified from the outside inward, by an argument that explained how it was a good thing that people should have allegiances that were less than universal.[12]

The ideas of justification and universality Williams sees as Socrates' tools for overcoming custom and tradition.[13] Although Williams is not committed to that Socratic tradition as intensely as many philosophers, another contemporary philosopher who is so committed to it, and who also appears in chapter 3 above, is Marcus Singer. The concluding paragraph of his already cited presidential address is unequivocal.

> [T]he ideal of rational morality has been made available to us only through the work of philosophers, and practically every element in the idea is due to this on-going, even sacred tradition. Without reflective thought on morality, which is moral philosophy whether practiced by professed philosophers or not, there would certainly have been morality, but there would have been no improvements in morality, hence no moral progress—this is true even though some instances of moral progress have been won only at immense costs in blood and pain. . . . It is the tradition of moral philosophy, and the practice of morality, that has made the idea of rational morality possible and available. We are the present beneficiaries of this work, often carried on in great agony of spirit, and we must also regard ourselves as carrying on a tradition which . . . will be in substance somewhat different . . . for our having assumed this responsibility. . . . I cannot think of any commitment or any calling that is higher, more noble, more exhilarating, or more important.[14]

The spirit of moral philosophy, centered around the ideas of universality and justification, and assuming a psyche divided between reason and passion, is captured almost perfectly in Singer's enthusiastic conclusion. John Dewey's assessment of this same tradition is less sanguine. According to Dewey, Western moral theorists have typically

> marked off Moral Reason from thought and reasoning as they show themselves in ordinary life and in science. They have erected a unique faculty

whose sole office is to make us aware of duty and of its imperatively rightful authority over conduct. The moralists who have insisted upon the identity of the Good with ends of desire have, on the contrary, made knowledge, in the sense of insight into the ends which bring enduring satisfaction, the supreme thing in conduct. . . . And yet, according to Plato, this assured insight into the true End and Good implies a kind of rationality which is radically different from that involved in the ordinary affairs of life. It can be directly attained only by the few who are gifted with those peculiar qualities which enable them to rise to metaphysical understanding of the ultimate constitution of the universe; others must take it on faith or as it is embodied, in a derived way, in laws and institutions.[15]

For Marcus Singer, the idea of a rational morality, morality as usually understood within philosophy, is a sacred tradition for everyone. For Dewey, that same idea is far removed from everyday life and is hence of little use. Dewey finds Western theoretical morality a limited achievement of a small number of people. Reflective morality, as Dewey conceives it, is available to all whether or not they have the desire or competence to read and understand Aristotle, Spinoza, Kant, Bentham, or Mill. These giants of philosophy Dewey sees as working in the same remote sphere of the intellect as theoretical physicists. Working men and women, in order to have satisfying and virtuous lives, need no more appreciate their work than they need appreciate the work of Galileo, Newton, Heisenberg, Einstein, Stephen Hawking, or Steven Weinberg in order to have competent interactions with their physical environment. Reflective morality is the province of everyone, but theoretical morality is no more the province of everyone than is theoretical physics. Removing philosophical theory about morality from the center of reflective thinking about how to live displaces also the ideas of justification and of the conflict between reason and passion.[16]

Another way of putting this point is to say that removing the idea of justification from the center of thought about morality removes also the need to make reason dominant over passion. Removing justification from the center removes also the need for a distinction between reason and desire as separate faculties that must somehow find reconciliation within every personality. Human deliberation need not involve justifying oneself to anybody or a conflict between reason and passion. Making these pragmatist moves in thinking about deliberation situations means bringing to the fore the more useful ideas of habit, imagination, and creativity.

One noteworthy difference is that strategies of deliberation become widely available and are no longer the domain of those who are intellectually talented. Another difference is that individual character and habit become central to individuals' responses in deliberation situations. Consideration of this second difference I leave to the chapter on moral education.

The first difference I discuss and illustrate more extensively in what follows. Although my opening examples in this chapter—the strange cat or the copperhead in my kitchen—make clear the particularity of deliberation situations and the idiomatic character of resources and resourcefulness, they do not capture the drama of the situations philosophers typically focus on when they think about deliberation. Consider the situation of a single woman who is pregnant in spite of her plans for a demanding career; a young homosexual who is tempted toward a Christian cure for his homosexuality; a young husband who is attracted to his secretary; and so on for myriad situations requiring decision. Thinking about such situations illuminates significant differences between conventional philosophical ways of dealing with them and a pragmatist way of dealing with them.

Two philosophers whose thought is appropriate for illuminating these differences are Alasdair MacIntyre, a Thomist who respects reason and believes rational argument is, and should be, central to all deliberation, and John Dewey, the pragmatist who inspires the view defended here.

ALASDAIR MACINTYRE,
THOMIST, VERSUS JOHN DEWEY, PRAGMATIST

Dewey and MacIntyre diverge decisively about what moral deliberation is and what it should be. MacIntyre retains the ideal of rational, discursive argumentation as inseparable from the moral deliberation that brings a satisfying and virtuous life, even though he rejects the embodiment of that style of thought in most modern and contemporary moral theory. MacIntyre believes that only rational thought, thought rooted in the most reliable moral theorizing of one's tradition, can supply appropriate guidance. MacIntyre sees living well as the project of appropriating rationally in one's own life the moral principles hammered out in the history of one's intellectual tradition. Thus, according to MacIntyre, the better one reasons the better one deals with situations that require moral deliberation. In remarking about Plato, Aristotle, and Aquinas, MacIntyre notes that

> [f]or them, of course, every moral agent no matter how plain a person is at least an incipient theorist, and the practical knowledge of the mature good person has a crucial theoretical component; it is for this reason that both Aristotle and Aquinas agree that we study philosophical ethics, not only for the sake of theoretical goals, but so as ourselves to become good.[17]

Dewey, in contrast, sees theoretical ethics and its patterns of discursive argumentation as largely irrelevant to making appropriate decisions.[18]

Thus, according to Dewey, Lekan's Jane Addams, Thomas Hardy's Gabriel Oak, and the Jane Doe of *Ms.* magazine, no matter how ignorant of moral theory they may be and no matter how inept at discursive argumentation they may be, may still deliberate well and live virtuous lives. Such ordinary people need not be theorists, nor need they be incipient theorists; they must, in Dewey's perspective, be imaginative and creative. They must be autonomous in using their imaginative skills, while still respecting their traditions, and they must seek imaginatively to bring out of their present a better realization of the values that define them and their hopes for a better future.

Specific decisions individuals make vary as good or bad according to the vitality of their deliberative skills. The more fertile are individuals' imaginations, the more successful are their moral deliberations. Dewey thinks of moral deliberation as a matter of following possibilities in imagination, following them so that they can be appreciated and understood while they remain possibilities. Unlike actual consequences, one need not shoulder the burden of consequences that are merely possible.

The contrast between these two perspectives becomes obvious in application to a specific morally difficult situation. Consider a young woman who must decide what to do about an unintended, unwanted pregnancy. Should she continue the pregnancy or get an abortion? On MacIntyre's account, what she should do is to seek the most reasonable premises bearing on her decision, those found through previous and ongoing community dialectic to be the most reliable, and then she must apply those premises in her own life. (Is the fetus a person, deserving of life in the same way she and others are persons deserving of life? What kinds of circumstances legitimately warrant depriving persons of their lives and futures? Do such circumstances obtain in this case of her unintended pregnancy? And so on.) The quality of the young woman's moral decision is a function both of her familiarity with community traditions and debates, and also of her own facility with techniques of rational dialectic. The better she reasons her way through the complexities of her moral tradition, the better she lives her life, for her life is a continuing series of such decisions.

On Dewey's account of deliberation, the young woman looks concretely into her future, and into the futures of those affected by her decision. She projects imaginatively, given her understanding of herself and her communities, the consequences of choosing one alternative over another. (How might bringing this fetus to term affect her, given her aspirations, hopes, and dreams? Will she be able to continue her education toward a career in medicine? Is her mother or sister competent or willing to share crucial responsibilities? Is there sufficient wealth to employ a nanny? Does the father love her? Is he responsible? Would she want to bear and bring to maturity the child of *that* man? How might her aborting detrimentally affect her self-image? How might her family, or her church community, be affected by what she chooses? And so on.) Dewey's commitment to this imaginative style of deliberation is evident throughout his work.

Imagination, creativity, and habit are central to a pragmatist understanding of deliberation. If I confront a copperhead on my kitchen floor at four in the morning; if I am Jane Addams dissatisfied with the course of my life; if I am an attorney who thinks there must be more meaningful work; or if I am a young woman unexpectedly and unfortunately pregnant—in all of these cases my being deliberate involves *as a matter of fact* all the resources of imagination and creativity I can muster. Such situations almost never involve resort to discursive argumentation. The exception to this claim is usually a resort to authorities whom those doing the deliberating think may be better situated than they are to make the relevant choices; in this kind of case, those doing the deliberating are reasoning discursively, inductively, from the authority of those to whom they appeal. Those who reason from authority do not thereby become the incipient moral theorists MacIntyre intends them to be; instead, they choose to surrender their autonomy to another they believe better qualified than themselves to decide what they ought to do.

Worth emphasizing again is the fact that *who one is* decisively determines how one negotiates every deliberative situation, from an urgent snap-decision situation to a more extended context for choice. And who one is, for pragmatists, is a matter of the web of habits that have come together through the defining interactions that have produced one's present self. Dewey remarks, "The essence of habit is an acquired predisposition to *ways* or modes of response."[19] Every detail of one's capacity to respond in decision situations is formed in one's social interactions—in family; in church, synagogue, or mosque; in school; in one's exposures (or lack thereof) to music, literature, history, and philosophy; and through all the myriad agencies of culture. Who one is, as one is shaped by all these contexts, defines one's abilities to confront situations of choice and action. Whether or not one is able to deal successfully with a copperhead-in-the-kitchen situation or with a situation of dissatisfaction about one's career prospects is a complex function of every detail of one's character.

Furthermore, one's character is in continual process of development in interactions with all of these agencies of culture. One becomes not who one already is but one becomes, perhaps paradoxically, who one becomes in consequence of these myriad interactions in which one is always an active participant. The seeming paradox in this claim may be mitigated by recourse to Dewey's way of expressing it.

We arrive at true conceptions of motivation and interest only by the recognition that selfhood (except as it has encased itself in a shell of routine) is in process of making, and that any self is capable of including within itself a number of inconsistent selves, of unharmonized dispositions. . . . Inconsistencies and shiftings in character are the commonest things in experience. Only the hold of a traditional conception of the singleness and simplicity of soul and self blinds us to perceiving what they mean: the relative fluidity and diversity of the constituents of selfhood. There is no one ready-made self behind activities. There are complex, unstable, opposing attitudes, habits, impulses which gradually come to terms with one another, and assume a certain consistency of configuration, even though only by means of a distribution of inconsistencies which keeps them in water-tight compartments, giving them separate turns or tricks in action.[20]

This developmental idea of selves is integral to pragmatism's understanding of belief and desire. Thinking of beliefs and desires as habits of action is thinking of them as more integral to selves, as more constitutive of selves, than they appear in typical philosophical thought about belief and action. For pragmatists, as for Continental existentialists, there are no ways to get at one's character or growth possibilities than by careful inquiry into one's tendencies, habits, and impulses, into the developmental history of those elements of character and their potentials for further development. For pragmatists, these dimensions of character and personality are intractably idiomatic; and the ways they might become less than idiomatic are themselves a function of culturally rooted tendencies, habits, and impulses.

Pragmatists' understanding of selves and actions are scientific understandings, in the sense of "scientific" in which William James distinguishes science from philosophy.[21] For this scientific understanding, one must become sensitive to what one seeks to understand, and attaining this sensitivity requires skepticism toward perspectives that normally constrain sensitivity. Hence, one must set aside the issues of justification, dualism, the nature of belief and desire, as well as other theories that limit understandings of these issues. Transcending typical philosophical issues and positions enables the sensitivity to phenomena required for an adequate scientific understanding of selves and actions, of beliefs and desires.

Transcending standard alternatives about action and deliberation makes possible full recognition of the facts about deliberation situations. In particular, one becomes able to recognize the idiomatic character of individuals' deliberations. One's resources and resourcefulness are distinctively individual, as are one's beliefs, desires, and character; these things are complex functions of one's native constitution and environments. One's ability to deploy imagination in being deliberate depends in complex ways on such things as one's parents, whether one lives with both rather than only with one, one's siblings and how many one has, what their gender is, and the temporal gap between oneself and them, the character of one's communities, the details of one's exposure to various media, and on one's literary, musical, and scientific training, as well as on many other dimensions of one's history. Recognizing the distinctive individuality of responses in deliberation situations is the beginning of wisdom in thinking about human action.

Failure to recognize the idiomatic character of possibilities for individual response in problem situations may encourage too theoretically systematic an account of deliberation. Even some thinkers who have great respect for the pragmatist tradition of philosophy err in giving too systematic an account, or too philosophical an account (in James's understanding of philosophy noted earlier), of deliberation and action. Todd Lekan appeared earlier as one who erred in just this way in his too systematic account of deliberation. Others who err in a similar way are Mark Johnson and Thomas Alexander. Consider their account of moral theory.

IMAGINATION

John Dewey acknowledges the centrality of imaginative projection in situations requiring deliberation. The passage from his 1932 *Ethics* cited above is representative of his thought about deliberation. The following passage from *Human Nature and Conduct* elaborates ten years earlier the same thematic content.

> [T]he thing actually at stake in any serious deliberation is not a difference of quantity, but what kind of person one is to become, what sort of self is in the making, what kind of a world is in the making. This is plain enough in those crucial decisions where the course of life is thrown into widely different channels, where the pattern of life is rendered different and diversely dyed according as this alternative or that is chosen.[22]

This passage captures precisely what is at stake in the lives of Jane Addams, Gabriel Oak, and Jane Doe. The significant forces in their moral lives are, on one hand, environing conventions, and on the other, their personal goals. The dialectic between these two forces is the anvil on which they hammer out their futures. Precisely how this dialectic works toward a conclusion in their lives is obscure. The same dialectic works toward unique conclusions in the lives of all individuals. The wealth of diversity among humanity in the way that dialectic works yields almost unlimited resources for human creativity. According to Dewey, that wealth of diversity is the locus of reflective activity that creates selves, families,

and communities. Such creations of futures yet undefined need all the reflective resources individuals can muster; they need imagination for
growth beyond what already is, and prudence for preservation of the realized good, and perhaps even theoretical reason for consistency. All these
modes of thought figure significantly into the reflective life, but there is
no algorithm, nor even method as ordinarily understood, for achieving
desirable results. No theory can capture the interplay among these moral
forces in individual lives.

Mark Johnson and Thomas Alexander, in seeking to bring theoretical
focus to Dewey's emphasis on imaginative projection as a style of
thought, fail to take seriously enough the methodological indeterminacy
in pragmatism's understanding of decision making. Instead Johnson and
Alexander see Dewey as suggesting a new direction for moral theory, a direction that takes imaginative projection as a style of moral deliberation
more seriously than does the dominant tradition. In seeing Dewey this
way, however, they succumb to the hope that they might achieve a successful alternative, but still systematic, theory of morality; to the extent
that they succumb to this philosophical hope, they fail to see Dewey's
commitment to respect the particularity of individuals and situations.

In *Moral Imagination*, Mark Johnson seeks to bring to the center of moral
theory Dewey's insight that imagination is central to deliberation. He
finds that traditional moral theories—those that see discursive reasoning
from principles to be the heart of moral thought, like the theories of Singer
and MacIntyre—overlook the fundamentally metaphoric structure of all
moral thought. The traditional "Moral Law Folk Theory," in Johnson's
view,

> misses the imaginative activity that is crucial to humane moral deliberation.
> What rules there are get whatever meaning they have only from our inter-
> pretation of them, and all interpretation is irreducibly imaginative in charac-
> ter.[23]

Johnson seeks to correct this oversight of traditional moralists by reconstituting moral theory around a metaphorical interpretation of moral concepts that brings imaginative projection as a style of moral deliberation
into theoretical prominence.[24] He sees this reconstitution of moral theory
as embodying a "Deweyan conception of Morality."[25] Part of his motivation appears to be the realization that the deliberation of ordinary life is
very different from the discursive reasoning assumed by traditional theories of morality. Traditional theories of morality, in Johnson's view, typically nurture the false "Moral Law Folk Theory," including the idea that
moral decisions are a matter of applying properly certified principles de-
ductively to problematic situations. Moving the application-of-principles

model out of the center and putting in its place the imaginative-extension-beyond-prototypical-cases model, Johnson argues, enables both a more adequate and a more useful undertaking of moral theory.[26] Thomas Alexander endorses the idea that Johnson's large-scale proposal "has direct implications for pragmatic ethical theory" and that "recent work suggesting the centrality of imagination—including that of MacIntyre and Nussbaum . . . points toward Dewey as providing an adequate theoretical framework within which most of the topics of ethical theory must be reconsidered."[27]

Johnson and Alexander see Dewey as suggesting a new direction for the development of moral theory, a direction that acknowledges the primacy of imagination and metaphor in moral deliberation. They suggest that taking metaphor seriously yields a systematic theory of morality by contrast with which the "Moral Law Folk Theory" appears inadequate and misguided. This new theoretical direction for "pragmatic ethical theory" they see to be more adequate as theory and more useful toward achieving successful lives. In seeing Johnson's imaginative-extension-beyond-prototypical-cases model as alternative to, and more adequate than, the application-of-principles model, they succumb to the idea that pragmatism competes theoretically with traditional theories of morality; in doing so, they fail to embrace pragmatism's respect for particularity.

Johnson's commitment to imaginative projection as the correct understanding of moral deliberation derives from his conviction that human understanding is intrinsically metaphorical. As he sees it, human understanding simply does not follow the course of deductive reasoning from premises to conclusions; rather it relies on "prototypical cases" as foundations for thinking about problems, and in problem situations it seeks to extend the prototypical cases to accommodate new situations. Recognizing this fact about human understanding, according to Johnson, requires "a new conception of moral theory itself."[28] Reconstituting moral theory in the way Johnson suggests and using Dewey's pragmatism to support such reconstitution in effect distorts Dewey's understanding of reflective living, and the deliberation characteristic of it, into the sort of systematic theoretical enterprise Dewey sought to transcend. On the pragmatist account presented here, Dewey's understanding of deliberation as imaginative projection does not compete with traditional accounts of deliberation as rationally discursive; rather it seeks to open human understandings of deliberative processes to the creativity Dewey sees to be inseparable from efforts at constructive living. Dewey would not approve Johnson's efforts to construct a different kind of theoretical system, nor should other pragmatists.

Dewey avoids systematic theorizing while Johnson succumbs to the temptation toward theory that is endemic to life in the philosophical world. In addition, Dewey embraces the relatively local ideal of democratic individualism and makes it integral to his ideal of reflective living. Dewey's reflective life, again, includes autonomy, harmony as well as creative tension with a nurturing community, and commitment to ideals both individual and communal. His commitment to democratic individualism is a frank commitment to all of these constituents of the reflective life, not as in any traditional way "universal" or "rational" or as rooted in "human nature" or "in the nature of deliberation" but as the fortuitous outcome of historical contingencies of which humans are beneficiaries.[29] Johnson's search for moral system, for better philosophical theory, is not Dewey's.

Johnson's rendition of "pragmatic moral theory," beyond the fact that it is phenomenologically more adequate than discursive accounts of moral deliberation, is subject to some of the same difficulties Johnson finds in Moral Law Folk Theory. For example, the problem of applying laws to problematic cases reappears in Johnson's reconfiguration of moral theory as the problem of finding the correct metaphorical extension to problematic cases. Johnson's optimism about this problem is puzzling.

> Fortunately, what we know about prototypes can supply what we need to make intelligent moral decisions. There are principles of extension (e.g., metaphor) from the central to the non-central members within a category. . . . Cognitive Science can study empirically the nature of prototype structure and the various kinds of imaginative extension to the non-central cases.[30]

An "intelligent moral decision" will apparently be a matter of finding the correct imaginative extension from some prototype situation to a problematic situation requiring a decision. But finding the correct imaginative extension and seeing how it is appropriate in a problematic situation will surely be no more straightforward than finding the correct moral law and seeing how it is appropriate in a problematic situation. Admittedly, the content of moral theory as Johnson envisions it will be different from anything in Moral Law Folk Theory, but applying that content will be just as problematic as he finds applying the content of Moral Law Folk Theory.[31]

A further problem in Johnson's presentation of his alternative theory is his assumption that moral theory, reconceived as he proposes, empowers individuals to achieve more intelligent decisions.

> To be morally insightful and sensitive thus requires of us two things: (1) we must have knowledge of the imaginative nature of human conceptual systems and reasoning. This means that we must know what those imaginative structures are, how they work, and what they entail about the nature of our moral understanding. (2) We must cultivate moral imagination.[32]

Surely nobody will challenge the suggestion that being morally insightful and sensitive requires the cultivation of moral imagination. The idea, however, that moral insight and sensitivity requires knowledge of some particular moral theory is beyond credibility, even if the theory in question is sensitive to the foibles of Moral Law Folk Theory and takes seriously metaphor and imagination. The idea is that Jane Addams, Gabriel Oak, or Jane Doe would have been better equipped to confront their problems if only they had known about, and taken seriously enough, some parts of contemporary cognitive science along with Johnson's suggestions about their relevance to moral theory. This idea resonates with the same inappropriate presumption found earlier in Allan Gibbard, Thomas Scanlon, and Alasdair MacIntyre.[33]

Johnson's enthusiasm for metaphor and imagination is laudable, but his effort to translate that enthusiasm into a new kind of moral theory is a misguided effort—similar to the one he finds in Moral Law Folk Theory—to bridge the gap between theory and life. From Dewey's pragmatist perspective, Johnson's effort is one more distraction from reflective confrontation with concrete problem situations, the kind of confrontation that is the heart of deliberation and reflective morality.

Moral theory, along with theories of deliberation that seek universality and conformity in the activity of being deliberate, misses the living thought that must find its way through the difficulties of life. Understanding beliefs and desires as habits of action, and acknowledging that the roots of these habits are in human communities, may enable the focus required for amelioration of the conditions that undermine human growth and the integrity of communities. Who, among pragmatists, adequately respects individuals and their cultures?

EXAMPLES OF PRAGMATIST DELIBERATION

Hilary Putnam exemplifies the deliberation encouraged by pragmatism. Putnam shuns theory of the sort that has been central to philosophy, but he nonetheless focuses on problematic issues in innovative ways. He expresses the autonomy, the creative tension with his dominant culture, and the ideal-guided thoughtfulness that are central to the reflective life; he exemplifies imaginative deliberation.

Putnam's "How Not to Solve Ethical Problems" expresses acute awareness of the failure of moral theory. Part of the problem Putnam sees is that moral theorists typically seek *solutions* to moral problems, and that they do so by relying on intuitions and on a priori arguments, in spite of the fact that those techniques lead to unacceptable results.[34] Putnam suggests that different metaphors might open different ways of dealing with such problems, in particular that the metaphors of *adjudication* and *reading* might serve more effectively than the scientific metaphor of problem and solution. His suggestion expresses Putnam's autonomy from his philosophical culture as well as his commitment to the ideal of democratic community.[35]

Putnam's metaphors allow him to reject ideologically rigid ways of dealing with social problems, in particular the problems of inflation, unemployment, alienation, and poverty. He rejects the Marxism-Leninism of his own past as well as the neoconservatism of Robert Nozick and Milton Friedman. These perspectives embrace social consequences that Putnam finds unacceptable. Marxism-Leninism accepts a revolution that yields only a different, but not a better, ruling class, and it does not avoid the same kind of social problems that motivated the revolution. Neoconservatism accepts disastrous levels of unemployment, especially among deprived youth, as the price of avoiding levels of inflation that burden the middle class. Both of these ideology-driven perspectives embrace unacceptable consequences because of their a priori commitments. Putnam sees that those commitments need to be replaced by a commitment to addressing "the problems of men" in "the moving present";[36] he insists on better outcomes than either of the ideology-driven perspectives offers.

> The fact is that we do not know that progress is impossible, any more than we know that progress is inevitable, and we never shall know either thing. A great Jewish sage once wrote that "It is not given to us to finish the task, but neither are we permitted not to take it up." . . . At our best we have always been a nation with an unfinished task and an unfashionable faith in progress. Let us return to our best.[37]

Putnam's commitment to pragmatism's reflective morality inspires his insistence that America can do better in efforts to address moral and social problems than is allowed by ideologically driven "solutions" that embrace unacceptable consequences.[38]

Richard Rorty expresses this same spirit. His "Human Rights, Rationality, and Sentimentality"[39] captures as well as does Putnam's essay Dewey's focus on human problems. Rorty's concern is to bring into focus a way of seeing why humans frequently behave in xenophobic ways, why they frequently treat other humans as less than human. Rorty believes our philosophical tradition, especially in its theoretical concerns with morality, has reinforced undesirable xenophobic tendencies.

> Plato set things up so that moral philosophers think they have failed unless they convince the rational egoist that he should not be an egoist. . . . But the rational egoist is not the problem. The problem is the gallant and honorable Serb who sees Muslims as circumcised dogs. It is the brave soldier and good

comrade who loves and is loved by his mates, but who thinks of women as dangerous, malevolent whores and bitches.[40]

Rorty thinks that these xenophobic tendencies are a more proper focus of intellectual effort than are the epistemological problems that drive efforts to answer the rational egoist. His own proposal for addressing the problem is to focus on helping people feel more secure and helping them toward greater sympathy for others. "By *security* I mean conditions of life sufficiently risk-free as to make one's difference from others inessential to one's self-respect, one's sense of worth."[41] Rorty's suggestion is the psychological suggestion that insecurity fuels xenophobia because it undermines self-respect. He recommends a redirection of attention from traditional moral theory toward a wider realization of conditions that contribute to personal security and to sympathy with others. In his focus on human problems rather than on problems of moral theory and in his suggestion of concrete proposals for addressing them, Rorty embodies the spirit of pragmatism. The ideal of the widest possible community, part of the democratic ideal as Dewey conceived it, motivates Rorty.[42]

Putnam and Rorty embody Dewey's respect for reflective living. Each of these thinkers shares Dewey's commitment to the reflective life, a commitment that guides their responses to problem situations. Each rejects moral ideologies that hinder productive responses to problem situations. Their deliberations show how the respect for particularity embedded in traditional pragmatism may constructively address large human problems, and they show how philosophers may address those problems apart from moral theory.

This chapter has considered traditional philosophical issues about deliberation and has explored different contexts for deliberation. My conclusion is that thinking about deliberation making use of the constructs of habit, imagination, resourcefulness, and creativity is more adequate to phenomena of deliberation than are the more characteristic, traditional constructs of belief, desire, reason, and passion. The former constructs, rooted in philosophical traditions of pragmatism, open toward more constructive tasks than the defensive, apologetic tasks of conventional philosophy. The next chapter considers one of these more constructive intellectual tasks, the task of moral education.

NOTES

1. For an extensive and generalized account of this idea of habit and the deliberation normally accompanying it, see Todd Lekan, *Making Morality* (Nashville,

Tenn.: Vanderbilt University Press, 2003). Chapter 1 of Lekan's book, "A Pragmatic Account of Practical Knowledge," is the relevant portion of his discussion.

2. Elijah Millgram's survey of theories of practical reasoning for the Dictionary of Philosophy of Mind, www.artsci.wustl.edu/~philos/MindDict/practical reasoning.html, is evidence for this claim. According to Millgram, "Practical reasoning is no longer the handmaiden of ethics, and today theories of practical reasoning are not normally advanced merely as components of some favored moral theory. The fortification and defense of a very small number of entrenched positions inherited from the great dead philosophers has given way to a healthy profusion of competing and largely new views. Important ideas and arguments turn up annually or semi-annually—a rate that marks a philosophical subspecialty as rapidly developing." I do not share Millgram's enthusiasm for a profusion of new views about what is mistakenly called "practical reasoning" or for the rapid development of a new subspecialty in philosophy. These things are, in my view, symptoms of philosophers' refusal to take seriously the phenomenology of ordinary deliberation. Pragmatists do take seriously the phenomenology of deliberation.

3. See Lekan, *Making Morality*, especially 36–41.

4. I should acknowledge that Lekan declines to assert that the schema he presents on his page 37 is universal for all occasions of deliberation. He notes in footnote 27, 182, "I do not want to argue that every time a person deliberates, she must represent the event in precisely the way that I set out above. The important point is that the basic features of the deliberative event are somehow represented by the person." I remain convinced, however, that deliberative situations vary almost indefinitely in the kinds of urgency they present, as well as in the available resources and in the resourcefulness of the individuals involved in those situations. These dimensions of radical particularity in deliberative situations and in the persons in those situations undermines the idea that general schema for such situations might be philosophically or intellectually useful.

5. Lekan, *Making Morality*, 37.

6. LW7:275.

7. See "How to Make Our Ideas Clear," in *Pragmatism: The Classic Writings*, ed. H. S. Thayer (Indianapolis, Ind.: Hackett Publishing Co., 1982), 79–100. For a clear discussion of Peirce's views about belief, see Douglas Anderson, *Strands of System* (West Lafayette, Ind.: Purdue University Press, 1995).

8. The use of the term "family resemblance" here is no accident; it should recall Wittgenstein's resistance to universals, or abstract characteristics, that may be subject to philosophical analysis of their "conceptual content."

9. John Dewey shares this understanding of habit, character, and virtue. See, for example, MW14, especially 16.

10. For accounts of these pragmatist perspectives, see Dewey, *The Quest for Certainty* (LW7), especially chapter 6, "The Play of Ideas"; see *Logic: The Theory of Inquiry* (LW12). A more contemporary figure with similar views about this issue is W. V. Quine; see *From a Logical Point of View* (Cambridge, Mass.: Harvard University Press, 1953).

11. For a traditional account that unfortunately respects this tension, see my "A Note on the Impossibility of Rationalizing Desire," *The Journal of Value Inquiry*, 18 (1984), 63–67.

12. Bernard Williams, *Ethics and the Limits of Philosophy* (Cambridge, Mass.: Harvard University Press, 1985), 14.

13. For Williams's larger account of this tradition, see chapter 1, "Socrates' Question," of *Ethics and the Limits of Philosophy.*

14. Marcus Singer, "The Ideal of a Rational Morality," *Proceedings and Addresses of the American Philosophical Association* 60, no. 1 (1986): 32.

15. LW7:262.

16. Recall the discussion in chapter 3 of the views of Allan Gibbard and Thomas Scanlon.

17. Alasdair MacIntyre, *Whose Justice, Which Rationality* (South Bend, Ind.: University of Notre Dame Press, 1988), 175.

18. This claim may seem too extreme. See, however, the sections of *Ethics* titled "Present Need of Theory" and "Sources of Moral Theory" for confirmation of it (LW7:176–80).

19. MW14:32.

20. MW14:96.

21. See lecture 18, "Philosophy," of James's Gifford Lectures, *The Varieties of Religious Experience* (New York: Longmans, Green, and Co., 1902).

22. MW14:150.

23. *Moral Imagination*, 31.

24. *Moral Imagination*, 77, 80, 125, 187–89.

25. *Moral Imagination*, xiv.

26. *Moral Imagination*, 190–91.

27. Alexander sees MacIntyre's emphasis on narrative to signify that he too shares Johnson's conviction about the need for a redirection of moral theory of the sort Johnson suggests. The discussion of MacIntyre's emphasis on reason presented in the immediately preceding section of this chapter, however, suggests that Alexander has overestimated MacIntyre's commitment to reconceiving moral theory in Johnson's idea of a Deweyan direction. *Moral Imagination*, 396–97.

28. *Moral Imagination*, chapters 2 and 3, especially 76–77.

29. Dewey himself mentions repeatedly that American democratic communities are a "gift of grace"; in this way Dewey explicitly embraces the radical empiricism evident in Richard Rorty's *Contingency, Irony, and Solidarity* (Cambridge: Cambridge University Press, 1989).

30. *Moral Imagination*, 190.

31. Johnson sometimes seems as loyal to Dewey as he is, given my portrayal here, disloyal, for he seems distinctly ambivalent between the desire for a theory more adequately applicable to "real life" than is "Moral Law Folk Theory," and the desire to acknowledge the uniqueness, and inaccessibility to theory, of problematic moral situations. The idea that there are "principles of extension" accessible to study by empirical science (190) issues from the first desire, while the second desire motivates apparently incompatible claims, for example: "The meaning, point, and force of a particular prototype will also depend in part on the various narrative contexts in which it is embedded. This holds both for the way the prototype originates in an individual's experience and for the way it is developed and applied in present situations" (191). This latter claim easily suggests the uniqueness, and inaccessibility to theory, of problematic situations. This same ambiva-

lence appears to pervade the text and makes for difficulty conceiving it as single-minded about what shape a Deweyan view should take.

32. *Moral Imagination*, 198.

33. See chapter 3 of this work for a broader discussion.

34. Hilary Putnam, "How Not to Solve Ethical Problems," *Realism with a Human Face* (Cambridge, Mass.: Harvard University Press, 1990), 179–80.

35. Putnam, "How Not to Solve Ethical Problems," 189.

36. John Dewey, "The Need for a Recovery of Philosophy," in *The Essential Dewey*, vol. 1, ed. Larry Hickman and Thomas Alexander (Bloomington: Indiana University Press, 1998).

37. "How Not to Solve Ethical Problems," 192.

38. Putnam's commitment to Dewey's reflective morality, evident in this essay, does not deter his criticism of Dewey on wider grounds. See "A Reconsideration of Deweyan Democracy," in *Renewing Philosophy* (Cambridge, Mass.: Harvard University Press, 2002), 180–200. Putnam thinks Dewey's commitment to instrumental rationality on the one hand and to consummatory experience on the other commit Dewey also to a Positivist-style bifurcation of experience. Thomas M. Alexander sees the error in this positivistic conception of Dewey's thought. See *John Dewey's Theory of Art, Experience, and Nature: The Horizons of Feeling* (Albany: State University of New York Press, 1987). Alexander is aware that the aesthetic dimension of experience is at the foundation of Dewey's thought.

39. "Human Rights, Rationality, and Sentimentality," *The Yale Review* 81 (October 1993): 1–20.

40. Rorty, "Human Rights," 11.

41. Rorty, "Human Rights," 14.

42. Again, Rorty's status as "a Deweyan" is as much in question as is Putnam's. Rorty declines to count himself "a Dewey scholar" and many who sympathize with Dewey's pragmatist thought believe that Rorty's views generally do not do Dewey justice. See, for example, Thomas Alexander, "John Dewey and the Moral Imagination: Beyond Putnam and Rorty toward a Postmodern Ethics," *Transactions of the Charles S. Peirce Society* 29, no. 3 (summer 1993). See also Herman Saatkamp Jr., *Rorty and Pragmatism: The Philosopher Responds to His Critics* (Nashville, Tenn.: Vanderbilt University Press, 1995); see especially the essays by Thelma Z. Lavine, James Gouinlock, and Susan Haack.

7

---—*vv*——

Education

Education is a problem. We want to do it better, and we want to do it more efficiently. How to accomplish these goals is a focus of attention for thousands of American educators and millions of citizens.

Dissatisfaction with the results of customary strategies of education has cast an aura of malaise over American education. Many think inadequate funding is the problem; others think the fault lies in teacher education; still others blame lack of rigorous standardized testing. Matt Miller, a senior fellow at the Center for American Progress, has recently blamed local control of education and proposed a more thorough nationalizing of American education; in his "modest proposal to fix the schools," Miller suggests we "First, Kill All the School Boards."[1] Since I am an educator only in the sense that I have taught college and university students for thirty years, I cannot pretend to have a solution to this problem. I offer simply a pragmatist, Deweyan reading of our current American situation, a reading that might suggest strategies for improvement. I begin with an extensive citation from a talk by John Taylor Gatto on the occasion of his accepting the New York City Teacher of the Year award on January 31, 1990.

> We live in a time of great school crisis. Our children rank at the bottom of nineteen industrial nations in reading, writing and arithmetic. At the very bottom. The world's narcotic economy is based upon our own consumption of the commodity; if we didn't buy so many powdered dreams the business would collapse. . . .
>
> Our school crisis is a reflection of . . . [a] greater social crisis. We seem to have lost our identity. Children and old people are penned up and locked

133

away from the business of the world to a degree without precedent—nobody talks to them anymore and without children and old people mixing in daily life a community has no future and no past, only a continuous present. In fact, the name "community" hardly applies to the way we interact with each other. We live in networks, not communities, and everyone I know is lonely because of that. In some strange way school is a major actor in this tragedy just as it is a major actor in the widening gulf among social classes. Using school as a sorting mechanism we appear to be on the way to creating a caste system, complete with untouchables who wander through subway trains begging and sleep on the streets.

Gatto, like me, has little more to back his reading of our educational situation than his experience teaching; his teaching, however, is in the New York City schools, probably one of the more challenging contexts a teacher might face. Gatto's remarks point to what seems to me—and I've shepherded four children through public and private schools in addition to counting John Dewey as my favorite philosopher—a critical dimension of America's educational problem: the idea of what education fundamentally is.

TOWARD A CONCEPTION OF EDUCATION

The conception of education that underlies the aura of malaise about schools is as vague as is our dissatisfaction with methods, goals, and outcomes of education. Part of our large American problem about education is conceptual. Our conception of education, our understanding of what it is and what it should do, is at best vague and at worst incoherent. Like Gatto, I sense that American culture has lost its way educationally; and like Gatto, I believe that the change we need is more radical than anybody, perhaps apart from isolated pockets of home-schoolers and "unschoolers," has yet considered. I do not, like Matt Miller, believe that killing off the school boards is the sort of radical change we need; instead, we need a different conception of education from the one that typically dominates our thinking about education.

Fortunately, the conceptual issue is one that pragmatists, following in the footsteps of John Dewey, can address. Dewey saw that education, in concept and in practice, was critical for American democracy; as goes our success at education, he thought, so will go our success at democracy. Dewey saw democracy's power in its enabling of individual growth, a growth coherent with integrity of community. This symbiotic integration between individuality and integrity of community is, in Dewey's understanding, the deepest attraction of democracy. This symbiotic integration needs, as Dewey also saw, an understanding of education that enables *both* growth of individuality *and* integrity of community. This symbiosis and tension between their individuality and their respect for their communities must saturate the lives of citizens. Citizens of a democratic community, Dewey believed, must be equipped to practice what he calls "reflective morality."[2]

Reflective morality requires an education that equips citizens to sustain their communities and values. Education must enable youth to respect themselves and their peers as responsible for embodying and conveying deep community values, and it must provide conditions for their growth toward their own futures of individual achievement. In this sense, all education is value education.

The currency of education must encourage the mature, reflective citizens required for democracy. Whatever educational institutions do or do not, they progress in this respect, or they regress; they contribute to the vitality of democratic culture or they detract from it. Dewey understood these relationships early in his career when his commitment to education became central to his philosophical concerns. Even before his great *Democracy and Education* of 1916, Dewey was committed to an understanding of humanity that required primary focus on education. Dewey's philosophy indeed is philosophy of education, or philosophy *as* education; it funnels to a focus on issues of human growth and education, especially as these are possible in a democracy.[3]

In order to get at the idea of education that intersects with pragmatism's commitments to individual growth and democracy, a review of pragmatism's worldview is helpful. This worldview is part of an understanding of education that is natural to pragmatism. The relevant dimensions are contextual individuality and contextual intelligence. Begin with the idea of contextual intelligence.

CONTEXTUAL INTELLIGENCE

Contextual intelligence is intelligence elicited in individuals' own situations; it is the habit, skill, and resourcefulness with which they confront challenges of experience. Intelligence, *qua* intelligence, has no specific content of talent, skill, or knowledge. Highly intelligent individuals may know nothing of calculus, algebra, or elementary mathematics. Such individuals may know nothing about how internal combustion engines work; they may know nothing of poetry or music; they may not know how to read. Similarly, such individuals may lack basic knowledge of geography, history, and alternative political arrangements.

Intelligence is potential for competent response to conditions within an environment, where the environment itself engenders skills for dealing with its challenges. Humans in many different cultural contexts may be highly and equally intelligent. African tribesmen may be as intelligent as Ph.D.s in philosophy; they may be equally suited to deal with the challenges of their different environments. Effecting a change of place between an African tribesman and a philosophy Ph.D. would no doubt result in disaster for both; neither would be able to survive in the other's environment. Without help from sympathetic others, each would perish in the other's environment, yet they may be as nearly equal in intelligence as any persons on the planet.

This contextual understanding of intelligence is basic to a pragmatist account of education. Environments themselves provide the measure of what intelligence is for those who live in them. Those environments provide also an appropriate understanding of what it means to measure up to their challenges, an understanding of what intelligent response is. The environments provide also means whereby the young and inexperienced may acquire the skills to confront their challenges. The educational practices prominent in any cultural environment are those that promote familiarity with traditions that have conferred significant chances for success at meeting challenges of that environment. Education is this transference of traditions from those who are mature and knowledgeable to those who are growing to maturity and are less knowledgeable. There are no doubt native differences among humans that account for differences in their abilities to assimilate the traditions conveyed by their education. These native differences are not fully responsible for success or failure at assimilating traditional ways of confronting environmental challenges. Education itself, the means whereby families and communities nurture their young to maturity, is also significant. The education offered—its means, strategies, and goals—is also decisive.

Within the American context, this idea of contextual intelligence means that education should enable our youth to acquire the skills required for success at meeting the challenges of life in America. American schools thus typically prepare students to function in an industrial, technological economy in which they must work in order to become self-supporting, politically literate citizens. Our youth must know mathematics to balance their income and expenses and to pay their taxes; they must be able to work at a job that provides sufficient income for financial independence from others; and they must be flexible in the work they are willing and able to do. They must have factual knowledge to the extent required for success at their employment. The real challenges of the American environment are those involved in wresting a living from the industrial, technological opportunities offered by American businesses. American culture offers an environment with its own challenges, challenges no different in principle from those of any other environment in the world.

The typical challenges Americans face are different from the challenges of other cultural environments. In principle, however, the content of the ideas of intelligence and education are not different for the American context from their content for any other cultural environment.[4]

CONTEXTUAL INDIVIDUALITY

A corollary of the pragmatist idea that intelligence is contextual is the idea that individuality is contextual; each individual comes to maturity within a context that defines what that individual might become. Each individual has a native constitution, a biological nature, but this native constitution responds in specific ways to environmental pressures and opportunities. Different developmental contexts in which similar humans reside yield mature individuals who differ in their abilities to respond to challenging situations. At one level, this observation is a truism. A boy growing up on an Indiana farm milking cows and cultivating crops may have a native constitution similar to that of a boy raised in New York City among the clang and bustle of millions. The two boys, for all of their native similarity, will become adults suited to meet different challenges and for different styles of life. At another level, however, this truism is subtle in ways that are best appreciated from the perspective of pragmatism.

For pragmatists, persons are biological organisms. As biological organisms, persons have no independence of their environments; in particular, they have no ontological or rational independence. Persons do have unique characteristics, including their intelligence, complemented by the language use that enables their social coherence. Their intelligence becomes evident, however, only in response to challenges; when it does become evident it does so in virtue of habits that enable differential responses. Individual intelligence may be nothing more than habitual disposition for recourse to infrequently used habits in response to novel situations. When one embraces a biological, Darwinian perspective, then one sees human uniqueness in terms of impulse, habit, and creativity; these ideas enable a fruitful understanding of what humans are in the sense that they enable effective approaches to engendering intelligent habits of response, a fundamental goal of education. This idea of contextual individuality may be reinforced by helpful words from Dewey:

Habit is however more than a restriction of thought. Habits become negative limits because they are first positive agencies. The more numerous our habits the wider the field of possible observation and foretelling. The more flexible they are, the more refined is perception in its discrimination and the more delicate the presentation evoked by imagination. The sailor is intellectually at home on the sea, the hunter in the forest, the painter in his studio, the man of science in his laboratory. These commonplaces are universally recognized in the concrete; but their significance is obscured and their truth denied in the current general theory of mind. For they mean nothing more or less than that *habits formed in process of exercising biological aptitudes are the sole agents of observation, recollection, foresight and judgment*: a mind of consciousness or soul in general which performs these operations is a myth.[5]

The portion of the quotation I have italicized exposes the pragmatist roots of the idea of contextual individuality. The idea that humans are biological organisms having biological aptitudes may be depressing from conventional religious perspectives, but it is decisively empowering for those who must address issues of education. Education becomes a matter of engendering habits, of habit-offering; and learning becomes a matter of acquiring habits, of habit-taking. When education is recognized to be thoroughly habit oriented, then issues of education become concrete, particular, and individual. Consider another quote from Dewey:

Concrete habits do all the perceiving, recognizing, imagining, recalling, judging, conceiving and reasoning that is done. "Consciousness," whether as a stream or as special sensations and images, expresses functions of habits, phenomena of their formation, operation, their interruption and reorganization.[6]

The idea that different environmental conditions yield different abilities is explicit in Dewey's words; every habit enables or disables individuals' aptitude for intelligent response in typical as well as in novel situations. Any situation or interaction with others is occasion for the acquisition of habits. Since concrete habits are dimensions of character and personality that enable, or disable, the potential for intelligent address of problems, anything that is habit-forming is part of education. To paraphrase Dewey, everything one is aware of is a function of habits, of their formation, of their operation, and of their successes, failures, and alterations. Functionally speaking individual persons are their habits. They are their impulses as well, but impulses are less definitive of character and personality than are ways of dealing with impulses, and ways of dealing with impulses are habits. Every aspect of an environment contributes in definitive ways to one's identity, to who one is and to who one aspires to become. The plasticity, or malleability, of individuality resolves through processes of interaction and habit acquisition into a concrete individual identity; habits become better defined with time and in interactions with others, and they yield largely predictable results.[7]

The musical and film *My Fair Lady* illustrates this pragmatist insight in the service of a delightful story. Professor Henry Higgins is a skillful linguist who has the ability to pinpoint individuals' birthplaces within five miles by attending carefully only to nuances in their manner of speech. The habits of speech, in all their subtle variety, are for Professor Higgins a consequence of learning speech in a specific environment; and Higgins knows environmental differences of speech patterns well enough to identify birthplaces with great accuracy. Higgins's skill in this respect is a highly developed skill we all have, the skill of guessing fairly accurately where a person has grown up, north or south, Boston or Manhattan, Minnesota or Mississippi. The large challenge Professor Higgins faces is to bring new, more decorous, habits of speech to Eliza Doolittle, whose initial habits of speech are, he thinks, a grievous offense to civilized ears. Higgins is finally successful in changing Eliza's speech, as well as other pervasive habits of her behavior—her ways of walking and of eating, among others. After serious, lengthy effort, Professor Higgins manages to change Eliza from a street urchin into a lady. The pervasive change of habits Professor Higgins engineers transforms Eliza into a different person. Eliza is one example of how the habits make the person. Eliza's transformation from street urchin to lady is the sort of transformation that is rare, but not completely unfamiliar.

Other transformations similar to Eliza's are familiar from various efforts to deal with difficult individuals. Our courts of law occasionally sentence repeat offenders of minor infractions to boot camps. The boot camps function to change destructive habits. Their inmates do not sleep until noon; they do not drink or smoke; and they are compelled to live in accord with more normally accepted habits of life. The hope is that these inmates will acquire constructive habits that enable them to live their lives without falling into criminal behavior. Other examples of efforts to change habitual patterns of behavior appear in organizations like Alcoholics Anonymous (AA). These organizations are designed to interrupt destructive habits. The fundamental assumption of all such groups is that individuals change by changing their behaviors and thus their habits. The hope of each member of AA is to become an analogue of Eliza Doolittle, to become transformed from an alcoholic to a (metaphorical) lady, and likewise for inmates of boot camps. These examples recognize that character change is change of habit, and that change of habit is change of behavior and of contexts for behavior.

Return to the point that environment contributes definitively to individuals' identity. A well-known example of this fact is the ability of humans to acquire language skills with relative ease at early ages. Children will learn to speak, read, and write a variety of languages when their neurological "language window" is open, when there is a specific plasticity in the development of their brains. After this language window closes, then language learning becomes more difficult. When children get to secondary school, the time when they are typically offered an opportunity to learn other languages, their aptitude for acquiring language skills is diminished. The general, widely recognized point is that early experiences and environment are definitive for individual development. One's early environment opens, through processes that engender habit, character, and personality, toward a limited set of possibilities for growth and development, and it closes other possibilities. The Indiana farm-boy will not become an academic professional; his city-bred cousin will not pursue agriculture. These are obvious examples of the ways environmental contexts constrain and limit, encourage and expand, opportunities for individual development.

The upshot of this pragmatist understanding of individual development is that everything in an environment is educational. Each aspect of a child's environment is relevant to habit formation; each practice in an environment acquires its inertia in the child; each regularity puts in place a regularity of expectation, a habitual expectation that becomes a value and may be definitive for the child's development. To awaken to the crowing of a morning rooster sets in place an expectation that becomes a value. To awaken to the sound of police sirens in a nearby part of one's borough sets in place different expectations. To feed chickens and gather their eggs every morning again puts in place habitual expectations that become values. To watch the cartoon channel where animated characters career about in psychedelic settings likewise puts in place habitual expectations that become values. Every nuance of an environment contributes its share to individual identity. Every nuance of regularity puts in place an expectation that contributes to character and shapes hopes for individual achievement.

To think of education as habit-formation is to think of it as socially and culturally pervasive. Everything that happens in a family and its various communities is education for every member of the family and especially for its children. Children hear from their grandparents about how things were "in the old days": the grandparents walked five miles to school and began working at age twelve, and "life was not easy back then." The grandparents are remarking about ways in which customary expectations have changed during their own lives, about ways basic values have changed. These "generation gaps" indicate differences in environmental conditions that are responsible for differences in values. A similar, but larger, expression of differences in environmental conditions, habits, and values becomes evident from acquaintance with life in earlier centuries. Literature is a good source for the acquaintance. A Charles Dickens novel, perhaps *Great Expectations*, expresses large cultural differences that evidence very different habitual expectations and values. Biographies of earlier historical figures have the same effect; Elizabeth Dodds's biography of Jonathan Edwards, *Marriage to a Difficult Man*, expresses differences of value in that early eighteenth-century context.[8] For pragmatists, these cultural and environmental differences produce different habits, different values, and different hopes—different individuals; pragmatists incorporate in their thought about education these connections between environments and the persons they make possible.

The habits, values, and hopes of individuals in their own cultural contexts are organic in the sense that they are characteristics of a complex biological organism in a specific environment. The mentality of humans, to quote Dewey again, "can be understood in the concrete only as a system of beliefs, desires, and purposes which are formed in the interaction of biological aptitudes with a social environment."[9] Humans' intellectual skill, their "minding" behavior in their various environments, is continuous with their biological natures. As human bodies interact with their environments in characteristic general ways—ingesting, excreting, respiring, and "livering"—those same bodies acquire habitual ways of interacting with their environments.[10] These characteristic modes of interaction include human intellectual skills, and they are biologically rooted in bodies having specific ecological contexts; they are continuous with the more bodily seeming, or "autonomic," habits of interaction. Another Dewey quote:

> Individuals with their exhortations, their preachings and scoldings, their inner aspirations and sentiments have disappeared, but their habits endure, because these habits incorporate objective conditions in themselves. . . . But no amount of preaching good will or the golden rule or cultivation of sentiments of love or equity will accomplish the [desired] results. There must be change in objective arrangements and institutions. We must work on the environment not merely on the hearts of men.[11]

Just as we think of our merely bodily interactions with our environments— respiring and ingesting—as conditioned by our biology and our environment, so we should think of "higher" faculties, our intellectual skills, as likewise conditioned by our biology and environment. The crucial differences among the organic habits that characterize humans have roots in the environmental contexts that engender those habits. Human intellectual faculties, along with the habits, values, and modes of operation that characterize them, are organic, and they are symbiotic with ecological and cultural environments. Think of Dickens's or of Jonathan Edwards's eighteenth century, and add also the more dramatic differences of contemporary African tribal cultures, ancient Chinese cultures, or others of imaginably greater difference. In all these different environments human intellectual abilities, along with their characteristic habits and values, are outgrowths of specific cultural contexts interacting with biologically native constitutions.

This emphasis on human continuity with the natural world may seem overdone. The danger, however, in not taking this continuity seriously enough is that we may not otherwise appreciate the enormity of the task of education. Education happens everywhere all the time, and especially to the young who have little established habit to resist the educational features, the habit-offerings, of their environments. Intentional education must take account of and address the dominant ways in which education happens. Families and communities must address intentionally the ways education happens to the young.

Only pragmatism, in recognizing the symbiosis of intellect, character, and personality with cultural environments, fully recognizes the ubiquitous education that pervades American culture. Pragmatism opens us to the fact that all dimensions of our environment—its visual and auditory media, its athletics, its automobiles, its supermarkets, its churches, its video arcades, its schools—*are* American education. These dimensions of our environment shape in detail the characters, habits, and values of all Americans, especially the young. Improving American education is seeking to shape in constructive ways all of these definitive dimensions of culture. Focus on funding, on teacher qualifications, and on testing procedures is but one way, a minor one, of shaping education.

The tasks of seeking improvement in education are daunting. Scholars of pragmatism are among those who realize how daunting they are. Bruce Wilshire, for example, in "Body-Mind and Subconsciousness: Tragedy in Dewey's Life and Work," expresses the enormity of the task of improving American education, and he shows that Dewey appreciated that daunting enormity. Wilshire acknowledges that confronting the facts about education brings him to conflicting reactions. The dominant reaction is toward despair, toward "[recoil] in the face of difficulties and complexities that seem insurmountable." The other reaction is to grasp the straw held out by the great pragmatists, their concurrence that

> [s]urvival depends upon the difficult feat of combining intelligence and hope. At times, we must hope against hope. For if we do not, if we do not try to ameliorate our situation, we are surely lost.[12]

Grasping the enormity of the task of responding intentionally to problems of education is a condition of whatever success might be possible. We must become aware that, as Wilshire puts it, "minding emerges within a background of human and prehuman organic habits that is never simply discarded and left behind." We must become aware that every aspect of the environment that is not intentionally addressed for how it shapes our dispositions may work against our own goals. I quote from Wilshire again to capture his realization of this fact:

I have just seen a movie—"Total Recall"—and have watched Arnold Schwarzenegger's character tear people's bodies to pieces as if they were excrement. Some children were in the audience. Just "protecting and enjoying first amendment rights"? Is that a convincing justification for such a spectacle? Do we have any idea of what we are doing with our technologies of communication, for example? Are we simply releasing dangerous impulses through "fictions" in a more or less safe environment? Or are we prompting acting out behavior in the "real world"? And aren't these alternatives simplistically framed? In their generalizing don't they gloss over the ineluctable particularity of particular people at particular moments in particular situations trying to cope with their particular subconscious or preconscious devils? In an ever shrinking and interdependent world how many technologically outfitted and precariously balanced madmen can the planet tolerate? I am as appalled as was Dewey when the lid is pulled off subconscious mind. Its too frequent "corruption" and "perversity"— brought on in large part by civilization itself—are clearly evident. Only with this in mind can we truly appreciate the adage, We have met the enemy and it is ourselves.[13]

Positioning ourselves to deal with the enemy who is us requires acknowledging our contextual individuality and contextual intelligence. These aspects of our human condition provide ways of understanding growth and development that are typical of pragmatism. Thinking explicitly about growth and development in ways that acknowledge our contextual individuality and contextual intelligence yields a focus on our environments that may enable a fruitful approach to education. Before discussing this context and habit oriented approach to education, I examine a more philosophical issue about the centrality of context in pragmatism's approach to intelligence and individuality.

CONTEXTUAL RELATIVISM? EMPIRICAL UNIVERSALISM?

The pragmatist emphasis on context does undermine philosophical tendencies to think in conceptual universals about the human condition. Thinking in this contextual way might suggest that there are no common needs, interests, or ambitions that support a constructive way of thinking about growth and education. The pragmatist response to this worry about context is twofold. First, this idea of context is genuinely incompatible with the largest ambitions of reason: the idea that there are rational principles for behavior and that the process of growth might be controlled by reason. Second, the commitment to context accepts and exploits the biologically universal aspects of human similarity. The context that pragmatists embrace sees humanity in all the ways science, observation, and experience allow;

but it rejects the philosophical understanding of humanity rooted in the Platonist-Cartesian axis of intellectual tradition.

This rejection of rational universalism is a rejection of the idea that dialectical, argumentative skill is central to growth and development, or to moral living. This rejection of rational universalism includes the rejection of common claims about growth and education, claims such as those made by Alasdair MacIntyre. A good education, as MacIntyre understands it, produces individuals who have highly developed dialectical skill, and who reason well from appropriate premises to sound conclusions they are willing to act upon. Good moral people, in this account, are either good theorists or are willing to accept guidance from good theorists. For John Dewey and others who take context seriously, good moral people are creative, imaginative, and resourceful in approaching challenging situations. Since only very different educational processes are likely to yield these different kinds of persons—those who are dialectically skillful as opposed to those who are imaginatively creative—MacIntyre and Dewey make different recommendations about education. MacIntyre follows St. Thomas and gives dialectical skills priority:

> Generally in learning we ought to move from what is most easily apprehended in the light of what we already know toward what is more intelligible as such, but less easily apprehended by us immediately. But in some cases we cannot enter upon one type of enquiry until we have already mastered another, because the first has to draw upon the second. For this reason logic, although Aquinas thought it the most difficult of the sciences, has to be studied first. . . . After logic comes mathematics, and after that physics. Only by then will the student have reached a stage where the two conditions which were prerequisites for moral enquiry will have been satisfied: sufficient experience of action and judgment and a mind undistracted by the immediacies of passion. . . . What then will the course of introductory moral teaching be? . . . Here the questions follow a sequence in which we begin by asking what the ultimate end or good of human beings is. . . . We then ask what human actions are, so that we can understand which types of human action are directed toward what is good and best for us and which direct us toward what is less and other than that. It turns out that this requires us to understand the nature of the passions and the different parts which they can play in the genesis of action, a discussion which is a prologue to an account of what a virtuous habit or disposition is and correspondingly what vices and sins are. . . . Most notably only by reference to the existence and goodness of God can the ultimate end of human beings be specified.[14]

Dewey's emphasis is on the need for art, drama, literature, and sport as necessary preparations for moral living. These are activities that release and stimulate imagination; they "introduce variety, flexibility, and sensitiveness into disposition" and because of their "humanizing capabilities," they are "moral necessities"; they do what nothing else can do for human nature, "softening rigidities, relaxing strains, allaying bitterness, dispelling moroseness, and breaking down the narrowness consequent upon specialized tasks."[15] Literature and art are, Dewey argues in *Democracy and Education*, "agencies of appreciation," but again he sees them as moral necessities:

> They have the office, in increased degree, of all appreciation in fixing taste, in forming standards for the worth of later experiences. They arouse discontent with conditions which fall below their measure; they create a demand for surroundings coming up to their own level. They reveal a depth and range of meaning in experiences which otherwise might be mediocre and trivial. They supply, that is, organs of vision. Moreover, in their fullness they represent the concentration and consummation of elements of good which are otherwise scattered and incomplete. They select and focus the elements of enjoyable worth which make any experience directly enjoyable. They are not luxuries of education, but emphatic expressions of that which makes any education worthwhile.[16]

Dewey believes imagination is primary not only in growth and education but also in moral life and thought. Literature and art are necessities of education, and especially of moral education.

Dewey carries this theme about the importance of the arts to moral life and to all of human culture into his reflections about democracy in *Freedom and Culture*. He notes, "Emotion and imagination are more potent in shaping public sentiment and opinion than information and reason."[17] He finds support for this view in the historical appropriation of the arts by the Church as a way of consolidating its power over its subjects, and in their historical appropriation by totalitarian societies. Totalitarian regimes seek complete control over feelings, desires, emotions, and opinions; hence, they "must first of all, and most enduringly of all, . . . command the imagination."[18] A careful look at history, Dewey believes, reveals the pivotal function of the arts, broadly conceived, in all of culture, and it reveals also the lesser role of reason.[19]

This contrast between Dewey and MacIntyre about whether one should seek primarily rational, dialectical skill expresses a standard contrast between Dewey and many traditional philosophers. The contrast with MacIntyre in this respect is noteworthy, however, because MacIntyre rejects the concept of rationality involved in most modern and contemporary accounts of morality. Although MacIntyre agrees with Dewey in rejecting Enlightenment understandings of reason and morality, he holds fast to the idea that rational, discursive argumentation is the skill most likely to yield virtuous people. Dewey rejects this idea and insists on an ideal of reflective living that is independent of the theoretical traditions of philosophy.

Richard Rorty also sees literature and imagination as keys to achieving successful living and to deliberating about alternatives; in Rorty's account, too, rational argument and dialectical skill are of secondary significance. Rorty himself puts this point as follows:

> Criticism is a matter of looking on this picture and on that, not of comparing both pictures with the original. Nothing can serve as a criticism of a person save another person, or of a culture save an alternative culture. . . . So our doubts about our own characters or our own culture can be resolved or assuaged only by enlarging our acquaintance. The easiest way of doing that is to read books. . . . Ironists are afraid that they will get stuck in the vocabulary in which they were brought up if they only know the people in their own neighborhood, so they try to get acquainted with strange people (Alcibiades, Julien Sorel), strange families (the Karamazovs, the Casaubons), and strange communities (the Teutonic Knights, the Nuer, the mandarins of the Sung).[20]

Rorty endorses Dewey's perspective on morals and education; he thinks of literature and arts, because of their concreteness, as having eclipsed the discursive practices MacIntyre finds inseparable from living well.[21]

This idea that literature and art are moral necessities, basic equipment for successful living, is a recurrent theme in Rorty's as in Dewey's work. In expressing their commitment to this theme, Dewey and Rorty seek to remove a prejudice against literature and art, the prejudice that sees them as at best helpful in reinforcing what only reason can discover and establish. Dewey takes note of this prejudice in many ways, but this remark in *Freedom and Culture* is typical:

> Even those who call themselves good democrats are often content to look upon the fruits of these arts as adornments of culture rather than as things in whose enjoyment all should partake, if democracy is to be a reality.[22]

In seeking to remove this long-standing prejudice, Rorty cooperates with Dewey against MacIntyre. For Dewey and Rorty literature and arts are primary in education because they cultivate, sustain, and expand individuals' creative imaginations. Emphasizing the context of intelligence and individuality is integral to this pragmatist perspective.[23]

The emphasis on context does not, however, become an endorsement of philosophical relativism. The context pragmatists embrace is biological; it recognizes that humans have common needs, interests, and hopes. These commonalities among diverse groups of humans make possible general conclusions about growth, education, morality, and knowledge. These general conclusions, however, are empirically circumspect; they are sensitive to results of inquiry in psychology, biology, anthropology, sociology, sociobiology, and other science disciplines.

Pragmatism reaches toward empirical universality in its respect for facts about human development and its willingness to incorporate these facts into efforts to improve human growth and development. The work of child psychologist Bruno Bettelheim is an example of the science pragmatists respect. While some psychologists and philosophers may think of children as "black boxes" needing conditioning, Bettelheim thinks of them as having common needs; and he sees their needs, hopes, anxieties, and fears to be significantly addressed in fairy tales. The genre of fairy tale literature, according to Bettelheim, is rooted in oral traditions that address these typical dimensions of children's psyches.[24]

Children do have characteristic needs, hopes, fears, and anxieties. Addressing these unstable parts of their psyches constructively, so that children may imagine them into the larger context of their individual development, is surely a goal for their education. Enabling children to confront cathartically in their narrative imaginations their own anxieties about growing into adulthood, their fears about strangers and about the unknown in general, and their needs to imagine possibilities for development into adults, must be an educational goal. Bettelheim believes that fairy tales have the specific goal of addressing these childhood needs, and he believes that classical fairy tales are usually successful when employed in their unaltered forms. The message of fairy tales, in Bettelheim's words, is

> that a struggle against severe difficulties in life is unavoidable, is an intrinsic part of human existence—but that if one does not shy away, but steadfastly meets unexpected and often unjust hardships, one masters all obstacles and at the end emerges victorious.
>
> Modern stories written for young children mainly avoid these existential problems, although they are crucial issues for all of us. The child needs most particularly to be given suggestions in symbolic form about how he may deal with these issues and grow safely into maturity. "Safe" stories mention neither death nor aging, the limits to our existence, nor the wish for eternal life. The fairy tale, by contrast, confronts the child squarely with the basic human predicaments.[25]

Maliciousness, meanness, misfortunes of fate, deaths of family members, the unknowns of their own psyches, the unknowns of their own abilities and deficiencies, the unknowns of their inevitable maturity and sexuality, and many other dimensions of children's concerns are explicit in the narrative content of fairy tales. According to Bettelheim, fairy tales enable children to confront these issues in the privacy of their own psyches. In his explications of the meaning and intent of various fairy tales, Bettelheim shows how the classical tales serve children's psychological needs.

Some readers of Bettelheim may be disaffected by his recourse to Freudian theory. Whether or not one approves the theoretical constructs of id, ego, and superego, along with other more controversial dimensions of Freudian theory, one may nonetheless discern the constructive usefulness of undiluted fairy tale literature. There are such realities as the death of parents, thoughts of which unsettle children, as well as stepmothers or ineffectual fathers, with whom many children must cope; these possibilities fairy tales confront directly, and they demonstrate that even these radical misfortunes may be overcome by those who are determined, creative, and resourceful. Children need these reassurances.

These narrative needs of children are part of their condition as the perceptive, imaginative, but immature organisms they are. If these narrative needs are not met, if they encounter a "Pollyanna" response that seeks to "paper over" these real anxieties, then children will be unprepared, disabled, or incompetent when they face the realities for which the fairy tales seek to prepare them. Bettelheim takes note of psychological inadequacies in alternative styles of children's literature.[26] Whether or not one can approve Bettelheim's strong thesis about the psychological necessity of fairy tale literature, one must acknowledge the power of some parts of his argument. If there are biologically organic, psychologically universal concerns in young humans, then they include those Bettelheim identifies as those for which fairy tales, in his analysis, are appropriate narrative responses.

In this context of Bettelheim's account of the power of fairy tales to address these universal human concerns, think again of Bruce Wilshire's response to his experience of *Total Recall*, with its portrayal of viciousness in Arnold Schwarzenegger's character. Who can know, or guess, the impact of such powerful multiple media presentations on children's psyches? The simplicity and directness of the fairy tales, along with the simplicity of the fantasy whose sensible and emotional content those tales leave to children's imaginations, are in Bettelheim's view a measured response to universal dimensions of childhood anxiety. What are we to make of contemporary media in this respect? How are we to assess their effects on children? Wilshire's evident guess about the effects of such experiences is that they are significantly detrimental: "In an ever shrinking and interdependent world how many technologically outfitted and precariously balanced madmen can the planet tolerate?"

However we might guess about the effects of these powerful media experiences on children, we know they are not evaluated for their psychological effects on the children who consume them. Not only are films like *Total Recall* not assessed for their psychological impact, but neither are other media enterprises that seek a wide audience among the young. Video games and music recordings are some of these productions. All of these media are conceived as means of entertainment, as ways of escaping the stress of work. And, as Wilshire notes, they are typically conceived as expressions of constitutional rights enjoyed by corporations and individuals to act apart from interference by censorious others. Concerned parents and citizens fail in their indifference toward the impact of these media on the psyches of those who are finding their way to maturity among them.

We need to be able to estimate the educational effects of the habit-offerings of American culture. We need to know the effects on our psyches of the uncontrolled efforts of corporate enterprise to profit from our engagement with their products. To recur to Wilshire's concern, if our enemy is ourselves we need to know our enemy much better than we do.[27]

Another quotation from Wilshire expresses the need for systematic effort to find out how we educate American children, how we, largely unaware, engender values and form characters.

> If Dewey is right, our conscious attitudes arise within a matrix of unconscious organic adjustments conditioned from our earliest days on earth. It follows that our highest rational priority should be the earliest education that a child receives. We need a Marshall Plan for our own reconstruction, and a Peace Corps comprised of the best and the brightest of our college graduates who will devote themselves to teaching on the "lowest" levels. We must also, somehow, enlist the cooperation of parents, and we can do so, of course, only by not invading their privacy. Strategies must be worked out.[28]

Being fully aware of the integration of character, value, and intellect with biological and psychological development may enable the focus on growth and development required to better our educational efforts. Not only biology, psychology, sociology, anthropology, and sociobiology, but also philosophy, history, and literature have roles to play in the enterprise of being deliberate about how we are educating our youth.

THE CENTRALITY OF HABIT, VALUE, AND CHARACTER

The first change in our thought about education must be to replace the idea of knowledge as its appropriate outcome with the idea of constructive habits as its appropriate outcome. Moving our efforts at education toward practices designed to engender constructive habits of character, as well as basic intellectual skills, is the primary recommendation that flows from the pragmatist conception of education. This change involves replacing our idea of education as knowledge inducing with the idea of education as maturity inducing, since maturity is approximately the having of constructive habits of character and personality. Putting habit and character at the center of thought about education means thinking of it as oriented toward producing constructive stability in habit and character, toward producing maturity. Those in need of education are those who lack appropriate stability of habit and character. Particular items of knowledge, on this view, become a peripheral educational concern.

Teaching and learning, on this pragmatist view, pervade American culture. Becoming intentional about the habits, values, and characters embedded in that culture is possible only through seeing the pervasiveness of teaching and learning throughout American culture. Professional educators, and all who are concerned about the educational environment, must put at the center of their thought the ideas of habit and character. Education is habit-offering and habit-taking; everything else is secondary. How may we offer constructive habits and make likely their acceptance? This issue is difficult in many ways. Consider briefly what habit-oriented education looks like.

Putting habit in the center of our understanding of education means intentionally conceiving of education in our schools as habit-offering. We must think of mathematics as the offering of techniques of calculation and manipulation of numbers; "number-facts" are useful only to the extent that they enable the manipulation of numbers. We must think of literature as the offering of techniques of reading, writing, and analysis; knowledge of facts about authors or items of literature, again, is useful only to the extent that such facts enable and augment those skills. History and social studies must be the offering of techniques for appropriating human culture and its past; factual knowledge of dates and names, again, is useful only to the extent that it enables use of those techniques. Of the many other items of curriculum that might be mentioned, all must be conceived around their contribution to habit and character.

This orientation around habit-offering and habit-taking suggests some conclusions about education. The *first* is that factual knowledge is not a primary educational goal. Being skillful in mathematics is not knowing number facts or standard formulas, though for those who are interested because of native aptitude those facts and formulae will become natural tools for use in satisfying activities. A *second* conclusion is that sitting and listening to lectures about specific topics—the periodic table, England in the eighteenth century, municipal government, and so on—is of little educational value; no constructive habits derive from those activities, largely because they are "passivities." Students subjected to such strategies may, however, benefit if their interests cohere with topics addressed. The *third* is that teachers, those in charge of carrying out conventional strategies of education, are useful for students to the extent that they are compelling models of good character or of vital interest; interactions with these teachers may be educationally useful. Teachers' breadth and depth of knowledge about their subject matters is not especially relevant to their effectiveness; what constitutes teacher effectiveness is teachers' characters and their engagement with their subject matters. Chemistry may be boring for most students, but what saves chemistry and other subjects that bring boredom is the character and personality of the compelling model, the teacher.

Making habit and character central to education means there is no controversy about value education. All education is value education. All of life is value education. All interactions with individuals, with corporations and bureaucracies are value education. The issue of education is the issue of how to produce maturity, how to produce a significant degree of constructive habit in maturing individuals. Only pragmatism puts this habit-oriented way of thinking at the center of education.

ISSUES FOR FURTHER THOUGHT

Putting habit and character at the center of thought about education has implications for specific issues in education. I conclude by mentioning some.

Science and Religion

The conflicts about whether to teach only evolution in biology classes become of little interest. Creationism too becomes of little interest. These views are significant only on a view of intelligence and intellect that makes true belief a leading educational goal. True belief or factual knowledge is of marginal interest when educational focus is on habit and character. Biology becomes not a study of facts about evolution and biological development, but the acquisition of skills and habits that equip one to address biological issues. These skills and habits include laboratory techniques that have developed during the history of biology to become important tools for addressing basic needs both human and intellectual. These skills and habits include habits of mind prominent in astute practitioners of biology during its historical development. Reading biographical accounts of individuals prominent in the history of biology, of the particular issues they confronted, and of how they tried to resolve them is especially useful. Intellectual biographies or autobiographies of prominent figures feature not just their conclusions, but their skills and habits. Darwin is of course a central figure in biology and is properly central to the study of biology. Francis Crick and James Watson are contemporary figures about whom interesting accounts are available, including their own *The Double Helix*. Also important are historical accounts of professional controversies surrounding the work of such prominent figures. Darwin's work was controversial from the moment it became known, and figures such as Harvard's Louis Agassiz and his colleague, Asa Gray, struggled with the religious implications of Darwin's theory; Agassiz's and Gray's story is also one those interested in biology ought to know. Mendel's work too is critical to the development of biology. The study of biology that coheres with understanding education as the process of producing intellectually mature individuals emphasizes the historical development of the discipline. Knowledge of fact and laboratory technique, when these are the primary goal of biological education, are husks of the science of biology. Biology *is* the battery of issues prominent in the history of the discipline and the characters who addressed those issues along with how they did so.

A similar conclusion can be drawn about every part of science study. Putting habit and character in the center of science education relieves conflicts between disciplines and their conclusions, on one hand, and religious or moral beliefs on the other.

Size and Local Control

Since the goal of education is to cultivate mature individuals, greater rather than less integration among students of models of maturity is desirable. Large schools and classes militate against that goal of greater integration of appropriate models of maturity. When educational processes leave students largely to their peers those processes capitulate to the de facto education carried out by other cultural institutions. Addressing students as individuals and having explicit concern for their habits, values, and character are the heart of education. Large schools and large classes increase, in ratio to their increasing size, the difficulties of addressing students as individuals and of having appropriate concern for their character development. When public school districts build larger schools to be more efficient in using public funds, they work against their own educational goals.

Physical Education

Physical education is a secondary concern when the primary emphasis of education is on knowledge acquisition. Indeed, physical education is an afterthought, an addition to curriculum justified by the need to be healthy and to have a healthy body as a condition of doing the intellectual work of accumulating knowledge. This idea is deeply rooted in Western philosophical traditions according to which one *has* a body but one's body is not strictly speaking part of one's identity; it is part of our inheritance from the Platonist-Cartesian thought that dominates Western culture. Physical education becomes at best something one must do in order to keep one's mind up to standard; or it is a matter of proper stewardship over one's body. Physical education has become something one does to stay healthy, not to become educated.

Pragmatist thought about education as cultivating maturity, especially given the idea that maturity is a development of organic individual potential, makes physical education integral to education. Physical education becomes not an addendum or an afterthought, but a vital part of educational development. Pragmatism does not underrate our bodies, because it sees that we *are* our bodies and their potentials. The idea that humans are biologically organic units means that physical development is as important a part of maturation as is intellectual development. Care for our physical selves *is* care for ourselves. Engendering good habits, including good "physical" habits, is integral to the goal of education.

Taking seriously this idea that we are our bodies and our bodies' habits means no longer thinking of physical education as an afterthought. In some other cultures, this wisdom is readily available.

Eastern disciplines such as yoga, tai chi, and karate integrate body discipline into the very idea of human growth and development. Study of these disciplines may begin at an early age and it brings a sense of accomplishment and peacefulness, as well as a sense of unity with one's body and harmony with others. Such disciplines may bring a balance to living that enables their practitioners to avoid many excesses of behavior that characterize individuals in Western cultures. The balance and peacefulness that come with consistent practice of disciplines is part of the organic maturity that should be the goal of all education. These disciplines engender the balance and discipline that bring integrity and maturity to the tasks of daily life; they keep in perspective the native and sometimes destructive impulses that frequently hinder growth toward maturity. When one no longer thinks of "physical education" as an inessential additive to education, then one may think in an integrated way about educational activities; one may naturally think of disciplines like yoga as a central part of education.

(I add parenthetically that in my experience of educational practices in the lives of my own children, their physical education in the schools is a better source of the maturity-inducing habits that, in a pragmatist understanding, *are* genuine education.)

Issues of education are central to life in a democracy. The democratic hope is partly a hope for successful strategies of education. The point of this chapter is that our conception of education is inseparable from our ideas about how to achieve the goals of education and about how to aim at those goals. A thoroughly pragmatist concept of education is a constructive alternative to dominant current conceptions. Putting habit and character at the center of our concept of education, and conceiving these as biologically organic, can bring constructive change to our strategies of education.

What this discussion of education makes clear is that all institutions of American culture are educational institutions, and that all such institutions need deliberate, reflective thought about how they contribute toward constructive goals and about how they may better achieve such goals. Our religious institutions are such institutions, and they embody values that in many ways conflict with values evident in American commercial culture. Religious institutions also have cultural roots much deeper than the institutions of American commercial culture. The tensions that are natural to the relations between these two institutions yield a promising perspective from which to consider issues about values and about how to ameliorate the de facto education offered in American culture. This promising perspective requires an understanding of religion and its value that is consistent with pragmatism.

A constructive account of institutions of religion is natural to pragmatism in spite of the fact that many are distrustful of pragmatism because they believe it has nothing constructive to offer. From the time of Dewey's *A Common Faith*, pragmatism has frequently been seen as a polite disguise for secularism. Mortimer Adler's "God and the Philosophers" lumps the pragmatists with the positivists who reduce religion to emotion and wish fulfillment.[29] Is pragmatism simply positivism in clever or not so clever disguise? What is pragmatism's constructive contribution to religion? And how may religion be or become part of the reflective life?

NOTES

1. *The Atlantic*, January/February 2008, 92–97.

2. For an account of reflective morality as Dewey conceives it, see LW7:162–66.

3. For an excellent secondary account of Dewey's views about education as these are integral with his philosophy in general, see James W. Garrison, "John Dewey's Philosophy as Education," in Larry A. Hickman, *Reading Dewey: Interpretations for a Postmodern Generation* (Bloomington: Indiana University Press, 1998), 63–81.

4. John Stuhr reviews some of these unique challenges for education in the American democratic environment in "Democracy as a Way of Life," his contribution to his *Philosophy and the Reconstruction of Culture: Pragmatic Essays after Dewey* (Albany: The State University of New York Press, 1993), 37–58. Stuhr also sounds the same note of pessimism about American education that has become common among commentators: "This democratic educational principle receives little more than lip service from the most powerful educational institutions in America today—the economic system, the government, the military, the media,

the family and neighborhood, and the school. To this extent, remarkably, America today is committed neither to democratic education nor to democracy" (53).

5. MW14:123.

6. MW14:124.

7. The perspective I here identify as pragmatist coheres well with the large-scale, anthropological investigations of Jared Diamond. Diamond provides historical confirmation of the general point I make here in terms of contextual individuality and contextual intelligence. See his *Guns, Germs, and Steel: The Fates of Human Societies* (New York: W. W. Norton and Company, 1997). Diamond courteously provides a one-sentence summary of his results: "History followed different courses for different peoples because of differences among peoples' environments, not because of biological differences among the peoples themselves." See also his account of differences between the Moriori and the Maiori peoples of Polynesia (54–57). I take his views as large-scale empirical confirmation of the theses I here call contextual intelligence and contextual individuality.

8. Elizabeth Dodds, *Marriage to a Difficult Man* (Santa Ana, Calif.: Westminster Press, 1981).

9. MW14:4.

10. The use of the term "livering," in this kind of context, originates, so far as I know, with John McDermott in "The Aesthetic Drama of the Ordinary," reprinted in *Pragmatism and Religion: Original Sources and Contemporary Essays*, ed. Stuart Rosenbaum (Urbana: University of Illinois Press, 2003).

11. MW14:20.

12. Stuhr, *Philosophy and the Reconstruction of Culture*, 271.

13. Stuhr, *Philosophy and the Reconstruction of Culture*, 270.

14. For remarks similarly suggesting that dialectical skills are the most fundamental for the moral life, see also Alasdair MacIntyre, *Three Rival Versions of Moral Iniquity* (South Bend, Ind.: University of Notre Dame Press, 1990), 129–30, 201–2; but also many of the sources mentioned in note 1 suggest the necessity of the kind of education traditionally taken to be appropriate for producing dialectical skills: logic, mathematics, and the kind of dialectical inquiry typically associated with classical philosophy, the sort especially evident in Plato's dialogues.

15. MW14:111–12.

16. MW9:238.

17. LW13:70.

18. LW13:70.

19. For further statements of Dewey's view about this issue, see *Human Nature and Conduct* (MW14:108), and *Art as Experience* (LW10:348).

20. See Richard Rorty, *Contingency, Irony, and Solidarity* (Cambridge: Cambridge University Press, 1989), 80. "Ironist" is Rorty's term for people who are aware of the contingency of their final vocabularies, the vocabularies in which they explain to themselves how their lives and their communities are significant, or how they figure in the grand scheme of things. Ironists in this sense have given up on the Enlightenment project of grounding their ways of seeing themselves in reason, God, or the moral law within, and seek only to expand their familiarity with alternative concrete possibilities.

21. Rorty, *Contingency, Irony, and Solidarity*, 192. Martha Nussbaum is another contemporary writer about these topics who endorses Dewey's idea of the significance of literature for moral life and thought. Improbably (or so it seems to me) she finds this theme deeply rooted in Aristotle's moral thought. Perhaps it's fair to say that Nussbaum seeks to straddle the gulf between Dewey and MacIntyre on the issue of what moral thought properly involves and to do so on the authority of Aristotle. Though her view is appealing in many ways, her effort to straddle the gulf between these views seems ungainly, but I cannot here consider her unique contribution. Her view is controversial, especially as regards its interpretation of Aristotle, but she argues it with such grace and deftness as guarantee it wide popularity. I heartily recommend her essays in *Love's Knowledge*, especially "The Discernment of Perception: An Aristotelian Conception of Rationality" (Oxford: Oxford University Press, 1990), 54–105. For an opposing view, see John M. Cooper's review of her earlier book, *The Fragility of Goodness: Luck and Ethics in Greek Tragedy and Philosophy*, in *The Philosophical Review* 97, no. 4 (October 1988): 543–64, especially 562–63.

22. LW13:69.

23. Another source, ostensibly external to philosophy and its concerns, that confirms these ideas of contextuality of intelligence and individuality is Morris Berman's *The Reenchantment of the World* (Ithaca, N.Y.: Cornell University Press, 1981). See especially Berman's chapter 5, "Prolegomena to Any Future Metaphysics." Berman also insists on what I have called the biologically organic character of human intellectual skill.

24. Bruno Bettelheim, *The Uses of Enchantment: The Meaning and Importance of Fairy Tales* (New York: Random House, 1977).

25. Bettelheim, *Uses of Enchantment*, 8.

26. Bettelheim's analysis of these inferior stories appears throughout his text as part of his ongoing commentary on the classical fairy tales; but for explicit remarks detailing inadequacies in contemporary children's literature, see 130ff.

27. Some relevant aspects of the enemy who is ourselves are fairly well-known. In the collection of essays, *Pornography*, ed. Robert Baird and Stuart Rosenbaum (Buffalo, N.Y.: Prometheus Press, 1993), some essays by social scientists point toward decisive evidence that violence is a much more baleful media influence on individual development than is, for example, nakedness or explicit sexual activity.

28. Stuhr, *Philosophy and the Reconstruction of Culture*, 271.

29. The account of Adler's speech along with Dewey's response to it by Robert Westbrook is useful. See Robert Westbrook, *John Dewey and American Democracy* (Ithaca, N.Y.: Cornell University Press, 1991), 519–23.

8

─⌇⌇─

Ecumenism

The reflective life respects tradition while it enables transcendence of tradition toward a better future; the guidance toward the future it provides comes through the ideals that are rooted in the traditions individuals imaginatively rely on. These ideals are the concrete representations— "saints" in the language of the earlier chapter—captured and preserved in cultural institutions. Recurring to the earlier discussion of the reflective life, the reflective life brings together the ideas of individual autonomy, respect for community, and ideals that guide our striving toward a better future. The content of the reflective life, again, is its commitment to autonomy, community, and ideality.

Since the ideals that guide the reflective life are embodied concretely in human institutions and traditions, they are shared among those who are shaped by and who sustain those institutions and traditions. Values are functions of the institutions and traditions that sustain them, as well as of the individuals who are embedded in them. For thoughtful people who acknowledge these facts about values, the feeling of responsibility for their own and the common human future can become weighty, even oppressive. The ideas of contextual intelligence and contextual individuality along with Bruce Wilshire's dismay about the profit-oriented exploitation of the American economic culture may heighten the sense of responsibility. This feeling of responsibility is appropriate.

Values and ideals are not, for pragmatists, ontologically transcendent; they do not present the epistemological difficulties that troubled modern and twentieth-century thinkers. Values and ideals are as concrete as the humans who hold them. The most important consequence for this understanding of values is that they do not reside in a nonhuman power to which humans must defer. Values and ideals are human responsibilities as much as they are human traditions; their roots in sustaining institutions do not exempt them from thoughtfulness about how they might be changed for better service. Indeed, the very fact that they are rooted in human institutions, along with our knowledge of the vicissitudes of such institutions, encourages the idea that they are as malleable as other dimensions of culture. The possibility of ameliorating every dimension of human life, including its values and ideals, is real. The goal of this final chapter is to suggest that this pragmatist conception of ideals and values encourages an expansive ecumenism and continues the egalitarian, cosmopolitan thinking of classical pragmatists, especially William James and John Dewey. Begin with the idea of ecumenism; what is it?

ECUMENISM DEFINED

Ecumenism is the goal of a shared understanding of values, even though these values may be rooted in very different traditions. Ecumenism is frequently thought of in connection with religion, where the ecumenical goal is to unite diverse religious perspectives into a more unified perspective. In one extreme scenario, one might imagine the unification into one religion of those rooted in the progeny of Abraham of the Hebrew Bible; thus Christianity, Judaism, and Islam might, in this scenario, come together into religious unity. A more extreme scenario might imagine a unity that includes not only the Abraham-centered religions, but also others of more diverse origin, including Hinduism, Buddhism, Confucianism, Shinto, and others even more diverse. More modest ecumenical scenarios may seem more realistic than more extreme ones. One might imagine more easily overcoming obstacles to ecumenical unity between Catholics and Episcopalians, Lutherans and Episcopalians, or Congregationalists and Baptists.

Institutions and traditions sustain these diverse religions. Muslims, to take one example, have their holy places, mosques, imams, the Koran, and the Prophet Mohammed, all coming together into a coherent vision of what religious life should be. Such institutions and traditions have cultural inertia; like physical objects, they tend to continue moving along the same cultural paths they have traversed for many years. Institutional inertia is an obstacle to religious ecumenism, and it may take various forms in individual psyches, including how the faithful are to interact, how they are to participate in rituals, and many others. Ecumenism is the idea of overcoming institutional inertia in the direction of unity with other religious institutions, whether they are different denominations of a single religion (e.g., Congregational and Baptist) or different religions entirely (e.g., Hindu and Muslim).

Ecumenism applies not only to the institutions of religion, but also to other venues of culture, including morals, economics, politics, and even etiquette. Democracy as a political system, for example, differs from monarchy, oligarchy, anarchy, and other political systems. Each political system, like each religion, has institutional inertia. And in the political realm, as in the religious, ecumenism is possible. In the political as in the religious realm, ecumenism means overcoming institutional inertia in the direction of a unity of political practice that is agreeable to participants in the different practices. This point about institutional inertia and ecumenism can be made again and again with respect to every venue of traditional culture, be it morals, economics, etiquette, or other more specialized venues of culture.

Consider philosophy. Philosophy is a specialized venue of culture that, like religion, has institutional inertia. When non-Western philosophers complained at the 1998 World Congress of Philosophy that Western philosophers did not respect their non-Western traditions, they were complaining about the absence among Western philosophers of an ecumenical perspective toward other philosophical traditions;[1] they felt discriminated against by adherents of a philosophical tradition larger and more powerful than their own. An appropriately ecumenical perspective, in their view, would acknowledge different philosophical traditions and methodologies, and would seek ways of integrating those different traditions and methodologies.

Science too is a specialized venue of culture that has institutional inertia. Western scientists, much as do Western philosophers, assume that their own scientific traditions *are* science, that other traditions of practice oriented toward knowledge and control of human environments are primitive, mythological, religious, or something other than science. Chinese medical traditions, including acupuncture and herbal treatments, Western scientists think are not scientific. Again we might imagine non-Western scientists seeking from their Western colleagues a more generous ecumenical spirit.[2]

In all venues of culture, whether large and pervasive like morals and religion, or more specialized like science and philosophy, ecumenism is the idea of overcoming cultural inertia in the direction of greater inclusiveness. The inertia of institutions does preserve them, but only at the cost of excluding different others who are shaped by different traditions. Western scientists exclude practitioners of different modes of knowledge and control of nature by thinking of them as not at all scientists. Western philosophers exclude practitioners of styles of intellectual discipline different from their own as not philosophers. These strategies of exclusion are recognizably similar to common strategies of moral and religious exclusion. Recall, for example, G. E. Moore's recourse to the intuitionist strategy of labeling as morally blind those who were not intuitively in touch with the good itself.[3] And recall the common exclusionary strategy of recourse to a special revelation that confers privileged knowledge on only a single religious group. All these strategies of exclusion work to sustain institutional inertia; that they are not intentionally designed for that purpose is irrelevant. Are such exclusionary strategies legitimate?

EXPLANATION AND JUSTIFICATION AGAIN

The question of the legitimacy of exclusionary strategies brings us back once again to the earlier question about explanation and justification, the question which of these intellectual strategies is more fundamental?[4] Consider how this issue arises in the current context.

The issue of the desirability of ecumenism is the issue whether or not it is desirable to try to overcome institutional inertia on behalf of greater inclusiveness. Exclusionary strategies justify institutional inertia and prevent change toward greater inclusiveness. Thus many Western philosophers see non-Western philosophy as not philosophy; many Western scientists see non-Western science as not science; many Muslims see that there is only one God, Allah, who has only one Prophet, Mohammed, and that all other gods are not God; many conservative Christians see that their God is the only God, a God who does not countenance the religious practices of others; and many American citizens see that all forms of political structure are inferior to their own democracy. Each of these exclusionary strategies is rooted in a legitimacy claim, a justification claim designed to sustain the inertia of the institution. These legitimacy claims perpetuate an intellectual culture oriented around issues of justification.

The premier issue for philosophers of science throughout the twentieth century, for example, was how exactly the practices of Western science are superior in achieving knowledge of the natural world; what is it about Western science that makes it cognitively special?[5] For Western political theorists, a similar issue was why democracy is in principle preferable to other political systems.[6] For Christian philosophers, a similar issue has been apologetics, the enterprise of defending and justifying a conventional Christian concept of God against intellectual objections. This ubiquitous focus on issues of justification perpetuates institutional inertia and the exclusiveness joined with it. When challenges come they become central tasks for intellectuals committed to sustaining the integrity of the institution. Thus, the activity of justification becomes an agent—usually in the form of philosophical inquiry—of exclusivity and institutional inertia.

An almost parenthetical remark in support of this idea that there is a connection between the enterprises of justification and the exclusivist inertia of cultural institutions is that those who participate even as critics or skeptics are in effect supporters, intentionally or not, of that same institutional inertia. This connection between skepticism and the conservatism that defers to institutional inertia is frequently noticed. From ancient skeptics such as Sextus Empiricus to modern skeptics such as David Hume and even the Catholic counter-reformer Erasmus, their inability to achieve real knowledge led them to defer to the inertia of social institutions already in place.[7] Those who question the claims on which an institution of culture rests usually end their critique as much in support of the institution as those who defend the claims, an ironic result.

To participate in the activity of investigating the justification of claims on which cultural institutions rest, whether as apologist or as skeptic, is in effect to support those institutions, implicitly if not explicitly. The continued inertia of those institutions, along with their exclusivist, anti-ecumenical tendencies, is the net result of those philosophical activities. The alternative to those activities centered on the idea of justification is the *scientific* inquiry that seeks comprehensive understanding of the roles of such cultural institutions in addressing human needs and interests. Such scientific inquiry is the alternative of trying to understand the role of particular institutions in serving human needs and interests.

This scientific, explanatory alternative enables a more comprehensive understanding of institutions as they address typical needs and interests. The perspective encouraged by this scientific understanding of institutions is amenable to experimentation on behalf of a more inclusive perspective. Seeing how different contexts yield different institutional ways to address human needs and interests suggests that one's own way of addressing them may be optional or at least malleable.[8] The disposition that seeks to understand humans and how their institutions flourish in various environments understands that those institutions might have been different and that they might change. This disposition respects institutions precisely because they serve specific needs and interests, but it sees beyond those institutions to a future arrangement in which they might better serve those needs and interests. For this disposition, greater inclusiveness, as well as genuine ecumenism, becomes possible.

The upshot of this discussion is that the contexts of inquiry in which explanations are primary are contexts favorable to inclusion and ecumenism. Likewise, contexts in which justification is primary are contexts unfavorable to inclusion and ecumenism because they yield impetus to the natural inertia of institutions toward exclusivity.

As in previous discussions of the explanation-justification dichotomy, I observe again that no argumentative strategies can show one of these modes of intellectual technique to be superior to the other; each has re-course to strategies showing that it should be preferred over the other.[9] At best, sponsors of these different strategies must arrive at argumentative stalemate. In the present instance, however, it may be evident that greater virtue lies on the explanation/genealogy side of this dichotomy.

To understand humans as integral parts of their natural world, and to see them as having developed in diverse, geographically different communities but also as having, because of shared biology, common needs and interests—to understand humans in these ways is to understand also that there are possibilities to overcome diversity in the direction of greater integration and harmony. Whether in the cultural venues of religion, morality, politics, or economics, to understand institutions genealogically is to understand that there are possibilities for greater inclusiveness.

The inclusive and ecumenical opportunities that naturally arise as part of the genealogical understanding of institutions may be the best rationale for the idea that explanation is more fundamental than justification. That the context of explanation encourages movement away from the inertia of human institutions in the direction of greater inclusiveness signals that the context of explanation can encourage greater unity while still preserving integrity. Genealogy may become as constructive as it has frequently been, in the hands of many of its proponents, deconstructive. Perhaps no stronger rationale than this is needed to favor privileging genealogical strategies over strategies of justification.

In any case, explanatory, genealogical strategies are characteristic of the American pragmatist tradition. Whether one considers William James or John Dewey, as well as others, one sees deep and abiding concern to understand the cultural contexts of human institutions. From James's *The Varieties of Religious Experience* to Dewey's *Art as Experience*, one finds subtle and sophisticated genealogical strategies in the service of efforts to understand the human world in all of its variety and intricacy.[10] In addition to its commitment to genealogy, one finds also in the pragmatist tradition a radical, ecumenical idealism. The classical American pragmatists were committed to values and ideals they saw to be vital for all humanity.

DEMOCRATIC IDEALISM

John Dewey is the philosopher of democracy; he saw democracy, in the American context, as expressing the most fundamental aspirations of all humanity. Democracy maximally enables individual growth and autonomy; it embodies ubiquitous ideals of community living; and it encourages ideals of community integrity and individual achievement that are discouraged in other contexts.

Dewey's idealism is evident throughout his life and work. In fact, probably the strongest thread of continuity that runs through his life and work from beginning to end is his commitment to democracy as a comprehensive ideal of human living. Distinctive expressions of his democratic idealism appear with regularity in Dewey's work. Here is one such expression familiar to all Dewey scholars:

> Democracy is a way of life controlled by a working faith in the possibilities of human nature. Belief in the Common Man is a familiar article in the democratic creed. That belief is without basis and significance save as it means faith in the potentialities of human nature as that nature is exhibited in every human being irrespective of race, color, sex, birth and family, or material or cultural wealth. This faith may be enacted in statutes, but it is only on paper unless it is put in force in the attitudes which human beings display to one another in all the incidents and relations of daily life. . . . The democratic faith in human equality is belief that every human being, independent of the quantity or range of his personal endowment, has the right to equal opportunity with every other person for development of whatever gifts he has.[11]

This passage is from "Creative Democracy: The Task Before Us," prepared in 1939 on the occasion of Dewey's eightieth birthday. One might read this essay many times over and never tire of its inspired and determined commitment to the democratic ideal. All the elements of Dewey's democratic faith come together here in clean compact prose, prose that is more poetry than prose for those familiar with his work. Respect for individuals; respect for the communities that nurture and sustain them; and commitment to pervasive ideals of individual and community living—all these elements of Dewey's democratic faith ring resolutely throughout his work. In this brief essay, Dewey's statement of that faith becomes a panegyric to democracy worthy of an Emerson or a Whitman.

Dewey's democratic faith, as he consistently expresses it, embodies a strong commitment to the reflective life; it embraces individual autonomy, integrity of community, and commitment to ideals both individual and social. Autonomy, community, and ideality come together in Dewey's democratic idealism into a hope for the future that finds appropriate contrast only in other large, hopeful ideals focused on the human future.[12]

Dewey's 1939 volume, *Freedom and Culture*, is an extended discussion and defense of his democratic idealism. One sees in that volume, and even in its title, Dewey's commitment to the reflective life; freedom and culture are symbiotic dimensions of the democratic ideal. Freedom is inseparable from an appropriately sustaining culture, a culture whose integrity depends upon each individual's commitment to the ideals that enable it. The possibility of the democratic whole depends on the coherence of its parts. Once one sees what Dewey's vision of democracy is, it does indeed appear a vision of human possibility as noble and compelling as any in history. As an ideal end, Dewey's democracy requires as much individual commitment as does any ideal end. As Dewey puts this requirement, "The struggle for democracy has to be maintained on as many fronts as culture has aspects: political, economic, international, educational, scientific and artistic, religious."[13] On all these fronts, the struggle for democracy must be democratic. Only democratic means respect democratic culture; only democratic means respect the autonomy of the individuals who make democratic culture possible; only democratic means can move along the slow and difficult path toward a fuller realization of the democratic ideal.

Democracy is impossible without a sustaining culture that nurtures the freedom that is impossible apart from an accompanying responsibility for the integrity of that sustaining culture. The symbiosis between individual freedom and community integrity, along with the democratic ideals without which neither of these is possible, is complete in Dewey's work. Insofar as the debate between liberalism and communitarianism is broached in contemporary philosophy so as to assume some incompatibility between democratic individualism and community integrity, that debate moves in disregard of Dewey's democratic idealism. Alasdair MacIntyre, Stanley Hauerwas, and many others are guilty, insofar as they carry on their jeremiads against democracy or individualism, at least of question-begging presumption in their failure to take account of the democratic idealism of American pragmatism, especially as that idealism finds expression in the life and work of John Dewey.[14]

In the present context, two questions are pressing: (1) what is the source of Dewey's democratic idealism? and (2) what is the concrete ideal that informs Dewey's democratic idealism? A single answer suffices for both questions.

"CHRISTIANITY AND DEMOCRACY"

Dewey's 1892 essay, "Christianity and Democracy"—Robert Westbrook calls it a "lay sermon"[15]—declares Dewey's turn from Christianity toward democracy. At this point Dewey finds it no longer worthwhile to defend any specific creedal content characteristic of Christian orthodoxy. Dewey has become by the time of this essay, at least in his thinking about Christianity, the pragmatist who becomes increasingly evident in his later work.[16] What makes for Dewey's pragmatism even at this early point in his career is his turn toward the idea that individual and community practices are the fullest measure, indeed the only measure, of individual and community values and ideals. Thus does Christianity morph into democracy. Dewey's democracy is Christianity "naturalized."[17] Let me quote from Rorty the passage from this essay that he singles out for attention:

> It must have seemed strange to the University of Michigan's Christian Students Association to be told, in 1892, that "God is essentially and only the self-revealing" and that "the revelation is complete only as men come to realize him."
>
> Dewey spelled out what he meant by going on to say, "Had Jesus Christ made an absolute, detailed and explicit statement upon all the facts of life, that statement would not have had meaning—it would have not been revelation—until men began to realize in their own action the truth that he declared—until they themselves began to live it."[18]

This passage from Dewey's essay makes explicit his practice-oriented understanding of Christianity: You can detect the meaning of Jesus Christ for individuals only to the extent that they live that meaning in their lives, and such meaning exists only as individuals live that meaning in their relationships and communities. Dewey is appealing to the test of practice, and this appeal is his naturalizing of the idea of Christianity. An idea, a value, or an ideal has traction in an individual life only to the extent that the individual lives that idea, value, or ideal. John Dewey's 1892 test of the meaningfulness of Christianity to any individual is whether or not that individual's practice, habits, and character conform to Christianity's historical exemplar, Jesus Christ. This commitment to locating individual character, values, and ideals in habit and action signals Dewey's pragmatism.

Dewey here abandons his earlier efforts to hold together some remnant of creedal Christianity with his commitments to science and democracy. Now Dewey seeks simply the practice of Christianity, meaning that his Christianity has "morphed" into democracy. But to say that Christianity morphs into democracy is not to say simply that it mutates into democracy. A mutation is a change in which something vital is left behind; a morphing is a change in which nothing vital is left behind.[19] Dewey's democracy is as filled with his Christianity as his Christianity is filled with his democracy; indeed, given his practice orientation, these things may not be distinguishable. Democracy, in Dewey's conception of it, is Christianity in practice; it is the systematic practice of Christianity in our moral, political, social, and cultural worlds. Steven Rockefeller captures Dewey's understanding of this relationship between Christianity and democracy as follows:

> For Dewey, the identification of Christianity and democracy, of religious life and everyday life, was a protest both against forms of institutional and personal religion that were empty of vital meaning and against forms of social and economic life that were unjust and dehumanizing.[20]

To gloss Rockefeller's remark in a way that may not be entirely consistent with his comprehensive treatment of Dewey, one might say that democracy for Dewey transcended the historical limitations of Christianity as theologically and philosophically conceived. In any case, Rockefeller's remark supports the idea that the source of Dewey's commitment to democratic idealism is Christianity. And the concrete ideal on which that democratic idealism rests is the life of Jesus. Dewey's abandonment of theology, of ontology, and of the supernatural is not his abandonment of the concrete historical ideals that have largely motivated Western thought about religion. Dewey's turn toward practice frees those ideals from theoretical conundrums and moves them fully into the world of practice. Another look at the passage from Dewey's 1939 essay, "Creative Democracy: The Task Before Us," reveals his ongoing commitment to a democracy fully infused with his Christianity of practice. I am tempted to quote again the same passage that appears earlier, but I refrain here in the interest of efficiency.

The democratic faith of which Dewey speaks must be "put in force in the attitudes which human beings display to one another in all the incidents and relations of daily life." The test of whether or not one has the democratic faith is the test of practice: what are the attitudes one displays toward one's fellows? One believes that "every human being . . . has the right to equal opportunity with every other person for development of whatever gifts he has" only if one has or cultivates, in oneself and others, habits of behavior that support this democratic faith. The bottom line for Dewey in this issue of having democratic faith is the test of practice. What does one do? What is one disposed to do? What does one seek to encourage in others? At this point in his thought, Dewey is unwaveringly committed to the Peircean, pragmatist understanding of belief as habit of action; any belief is a disposition to act. Faith has become a matter of practice, habit, tendency, and disposition. Dewey's democratic idealism is his faith in Christianity as practice; it is Christianity naturalized, where this means Christianity has become a concrete ideal—democracy—for guiding human practice.[21]

What of religious significance did Dewey leave behind when he made democracy the center of his commitments? One natural answer to this question is that he left behind the supernaturalism that appears not only in popular thought about Christianity but also in standard Christian creeds. That Dewey did leave behind the supernaturalism of the Christian metaphysical tradition is not in question. He did. The question is whether his leaving it behind was a leaving of anything vital for either Christianity or democracy.

Dewey's leaving behind Christian supernaturalism is symptomatic of two distinctive characteristics of his religious perspective. The first is that

Dewey takes more seriously than any previous thinker the idea that practice is fundamental in understanding personal commitments. The fullness of Dewey's commitment to understanding humanity in terms of organic habit, tendency, and disposition leaves behind any hiddenness of personality or character; no longer may humans think of themselves or of others as hidden behind veils or guises that conceal their real selves. Our real selves are what we do, or more modestly, what we tend to do, are disposed to do, or what we habitually do; our real selves are a matter of the engrained practices that make us who we are. The souls or minds of seventeenth- and eighteenth-century philosophy, and even of much current Christian thought, have disappeared and may no longer provide solace for those who worry about their eternal destinies. Ontology can no longer posture as a source of comfort for the fully human creatures of our natural world. Dewey's commitment to practice is, in this respect, simply a systematic recourse to the same idea that finds expression throughout the American tradition from Jonathan Edwards to Richard Rorty: "By their fruits you shall know them."

The second unique characteristic of Dewey's religious perspective is that his God has become, conceptually speaking, a God of practice. "The unity of all ideal ends" is Dewey's conceptualization of God in *A Common Faith*. As mysterious sounding as Dewey's account of God is to those accustomed to thinking of God as "the being than which no greater can be conceived," it nonetheless has the virtue of pointing toward the significance of practice for the religious life. The point of the religious life, for Dewey, is to live toward God, and his concept of God expresses that point. The Anselmian formulation is no better than a distraction from that understanding of religious life, for it mires one in epistemological and ontological conundrums.[22] But Dewey, as much as does even Jonathan Edwards,[23] sees that the whole point of the Christian life is practice. Democracy, in Dewey's thought, is Christianity as practice. One might also observe that for Dewey, as much as for Jonathan Edwards or St. Anselm, the sovereignty of God remains intact; that sovereignty in Dewey, however, becomes indistinguishable from the sovereignty of the democratic ideal.

Some contemporary pragmatists have seemed to argue, in apparent opposition to the view I sketch here, that Dewey's commitment to democracy is not a reconstruction of Christianity around the ideals that center in the person of Jesus, and they are reluctant to acknowledge that those same ideals might be the moral and religious backbone of democracy. These scholars seem to hold that, without their supernatural commitments, conventional religious institutions become pointless epiphenomena of culture, institutions no longer needed by a culture able to discern the genealogical roots of those institutions' supernaturalism.

PRAGMATISM AND RELIGIOUS INSTITUTIONS

Many scholars of pragmatism are skeptical about religious institutions. Dewey himself expresses the view that the church should "universalize itself and pass out of existence,"[24] in much the same way he suggests that an ideal educational system would not involve anything recognizable as a school.[25] These utopian remarks probably should not be read as evaluative commentary about existing cultural institutions; nevertheless, skepticism about institutions of religion among scholars of the pragmatist tradition is pervasive.

Alan Ryan, for example, comments that

> there is perhaps something too *briskly* pragmatic about . . . [Dewey's] endorsement of the utility of talking about "God."
>
> As myself an aggressive atheist, I am not persuaded that the *usefulness* of such ways of talking has much bearing on their *truthfulness*; to put it unkindly, one might complain that Dewey wants the social value of religious belief without being willing to pay the epistemological price for it. To put it less unkindly, we may wonder whether in fact, it is possible to have the *use* of religious vocabulary without the accretion of supernaturalist beliefs that Dewey wishes to slough off. What holds for belief might be thought to hold for institutions. That is, if the religious attitude is to be inculcated as a generalized social sentiment of cosmic confidence, we can inquire whether special institutions, rites, liturgies, and rituals are plausible expressions of that confidence and whether some are particularly effective in strengthening that outlook.[26]

Other scholars appear to sympathize with Ryan's skepticism about religious beliefs and religious institutions.[27] Two responses to this skepticism about religious belief and institutions seem appropriate.

The first response is that to think, as does Ryan, that one must pay an epistemological price for the social value of religious belief is to embrace at best only half-heartedly the fundamentals of Dewey's pragmatism. I mean by this comment that Dewey's God does not pay *any* epistemological price. A large part of the point of *A Common Faith* is to raise God above epistemology. Or if the metaphors of above and below seem inapposite here, then that same large point of *A Common Faith* is to remove from thought about God the issues about justification and epistemology that have systematically clogged Western thought about God. Once one understands that epistemology is systematically a "spectator sport" of the sort Dewey had shown as early as 1896 to be an inappropriate model for human knowing,[28] then one must see also that Dewey's conceptual innovation about God in *A Common Faith* does not invite epistemological controversy. Contrary to Ryan, no epistemological controversy infects

Dewey's God. The human activities of knowing and acquiring knowledge are all the myriad activities that make up the practices of science, in all the guises in which those practices appear. Epistemological issues, in any recognizable sense of epistemology as that intellectual discipline appears in philosophy, are not part of those practices; they are also not issues for Dewey's understanding of God or for the institutions of religion that are ubiquitous in human societies.

Another way of seeing this point about God, religious institutions, and epistemology is to reflect again on the pragmatist understanding of belief to which Dewey is committed. Beliefs are habits of action, or more subtly, beliefs are habits, tendencies, and dispositions. As habits, tendencies, and dispositions, beliefs are more or less distinct, more or less diffuse, and more or less well defined; they are more or less justified to the extent that one is inclined to engage in explicit behaviors that manifest those habits, tendencies, and dispositions. To think of beliefs as justified or not in some absolute way, to think of them as epistemologically responsible or irresponsible relative to a body of evidence, is to think of them as other than habits of action, as fixed items, perhaps propositions, that one may accept or reject for good or bad reasons. This way of thinking about beliefs as epistemologically justified or unjustified, as rational or irrational, reintroduces into pragmatist thought the conundrums of traditional epistemology. But Dewey works very hard in his entire corpus to avoid this result.[29] To take pragmatism seriously is to refuse to waver in one's embrace of the fullness of its orientation toward practice, and also toward science conceived as well-established cognitive practices. Ryan's embrace of Dewey and of pragmatism, again, is only half-hearted; and his own epistemological suspicions, as well as his aggressive atheism, are symptomatic of his half-heartedness.

The second response to Ryan is that as things now stand culturally— short of a utopia in which churches might universalize themselves and disappear—religious institutions are an integral, even necessary, part of human culture. Such institutions are as integral to human society as are institutions of knowing, learning, trading, and politicking. Each such institution is vital because it answers to a certain range of human needs and interests; indeed, the foundation of each institution is its address of some basic range of needs and interests. The various sciences, for example, are rooted in a basic desire to relate in more effective cognitive ways to our natural environment; more effective cognition empowers humans in relation to their environment, so that food, shelter, and virtually every dimension of life becomes better. Each institution of culture functions to empower individuals in their efforts to address basic needs. What of religious institutions? What needs and interests do they address?

Jonathan Ree puts his finger nicely on some of those needs and interests.[30] Ree agrees with pragmatists that metaphysical and theological issues—"divine and satanic inspiration, let alone the finer points of transubstantiation, angelology, resurrection, or divine rewards and punishments"—are irrelevant to religious life. What is not irrelevant to religious life is "the brevity and oddity of each individual existence, what might be called the tombstone facts of life." As Ree puts the point,

> It is religion that has supplied practically all the phrases, concepts, stories, and images that help us with such impossible tasks as remembering the unthinkable, forgetting the unforgivable, and lingering for a while over a fleeting instant of time. Religions have created prayers and liturgies and buildings and open spaces that may help us see our griefs and perplexities in their indissoluble individuality, but without forgetting their continuities with those of other people and generations. The shocks and aftershocks of love and death call for occasional suspensions of our daily, weekly, and annual rounds; and off the top of our heads we are unlikely to dream up new forms of interruption as well suited to our needs as those that we have inherited from religions.[31]

Much can be said about these needs and interests that are addressed more and less effectively by religious traditions. What is implausible is to think that these needs and interests might somehow be transcended by the effective workings of another institution—science for example. When one puts aside the metaphysics and epistemologies of supernatural religion one remains simply human. No matter how effective science—medical science for example—has become in recent decades it has not allowed humanity to finesse "the tombstone facts of life." These tombstone facts of life are among the needs religious institutions address. Transcending supernatural religion is not transcending these needs.[32]

The understanding of pragmatism that best captures the spirit of pragmatism and of Dewey's work transcends epistemological worries about God and religious institutions as well as similar philosophical worries about the foundations of morality or other human institutions. But apart from their address of what Ree calls the tombstone facts of life, another dimension of religious institutions speaks in their favor, especially in the context of contemporary American democratic culture.

As I noted in the previous chapter, human institutions are expressions of human values. Indeed, the relation between values and institutions is much closer than is captured by saying that the former are expressions of the latter; human institutions are human values, and they enable the individuals who come to maturity among them to realize their various potentials. Just as these institutions empower and enable their human charges, they also restrict and restrain them. Individual human potentials, as much as human values, are functions of the institutions that bring individuals to maturity and sustain them.

DEMOCRACY, INSTITUTIONS, AND VALUES

Religious institutions are loci of human values. As such loci of value, religious institutions enable and sustain some of the nobler values in history.

When Martin Luther King Jr. wrote "Letter from a Birmingham Jail," he appealed to his fellow clerics to take seriously, as violations of their own declared Christian faith, the injustices their fellow black people struggled with in their daily lives. Nonviolent resistance was the Gandhian and Christian ideal that King took into the civil rights struggles of the mid-twentieth century. His Christian commitment was the proclaimed ground on which rested his civil disobedience on behalf of justice for his countrymen. Where would Martin Luther King have been in a culture that, in all of its commercial capitalism, represented as uniquely worthwhile only the "bottom-line" economic dimensions of human activity? Could the person we know as the heart of the civil rights movement have been possible without the religious institutions that gave contemporary substance to his values?

King's "I Have a Dream" speech during the march on Washington in 1963, his 1964 Nobel Prize acceptance speech, and many of his rhetorical contributions to contemporary society would have been impossible without the Christian church that nurtured him to maturity. The Christian churches and the other religious institutions of American culture are the locus of vitally important values.

Self-sacrifice, respect for all, forgiveness, charity, fraternity, and other values vital for human communities have their most significant locus in religious institutions. For Christians, the person of Jesus expresses those values that are captured succinctly in the parables of the New Testament. The parables are simple stories, but they are psychologically powerful and compelling stories that invite considerate thought, and application in one's life. As stories, they are psychologically compelling in just the way Bruno Bettelheim suggests the traditional fairy tales are psychologically significant for individual mental health. Such simple and powerful narratives find their way into human psyches where they take up residence to guide human behavior into constructive paths. When one contrasts such stories with the many that are typical in American media culture—the ubiquitous sort, for example, that produced distress and despair in Bruce Wilshire when he experienced *Total Recall* (see the previous chapter)—one sees that values of the sort that motivated Martin Luther King Jr. find expression only in limited cultural spaces. Our religious institutions are those limited cultural spaces where such values are expressed and sustained. That they express and sustain vital moral values is another reason religious institutions are not optional even for sophisticated and knowledgeable intellectuals. John Dewey realized this fact about religious institutions, and he may even have been aware in his later work, especially in *A Common Faith*, that his youthful remarks about the churches universalizing themselves and passing out of existence were indeed utopian and unrealistic given the current state of human culture. Religious institutions are loci of noble ideals, ideals that enable community, integrity, and progress.

This fact of the cultural need for religious institutions is another part of the response to Alan Ryan's skepticism about religious beliefs and institutions. Religious institutions serve vital human needs and interests.

Also worth suggesting is that John Dewey's discomfort with laissez-faire capitalism and his doubts about its coherence with democracy may be enlightened by thinking, as I emphasize here, of his democracy as rooted in his Christianity. Dewey's treatment of the relation between capitalism and democracy in *Freedom and Culture* expresses his reservations about the values of capitalism.[33] The problem is that capitalist economic culture expresses only a limited range of values, values that when pursued in the ways prized in capitalist culture become incoherent with central values of democratic culture. (See again the passage from "Creative Democracy: The Task Before Us" that I quoted earlier in this chapter.) The values of capitalism and the values of Christianity are in serious conflict; thus the values of capitalism and the values of democracy are in serious conflict.[34] Seen in this way, Dewey's later support of religion coheres both with his reservations about capitalism and with his commitment to democratic idealism.

The democratic idealism in Dewey is respectful of religious institutions, and it is ecumenical. Richard Rorty's reservations about the ecumenism of classical pragmatism, apparently rooted in his own commitments to pragmatism, deserve attention in this context.

RICHARD RORTY AND ECUMENISM

Richard Rorty shares Dewey's democratic idealism. Rorty shares also Dewey's aversion to nondemocratic means for pursuing the democratic ideal. The Christian roots that hold in place Dewey's democratic idealism, however, Rorty does not share.[35] Nevertheless, the content of the democratic ideal is virtually identical in the thought of each. Autonomy, community, and ideality are recognizably central commitments in Rorty as much as they are in Dewey. The issue of ecumenism is more difficult in Rorty, however, than it is in Dewey.

The classical, liberal divide between the public world of political, social, and moral activity on one side, and the private world of religious, artistic, scientific, and other idiomatic interests becomes in Rorty's work a normative constraint on all culture. That divide militates against the ecumenical possibilities of the democratic ideal in Dewey's, and in my own, conception of it. I cannot do better presenting that liberal divide than Robert Westbrook has done in the epilogue to his 1991 *John Dewey and American Democracy*:

> Pressed by critics to make clearer his moral and political commitments, Rorty has said enough of late to suggest that his "social hope" as well as his view of the responsibilities of philosophy differs significantly from Dewey's. Refusing to accept the ethical postulate conjoining self-realization and the social good which was at the heart of Dewey's ethics throughout his career, Rorty has argued for a "liberal utopia" in which there prevails a rigid division between a rich autonomous private sphere that will enable elite "ironists" like himself to create freely the self they wish—even if that be a cruel, antidemocratic self—and a lean, egalitarian, "democratic" public life confined to the task of preventing cruelty. . . . For Dewey, of course, democracy was a "way of life" not merely a way of public life—an ideal that "must affect all modes of human association"—and he would not have accepted Rorty's contention that "there is no way to bring self-creation together with justice at the level of theory" for that would have required him to give up a principal article of his democratic faith. Rorty contends that the belief that "the springs of private fulfillment and of human solidarity are the same" is a bothersome Platonic or Christian hangover. If so, Dewey suffered from it.[36]

Westbrook explains here the apparent gap between Dewey's democratic idealism and Rorty's democratic idealism. As Rorty presents the issue, he appears on the more realistic side of the gap, while on the other, more optimistic side is Dewey. Dewey, in short, appears more comprehensive and inclusive in his democratic idealism than does Rorty. In "Religion as a Conversation-Stopper" Rorty points out that nobody in a liberal democratic society should expect orthodox, Christian antiabortionists to put forward their sectarian reasons for their antiabortionist position, and that furthermore those Christian antiabortionists should see that their sectarian reasons are conversation-stoppers. Rorty wonders how "we atheists," who base our political views on Enlightenment philosophy, might respond so as to engage meaningfully our sectarian opponents' reasons for their antiabortion position?[37] In Dewey's liberal democratic society Enlightenment atheists as well as orthodox Christians may seek a

common democratic standard for behavior in cases of unintended, unde-
sired pregnancies, and they may seek also a common and mutually satisfying legislative and judicial approach to social and political policy involving abortion rights.[38]

I find it difficult not to be sympathetic with the realistic pragmatism
that moderates Rorty's democratic idealism. The conservative Christian
orthodoxy that motivates some political perspectives on many issues is
difficult to engage constructively. On the other hand, as Jeffrey Stout
notes, it is disingenuous to expect orthodox Christians to be dishonest in
expressing reasons for their political perspectives.[39] The classical liberal
political tradition, embodied in John Stuart Mill and H. L. A. Hart, is the
source of Rorty's realistic perspective about this issue, along with his
Nietzschean skepticism about large human ideals.[40] Even though classical
liberalism and Nietzschean skepticism undergird Rorty's perspective on
these matters, I believe Rorty's work shows him to be at least ambivalent
about his official perspective and to be drawn affectively toward Dewey's
more inclusive, democratic idealism. Insofar as he is drawn affectively toward the democratic idealism of classical pragmatists, Rorty is a suitable
representative of that pragmatism, in spite of the fact that many contemporary intellectuals regard him with suspicion.

A parenthetical remark about Rorty's perspective is that his embrace of
atheism is no more appropriate than is Alan Ryan's embrace of it in his
harsh critique of Dewey's *A Common Faith*. The God of Dewey's *A Common Faith* is a God conceptually appropriate for conveying the democratic, and implicitly Christian, idealism of practice toward an inclusive
human community. Again, atheism is a possible perspective about a God
of theory, a God of theology and philosophy, a God whose being must be
justified and defended; about a God of practice, a unity of ideal ends,
atheism is not a plausible perspective. Insofar as he embraces atheism,
Rorty, along with Ryan, fails to embrace the fullness of classical pragmatism's democratic idealism. The democratic idealism of the classical pragmatists is an idealism of practice in which institutions of culture are justified to the extent that they support the cultural integrity that makes
possible reflective lives. The account of God Dewey provides in *A Common Faith* is an integral part of that democratic idealism.

In any case, Rorty does appear ambivalent about his embrace of the
private-public dichotomy; he seems at least to wish it unnecessary. Consider, for example, the account Rorty offers of moral progress:

> The right way to take the slogan "We have obligations to human beings sim-
> ply as such" is as a means of reminding ourselves to keep trying to expand
> our sense of "us" as far as we can. That slogan urges us to extrapolate fur-
> ther in the direction set by certain events in the past—the inclusion among

"us" of the family in the next cave, then of the tribe across the river, then of the tribal confederation beyond the mountains, then of the unbelievers beyond the seas (and, perhaps last of all, of the menials who, all this time, have been doing our dirty work). This is a process which we should try to keep going. We should stay on the lookout for marginalized people—people whom we still instinctively think of as "they" rather than "us." We should try to notice our similarities with them. The right way to construe the slogan is as urging us to *create* a more expansive sense of solidarity than we presently have.[41]

This idea of moral progress is recognizably similar to Dewey's own. Moral progress for Dewey is ameliorating institutions of culture so that reflective lives might become more widely available. Moral progress for Rorty is the imaginative process of coming to see possibilities for solidarity with different others. In neither understanding of moral progress is there a fixed idea that makes such progress possible; each account of moral progress depends on the historically malleable institutions of democratic culture. Where moral progress is concerned, Rorty shares Dewey's democratic idealism.

The fear that Dewey's democratic idealism may be unrealistic, that it may be unrealizable because of contingencies of culture and circumstance, is the dimension of Rorty's thought that motivates his frequent capitulation to the liberal perspective expressed in his advocacy of a strong private-public distinction.[42] His ambivalence between the idealistic hope of the classical pragmatists and the caution grounded in a realistic assessment of human prospects motivates both Rorty's faithfulness to Dewey's democratic idealism and his guarded assessment of its prospects. Although Westbrook is right in insisting on significant difference between Dewey and Rorty, the difference he discusses is not systematic.[43] In spite of the deep misgivings of many contemporary intellectuals about his work, Rorty is a genuine representative of classical pragmatists' democratic idealism, and he is at least warily committed to the inclusive ecumenism that is part of that idealism.[44]

THE UNITY OF ALL IDEAL ENDS

Dewey's God is, conceptually speaking, a God of practice. Furthermore, since pragmatism is oriented toward practice rather than theory, it intimates that thinking about God in accord with Dewey's suggestion may encourage an orientation of human thought and inquiry toward, as Rorty frequently puts it, the human future rather than toward eternity. If conceptual distancing from the onto-theological tradition's God of theory and eternity is possible, then those human ideals expressed in the Christian, democratic, and pragmatist tradition might come to the forefront of human intellectual life.

Not only might those democratic ideals come to the forefront of human activity, but so also might those alternative ideals expressed in other cultures that have no historical association with democracy or its development. Muslim, Hindu, and Confucian cultures express institutions and values different from those that, in the democratic West, sustain possibilities for productive individual lives. The symbiosis between Western democratic culture and the ideal of the reflective life may appear, in some of those non-Western cultures, a cultural anomaly to be avoided. Understanding Western democratic idealism of the sort that was vital in John Dewey's thought might be a very large, and perhaps unsavory, undertaking for individuals in those cultures. Likewise, understanding Confucian culture, its values, and the intricate relationships among individuals and their various communities in Confucian culture might be a very large, again perhaps unsavory, undertaking for American democrats. In all of these cultures, specific traditions, institutions, and values mold individuals and open possibilities for their futures. How do the ideals of those alternative cultures differ from the ideals of American democracy? Are the ideals of those alternative cultures coherent with those of democracy? Or are those different ideals incoherent with those of democracy? Dewey's practice-oriented understanding of God invites these questions, and it simultaneously discourages the theoretical questions that have dominated thought about God in Western philosophy and theology.[45]

When these kinds of questions are entertained apart from questions of justification, apart from questions about correctness of theological or philosophical content or argument, then they may yield the thoughtfulness that might produce recognition of similarity. If, for example, Hindus, Confucians, and Christians become able to suspend the issues of theological correctness that typically dominate much of their thought, they might recognize similarities among the concrete expressions of their own values, institutions, and traditions and the apparently different expressions of other traditions.

Suppose, for example, that among Christians, Jesus, Jesus's life, his parables, and stories about him came to the center of their thought about their religion. Suppose likewise that among Muslims, Mohammed, Mohammed's life, his teachings, and stories about him came to the center of their thought about Islam. And suppose parallel things about other religious traditions. The stories that might then come to the fore have their own integrity; they have their own psychological power; and they have their own ability to reach deeply into our affective psyches. Insofar as they have their integrity, psychological power, and affective depth, such stories may be definitive for individuals' lives. Bringing these culturally different, concrete ideals into clear focus for individuals of different traditions invites deep thoughtfulness about similarities and differences. To become able to live intentionally among such similarities and differences, in full awareness of their significance, is to take a step along the path toward, in Dewey's language, the unity of all ideal ends. A condition of being able to take that step is to think of those ideal ends as concrete, as fully embodied in cultural traditions, as themselves possible to capture in nets of explanation, and as themselves expressible in affectively compelling ways that have spiritual depth. As has become evident in preceding pages, a condition of that significant step is putting aside the projects of justification that have become so intimately a part of Western thought about religion. Apologetics, as the theological, philosophical task of securing exclusive privilege for a particular tradition, must be set aside in favor of the more significant religious tasks of seeking the unity of ideal ends, of seeking God.

Many examples of this concrete expression are possible, but consider for brief illustration the parable of the Good Samaritan. The story is a vital moral ideal, or as some would prefer to put it, the story is a "concrete expression of" a vital moral ideal. Interestingly, this particular parable is Jesus's response to some lawyers who were hoping to extract from him a precise account of the content of the law; they wanted to know, about the commandment to love one's neighbor as oneself, who counts as one's neighbor. (To express a contemporary way of putting what they wanted, one might say that they wanted an analysis of the concept of neighbor so that they might appropriately apply this portion of the law.) Jesus's response was to tell the story of the Samaritan.[46] Noteworthy about Jesus's response in this context is his refusal to respond to the lawyers' invitation to offer an analysis of the concept of neighbor; he limited himself to telling the story. The concreteness of that parable, its integrity, psychological power, and affective depth, enables its capture for many Christians of the central content of Christianity.[47]

The power of such stories in our psyches is their truth. Their power enables them as deep human values, values that find expression principally, if not exclusively, in religious institutions. Such stories are the poetry of our phenomenal lives, the powers that enable our constructive engagement of our natural and social worlds and that knit us together into the families, communities, and individuals we are. Not surprising, then, is the poetry and literature that feeds on these deep human values and that intensifies them as values that sustain us individually and that knit us into families and communities that lean in hope toward our common and individual futures.

Walt Whitman's *Democratic Vistas*, Ralph Waldo Emerson's "The American Scholar," Robert Frost's "The Gift Outright," W. E. B. Du Bois's "The

Prayers of God," and e. e. cummings's "A Man Who Had Fallen among Thieves" are some poetic expressions that capture poignantly the phenomenal truth of American democratic idealism. Consider a few lines from Whitman that are quoted by William James in *The Varieties of Religious Experience*:

> And I know that the hand of God is the promise of my own,
> And I know that the spirit of God is the brother of my own,
> And that all the men ever born are also my brothers and the
> Women my sisters and lovers,
> And that a kelson of the creation is love.[48]

Not only do Whitman, Emerson, Frost, Du Bois, and cummings, working in the same idealistic American tradition as William James, John Dewey, and Richard Rorty, imaginatively grasp and express the democratic idealism that is the poetry of American phenomenal life, but so also do others who are not part of that American democratic tradition. Gerard Manley Hopkins, a mid-nineteenth-century Catholic poet, comes very close to capturing that same poetry in the last lines of "As Kingfishers Catch Fire":

> . . . Christ plays in ten thousand places,
> Lovely in limbs, and lovely in eyes not his
> To the Father through the features of men's faces.[49]

And that same poetry finds expression in the work of Russian poet Yevgeny Yevtushenko, who did much of his artistic work during the Communist years of the Soviet Union. Yevtushenko's "I Would Like" expresses the same spirit of democratic idealism that sings through the prose of the American philosophers, especially in James and Dewey.[50] That same poetry finds expression in every literate human culture; one finds it in Confucius, in Gandhi, in the Dalai Lama, and in many others.

The poetry of democratic idealism, the poetry of our phenomenal lives, whatever its particular content, is vital to us as the individuals and communities we are, even though we have different traditions. That poetry is not restricted to the American province; it is not restricted to the Protestant or to the Christian worlds. The large spiritual traditions that hold humanity, sustained in religious institutions in all cultures, are concrete truths of human lives and promises of a larger human future of greater integrity.

I conclude with the well-known last lines of Dewey's *A Common Faith*:

> The Things in civilization we most prize are not of ourselves. They exist by grace of the doings and sufferings of the continuous human community in which we are a link. Ours is the responsibility of conserving, transmitting,

rectifying, and expanding the heritage of values we have received that those who come after us may receive it more solid and secure, more widely accessible and more generously shared than we have received it. Here are all the elements for a religious faith that shall not be confined to sect, class, or race. Such a faith has always been implicitly the common faith of mankind.[51]

NOTES

1. See the discussion in chapter 1 of this World Congress.

2. Paul Feyerabend is probably as good a speaker for the cause of these non-Western scientists as any they might suggest. See Paul Feyerabend, *Against Method* (London: Verso, 1978).

3. G. E. Moore, *Principia Ethica* (Cambridge: Cambridge University Press, 1920).

4. See chapters 1 and 5 for treatments of this same issue in different contexts.

5. Some sources among many for this enterprise include works by Thomas Kuhn, Hilary Putnam, Edward Wilson, Ian Hacking, Rudolph Carnap, Willard Quine, and Paul Feyerabend.

6. John Rawls's early work, as I have commented earlier, fits this mold.

7. The literature on this phenomenon is voluminous. See, for example, Richard Popkin, *Skepticism from Erasmus to Spinoza* (Berkeley: University of California Press, 1979), and David Hiley, *Philosophy in Question* (Chicago:University of Chicago Press, 1988).

8. This almost reflexive response probably explains Richard Rorty's liberal ironist response to what he sees as the ubiquitous facts of contingency; more of Rorty's perspective later. In any case, a result of following up this idea of explanation is that alternatives become genuine possibilities.

9. See earlier discussions of this issue in chapters 2 and 5.

10. William James, in chapter 18 of *Varieties*, explicitly embraces science of religion in preference to philosophy of religion.

11. John Dewey, "Creative Democracy: The Task Before Us," LW14. This essay is reprinted in Stuart Rosenbaum, ed., *Pragmatism and Religion: Original Sources and Contemporary Essays* (Urbana: University of Illinois Press, 2003), 91–96. See page 93.

12. Karl Marx, almost a contemporary of Dewey's, may have had a similar ideal hope for the large human future. The ideal human communities envisioned by Dewey and Marx may be similar, and the influence of their youthful religious experience on their mature understandings of what that ideal human community should be like may also be similar. Significant differences in their historical and cultural contexts, however, undoubtedly made for decisive differences in their efforts to aim at that ideal community. The differences between Dewey and Marx are interesting, but one definitive difference lies in their different understandings of appropriate means that may be used toward achievement of an ideal end. Means of achieving any ideal end that do not respect the autonomy of others, the

integrity of their communities, and their own ideals—their stature as loci of the reflective life—are not coherent with Dewey's democratic ideal. Dewey himself puts
the contrast as follows: "If there is one conclusion to which human experience un-
mistakably points it is that democratic ends demand democratic methods for their
realization. Authoritarian methods now offer themselves to us in new guises.
They come to us claiming to serve the ultimate ends of freedom and equity in a
classless society. Or they recommend adoption of a totalitarian regime in order to
fight totalitarianism. In whatever form they offer themselves, they owe their se-
ductive power to their claim to serve ideal ends. Our first defense is to realize that
democracy can be served only by the slow day by day adoption and contagious
diffusion in every phase of our common life of methods that are identical with the
ends to be reached and that recourse to monistic, wholesale, absolutist procedures
is a betrayal of human freedom no matter in what guise it presents itself."
Dewey's point is that the democratic ideal and the democratic faith are not coherent with means that compromise that ideal and faith. Totalitarian or authoritarian
or paternalistic means, no matter how noble the end they aim to achieve, are not
acceptable in a democratic, or a democracy-aspiring, culture.

13. LW13:186.

14. Jeffrey Stout is aware of this lacuna in most contemporary discussions of
liberalism and communitarianism. His recent *Democracy and Tradition* (Princeton,
N.J.: Princeton University Press, 2004) is in large measure an effort to remedy this
defect of contemporary discussions about these issues. Robert Westbrook's excellent *John Dewey and American Democracy* (Ithaca, N.Y.: Cornell University Press,
1991) is historically informative in its discussions of Dewey's democratic idealism,
especially in its relation to alternative views of democracy; see in particular the
epilogue to Westbrook's volume, "The Wilderness and the Promised Land,"
537–52.

15. See Westbrook, *John Dewey and American Democracy*, 78.

16. Richard Rorty argues that Dewey's really thorough pragmatist turn comes
only after his 1925 *Experience and Nature*. I believe, however, that the most significant dimensions of that later work supporting Rorty's interpretation are instead
compatible with the more thorough pragmatism that I see even in this 1892 essay,
but I cannot here undertake the controversy about Rorty's interpretation.

17. I use this term, "naturalized," guardedly. In his turn toward pragmatism,
Dewey does indeed turn toward practice and away from theory, the kind of theory that in Western philosophy and theology focuses intellectual effort almost exclusively on ideas of the supernatural. I do believe that Dewey turns decisively
away from theory in this standard philosophical and theological way of thinking
about theory. His turn toward practice, however, I do not think of as an expression
of ontological preference for what in contemporary philosophy has come to be
called "naturalism." Theory, in Dewey's naturalism, becomes a mode of practice;
it has no hope of transcending human practices of thought in the direction traditionally imagined by metaphysical realism or by some versions of scientific realism. "Naturalizing" as I intend it here means nothing ontological; it conveys the
idea of a turn toward practice.

18. Richard Rorty, "Pragmatism as Romantic Polytheism," in *Pragmatism and
Religion*, ed. Stuart Rosenbaum (Urbana: University of Illinois Press, 2003), 122.

19. "Morph" as I use it here may be a neologism; I take it from the popular children's novel series about "animorphs," and I try to use it in the sense it has in that novel series.

20. Steven Rockefeller, *John Dewey: Religious Faith and Democratic Humanism* (New York: Columbia University Press, 1991), 164.

21. Jeffrey Stout gives an expansive, though brief, account of the emergence of democratic culture. See *Democracy and Tradition* (Princeton, N.J.: Princeton University Press, 2004), chapter 9, titled "The Emergence of Democratic Culture." The account I give here of Dewey's democracy as Christianity of practice I see as consistent with Stout's more expansive account, but it focuses deliberately on Dewey's commitment to democratic idealism.

22. Among twentieth-century theologians who would protest Anselm's formula for God, or any formula that would assume God to be a being who might be known, are Paul Tillich, Karl Barth, and William Dean. See Paul Tillich, *Systematic Theology* (Chicago: University of Chicago Press, 1973); Karl Barth, *Church Dogmatics* (Oxford: T & T Clark Books, 2004); and William Dean, *The American Spiritual Culture* (New York: Continuum International Publishing Group, 2002).

23. See Bruce Kuklick, *A History of Philosophy in America, 1720–2000* (Oxford: Oxford University Press, 2001). Kuklick explicates Jonathan Edwards's account of grace as follows: "God related to individuals through human experience, and he became, through Christ, the reason for behavior. For the elect, Christ, the personal wisdom of God, was the telos of history." See page 19.

24. "The Relation of Philosophy to Theology," *Essays, The Study of Ethics (1893–1894)*, vol. 4 of *The Early Works of John Dewey, 1882–1898*, ed. Jo Ann Boydston (Carbondale: Southern Illinois University Press, 1984).

25. Alan Ryan quotes a *New York Times* editorial from 1933 wherein Dewey wrote to this effect. See Ryan's *John Dewey and the High Tide of American Liberalism* (New York: W. W. Norton & Co., 1995), 275.

26. Ryan, *John Dewey and the High Tide of American Liberalism*, 274.

27. Some who appear to hold a similar perspective are Steven Rockefeller and Michael Eldridge. See Rockefeller's *John Dewey*; and Eldridge's *Transforming Experience: John Dewey's Cultural Instrumentalism* (Nashville, Tenn.: Vanderbilt University Press, 1998).

28. See "The Reflex Arc Concept of Experience," *The Essential Dewey*, vol. 2, ed. Larry Hickman (Bloomington: University of Indiana Press, 1998). Dewey's later great works about epistemology and metaphysics hew to this insight about human knowing that Dewey definitively expresses in this early essay.

29. The view I am attributing here to Dewey may appear to denigrate the practices of discursive reasoning that are undoubtedly an integral part of contextual justification, the activity of trying to produce good reasons in favor of a certain view. Denigrating such practices is no part of my intent, nor do I think it was any part of Dewey's perspective. What Wilfrid Sellars calls "the logical space of reasons" conveys an idea of justification that is thoroughly coherent with the perspective about reason I here seek to convey. Sellars's idea of justification, however, is the fullest understanding of that idea that coheres with Dewey's pragmatism. See Rorty's discussion of Sellars in *Philosophy and the Mirror of Nature* (Princeton, N.J.: Princeton University Press, 1979).

30. Jonathan Ree, "The Poverty of Unbelief," *Harper's*, July 2002, 13–17.

31. Ree, "The Poverty of Unbelief," 16.

32. Even so antithetical-to-religion a character as Sidney Hook appears to agree with my assessment—and Ree's—of the cultural indispensability of religious institutions. See, for example, Hook's introduction to the Southern Illinois University Press Edition of Dewey's *Experience and Nature*. See LW1:xvi. For more in the same vein by Hook, see *John Dewey: An Intellectual Portrait* (Amherst, N.Y.: Prometheus Books, 1995), 220.

33. *Freedom and Culture*, in LW13.

34. In this connection, Milton Friedman's classical and conflicting view about the deep coherence of capitalism and democracy is worth mentioning. See his *Capitalism and Freedom* (Chicago: University of Chicago Press, 1962).

35. Confirmation of these claims is ubiquitous throughout Rorty's work. See, for example, his autobiographical essay, "Trotsky and the Wild Orchids," *Philosophy and Social Hope* (New York: Penguin Books, 1999), 3–20.

36. Westbrook, *John Dewey and American Democracy*, 541.

37. Rorty, *Philosophy and Social Hope*, 172.

38. For a sketch of how this common judicial approach might be attained, see my "The Constitution, Metaphysics, and Abortion," *Journal of Church and State* 43 (Autumn 2001): 707–23. For additional commentary about Rorty's approach to this dichotomy of private and public life, see again Jeffrey Stout, *Democracy and Tradition*, 85–91.

39. See Stout, *Democracy and Tradition*, chapter 3, "Religious Reasons in Political Argument," 63–91.

40. See "Moral Universalism and Economic Triage," Rorty's keynote speech at the UNESCO conference, 1996.

41. "Solidarity," *Contingency, Irony, and Solidarity* (Cambridge: Cambridge University Press, 1989), 196.

42. Again, see Rorty, "Moral Universalism and Economic Triage."

43. In addition to the citation I have given here from Rorty's essay "Solidarity," see also "Philosophy and the Future," *Rorty and Pragmatism: The Philosopher Responds to His Critics*, ed. Herman J. Saatkamp Jr. (Nashville, Tenn.: Vanderbilt University Press, 1995), 197–205; and Rorty, "Looking Backwards from the Year 2096," *Philosophy and Social Hope*, 243–51.

44. For a more skeptical assessment of Rorty's views and of his ability to contribute constructively toward the classical pragmatists' democratic idealism, see David Hildebrand, *Beyond Realism and Anti-Realism: John Dewey and the Neo-Pragmatists* (Nashville, Tenn.: Vanderbilt University Press, 2003); see especially chapters 4 and 5, and 190–93.

45. Less sanguine assessments of Dewey's account of God are common. See, for example, Michael Eldridge's treatment in *Transforming Experience: John Dewey's Cultural Instrumentalism* (Nashville, Tenn.: Vanderbilt University Press, 1998); chapter 5, "Dewey's Religious Proposal" is the relevant portion.

46. This story appears in Luke 10:25–37.

47. Jerome Berryman, an Episcopalian priest in Houston, Texas, makes the story dimension of biblical literature the exclusive focus of his approach to Christian education; his work brings systematically to the forefront of thought about

Christianity that dimension of concreteness, practice, and narrative that, in my account, Dewey and the pragmatist tradition embrace. See, for example, Berryman's *Godly Play* (San Francisco: Harper, 1994). Another contemporary thinker who puts this approach at the center of his treatment of these issues of morality and religion is Henry Rosemont. See *Rationality and Religious Experience: The Continuing Relevance of the World's Spiritual Traditions* (Chicago: Open Court, 2001).

48. See William James, *The Varieties of Religious Experience* (New York: Modern Library Classics, 1999), 431.

49. Hopkins's Catholic theology is not compatible with the American tradition thought of as pragmatism; however, he comes very close in this poem to capturing the same idea of concreteness of value that is central to that American tradition.

50. Yevgeny Yevtushenko, "I Would Like," *Almost at the End* (New York: Henry Holt), 1–5.

51. LW9:58.

Bibliography

Alexander, Thomas M. "John Dewey and the Moral Imagination: Beyond Putnam and Rorty toward a Postmodern Ethics." *Transactions of the Charles S. Peirce Society* 29, no. 3 (Summer 1993).

———. *John Dewey's Theory of Art, Experience, and Nature: The Horizons of Feeling*. Albany: The State University of New York Press, 1987.

Anderson, Douglas R. "Peirce: Ethics and the Conduct of Life." In *Classical American Pragmatism: Its Contemporary Vitality*, edited by Sandra Rosenthal, Carl R. Hausman, and Douglas R. Anderson. Urbana, Ill.: University of Illinois Press, 1999.

———. *Strands of System: The Philosophy of Charles S. Peirce*. West Lafayette, Ind.: Purdue University Press, 1995.

Appiah, Kwame A. *Cosmopolitanism: Ethics in a World of Strangers*. New York: W. W. Norton, 2006.

Baier, Annette. "Doing without Moral Theory." In *Postures of the Mind: Essays on Mind and Morals*. Minneapolis: University of Minnesota Press, 1985.

———. "Theory and Reflective Practices." In *Postures of the Mind: Essays on Mind and Morals*. Minneapolis: University of Minnesota Press, 1985.

Baird, Robert, and Stuart Rosenbaum, eds. *Pornography*. Buffalo, N.Y.: Prometheus Press, 1993.

———. *Same Sex Marriage*. Buffalo, N.Y.: Prometheus Press, 1997.

Barber, Benjamin. "America Skips School: Why We Talk So Much about Education and Do So Little." *Harper's*, November 1993.

Barth, Karl. *Church Dogmatics*. Oxford: T & T Clark Books, 2004.

Berman, Morris. *The Reenchantment of the World*. Ithaca, N.Y.: Cornell University Press, 1981.

Bernstein, Richard. *Beyond Objectivism and Relativism*. Philadelphia: University of Pennsylvania Press, 1983.

185

———. *Philosophical Profiles*. Philadelphia: University of Pennsylvania Press, 1986.

———. "Pragmatism, Pluralism, and the Healing of Wounds." In *Pragmatism: A Reader*, edited by Louis Menand. New York: Vintage Books, 1997.

Berryman, Jerome. *Godly Plan*. San Francisco: Harper, 1994.

Bettelheim, Bruno. *The Uses of Enchantment: The Meaning and Importance of Fairy Tales*. New York: Random House, 1997.

Boisvert, Raymond. *Dewey's Metaphysics*. New York: Fordham University Press, 1988.

Calore, Gary. "Towards a Naturalistic Metaphysics of Temporality: A Synthesis of John Dewey's Later Thought." *The Journal of Speculative Philosophy* 3, no. 1 (1989): 12–25.

Caspary, William. "One and the Same Method: John Dewey's Thesis of Unity of Method in Ethics and Science." *Transactions of the Charles S. Peirce Society* 39, no. 3 (2003): 445–68.

Chisholm, Roderick. *On Metaphysics*. Minneapolis: University of Minnesota Press, 1989.

Cohen, Morris R. "Some Difficulties in Dewey's Anthropocentric Naturalism." *Philosophical Review* 49 (1940): 196–228.

Coles, Robert. "The Disparity between Intellect and Character." *The Chronicle of Higher Education*, September 22, 1995, A68.

Cooper, John M. "The Fragility of Goodness: Luck and Ethics in Greek Tragedy and Philosophy." *The Philosophical Review* 97, no. 4 (October 1998): 543–64.

Dean, William. *The American Spiritual Culture*. New York: Continuum International Publishing Group, 2002.

Dembski, William. *Intelligent Design: The Bridge between Science and Theology*. Downers Grove, Ill.: Intervarsity Press, 2007.

Dewey, John. *The Later Works, 1925–1953*. Vol. 1, *Experience and Nature (1925)*. Vol. 4, *The Quest for Certainty (1929)*. Vol. 5, *Individualism, Old and New (1929–1930)*. Vol. 7, *Ethics (1932)*. Vol. 9, *A Common Faith (1933–1934)*. Vol. 10, *Art as Experience (1934)*. Vol. 13, *Freedom and Culture (1938–1939)*. Vol. 14, *Essays, Reviews, and Miscellany (1939–1941)*. Edited by Jo Ann Boydston. Carbondale: Southern Illinois University Press, 1981–1990.

———. *The Middle Works, 1899–1924*. Vol. 5, *Ethics (1908)*. Edited by Jo Ann Boydston. Carbondale: Southern Illinois University Press, 2008.

———. "The Need for a Recovery of Philosophy." In *The Essential Dewey*, vol. 1, edited by Larry A. Hickman and Thomas M. Alexander. Bloomington, Ind.: Indiana University Press, 1998.

———. "The Need for a Recovery of Philosophy." *The Middle Works, 1899–1924*. Vol. 10, *Journal Articles, Essays, and Miscellany (1916–1917)*. Edited by Jo Ann Boydston. Carbondale: Southern Illinois University Press, 2008.

———. "The Reflex Arc Concept of Experience." In *The Essential Dewey*, vol. 2, edited by Larry A. Hickman. Bloomington: Indiana University Press, 1998.

Diamond, Jared. *Guns, Germs, and Steel: The Fates of Human Societies*. New York: W. W. Norton and Company, 1997.

Diggins, John P. *The Promise of Pragmatism*. Chicago: University of Chicago Press, 1994.

Dodds, Elizabeth. *Marriage to a Difficult Man*. Santa Ana, Calif.: Westminster Press, 1981.

Eldridge, Michael. *Transforming Experience: John Dewey's Cultural Instrumentalism*. Nashville, Tenn.: Vanderbilt University Press, 1998.

Feyerabend, Paul. *Against Method*. London: Verso, 1978.

Friedman, Milton. *Capitalism and Freedom*. Chicago: University of Chicago Press, 2002.

Garrison, James W. "John Dewey's Philosophy as Education." In *Reading Dewey: Interpretations for a Postmodern Generation*, edited by Larry A. Hickman. Bloomington: Indiana University Press, 1998.

Gibbard, Allan. "Why Theorize How to Live with Each Other." *Philosophy and Phenomenological Research* 55, no. 2 (1995): 323–42.

Gouinlock, James. *John Dewey's Philosophy of Value*. New York: Humanities Press, 1972.

——. "What Is the Legacy of Instrumentalism? Rorty's Interpretation of Dewey." *Journal of the History of Philosophy* 28, no. 2 (1990).

Guelzo, Allen. "American Philosophy's Uneasy Embrace of God." *Harvard Divinity Bulletin* 30, no. 4 (Spring 2002): 35–36.

Hall, David, and Roger Ames. *The Democracy of the Dead: Dewey, Confucius, and the Hope for Democracy in China*. Chicago: Open Court Press, 1999.

Hardy, Thomas. *Far from the Madding Crowd*. New York: Modern Library Classics, 2001.

Hickman, Larry A. "Dewey's Theory of Inquiry." In *Reading Dewey: Interpretations for a Postmodern Generation*, edited by Larry A. Hickman. Bloomington: Indiana University Press, 1998.

Hildebrand, David. *Beyond Realism and Anti-Realism: John Dewey and the Neo-Pragmatists*. Nashville, Tenn.: Vanderbilt University Press, 2003.

Hiley, David. *Philosophy in Question*. Chicago: University of Chicago Press, 1988.

Hollenbach, David. "Civil Society: Beyond the Public Private Dichotomy." *The Responsive Community* 5, no. 1 (Winter 1994–1995): 16.

Hollis, Martin. "The Self in Action." In *John Dewey Reconsidered*, edited by R. S. Peters. London: Routledge and Kegan Paul, 1977.

Hook, Sidney. *John Dewey: An Intellectual Portrait*. Amherst, N.Y.: Prometheus Books, 1995.

Hume, David. "Of the Reason of Animals." In *A Treatise of Human Nature*, edited by L. A. Selby-Bigge. London: Oxford University Press, 1888.

——. *A Treatise of Human Nature*. Edited by L. A. Selby-Bigge. London: Oxford University Press, 1888.

James, William. "The Chicago School." *Psychological Bulletin* 1 (1904): 1–5.

——. *Essays in Radical Empiricism*. New York: Longmans, Green & Co., 1912.

——. *The Varieties of Religious Experience*. New York: Longman, 1902.

Johnson, Mark. *Moral Imagination: Implications of Cognitive Science for Ethics*. Chicago: University of Chicago Press, 1994.

Kahn, Sholom J. "Experience and Existence in Dewey's Naturalistic Metaphysics." *Philosophy and Phenomenological Research* 9 (1948): 316–21.

Kant, Immanuel. *Foundations of the Metaphysics of Morals*. 1977.

Kestenbaum, Victor. *The Grace and the Severity of the Ideal*. Chicago: University of Chicago Press, 2003.

Kingsolver, Barbara. *The Poisonwood Bible*. New York: HarperCollins, 1999.

Kuhn, Thomas. *The Structure of Scientific Revolutions*. Chicago: University of Chicago Press, 1962.

Kuklick, Bruce. *History of Philosophy in America, 1720–2000*. London: Oxford University Press, 2000.

Lawlor, Philip. "A Life of Purity." *Wall Street Journal*, September 8, 1997.

Lekan, Todd. *Making Morality*. Nashville, Tenn.: Vanderbilt University Press, 2003.

MacIntyre, Alasdair. *After Virtue*. South Bend, Ind.: University of Notre Dame Press, 1981.

———. *Dependent Rational Animals*. Chicago: Open Court, 1999.

———. *First Principles, Final Ends, and Contemporary Philosophical Issues*. Milwaukee: Marquette University Press, 1990.

———. *Three Rival Versions of Moral Enquiry*. South Bend, Ind.: University of Notre Dame Press, 1990.

———. *Whose Justice, Which Rationality*. South Bend, Ind.: University of Notre Dame Press, 1988.

McDermott, John. "The Aesthetic Drama of the Ordinary." In *Pragmatism and Religion: Original Sources and Contemporary Essays*, edited by Stuart Rosenbaum. Champaign: University of Illinois Press, 2003.

———. "Pragmatic Sensibility: The Morality of Experience." In *New Directions in Ethics*, edited by Joseph DeMarco and Richard Fox. New York: Routledge and Kegan Paul, 1986.

Menand, Louis. *The Metaphysical Club: A Story of Ideas in America*. New York: Farrar, Straus, and Giroux, 2001.

Miller, Matt. "First, Kill All the School Boards." *The Atlantic*, January/February 2008, 92–97.

Miller, Perry. *Edwards*. New York: William Sloane Associates, 1949.

———. *Errand into the Wilderness*. Cambridge, Mass.: Harvard University Press, 1956.

———. *Roger Williams*. Indianapolis: Bobbs-Merrill Company, 1953.

Millgram, Elijah. "Practical Reasoning, Dictionary of Philosophy of Mind." Available from http://www.artsci.wustl.edu/~philos/MindDict/practicalreasoning.html.

Moore, G. E. *Principia Ethica*. Cambridge: Cambridge University Press, 1920.

Nagel, Thomas. *Mortal Questions*. Cambridge: Cambridge University Press, 1979.

Neville, Robert C. "A Peircean Theory of Religious Interpretation." In *Pragmatism and Religion*, edited by Stuart Rosenbaum. Urbana: University of Illinois Press, 2003.

Nietzsche, Friedrich. *On the Genealogy of Morality*. Indianapolis: Hackett Publishing Co., 1998.

Nussbaum, Martha. "An Aristotelian Conception of Rationality." In *Love's Knowledge*. Oxford: Oxford University Press, 1990.

———. "Non-Scientific Deliberation." In *The Fragility of Goodness*. Cambridge: Cambridge University Press, 1986.

———. "Perceptive Equilibrium: Literary Theory and Ethical Theory." In *Love's Knowledge*. Oxford: Oxford University Press, 1990.

Pappas, Gregory. "Dewey's Ethics: Morality as Experience." In *Reading Dewey: Interpretations for a Postmodern Generation*, edited by Larry A. Hickman. Bloomington: Indiana University Press, 1988.

———. "New Directions and Uses in the Reconstruction of Dewey's Ethics." In *In Dewey's Wake: Unfinished Work of Pragmatic Reconstruction*, edited by William J. Gavin. Albany: State University of New York Press, 2003.

Peirce, C. S. "Evolutionary Love." In *The Collected Papers of Charles Sanders Peirce*. Cambridge, Mass.: Harvard University Press, 1960.

———. "How to Make Our Ideas Clear." In *Pragmatism: The Classic Writings*, edited by H. S. Thayer. Indianapolis: Hackett Publishing Co., 1982.

Pinker, Steven. *The Language Instinct*. New York: HarperCollins, 1995.

Popkin, Richard. *Skepticism from Erasmus to Spinoza*. Berkeley: University of California Press, 1979.

Pratt, Scott. *Native Pragmatism: Rethinking the Roots of American Philosophy*. Bloomington: Indiana University Press, 2002.

Putnam, Hilary. "How Not to Solve Ethical Problems." In *Realism with a Human Face*. Cambridge, Mass.: Harvard University Press, 1990.

———. "A Reconsideration of Deweyan Democracy." In *Renewing Philosophy*. Cambridge, Mass.: Harvard University Press, 2002.

———. *Renewing Philosophy*. Cambridge, Mass.: Harvard University Press, 1992.

Quine, Willard O. *From a Logical Point of View*. Cambridge, Mass.: Harvard University Press, 1953.

———. "Three Grades of Modal Involvement." In *The Ways of Paradox*. New York: Random House, 1966.

Ree, Jonathan. "The Poverty of Unbelief." *Harper's Magazine*, July 2002.

Reichenbach, Hans. *From Copernicus to Einstein*. New York: Philosophical Library, 1942.

Robinson, Marilyn. "Hallowed Be Your Name." *Harper's Magazine*, July 2006.

Rockefeller, Steven. *John Dewey: Religious Faith and Democratic Humanism*. New York: Columbia University Press, 1991.

Rorty, Richard. *Contingency, Irony, and Solidarity*. Cambridge: Cambridge University Press, 1989.

———. "Dewey's Metaphysics." In *New Studies in the Philosophy of John Dewey*, edited by Steven M. Cahn. Hanover, N.H.: University Press of New England, 1977.

———. "Ethics without Principles." In *Philosophy and Social Hope*. New York: Penguin Books, 1999.

———. "Human Rights, Rationality and Sentimentality." *The Yale Review*, October 1993, 1–20.

———. "Looking Backwards from the Year 2096." In *Philosophy and Social Hope*. New York: Penguin Books, 1999.

———. "Moral Universalism and Economic Triage." Keynote speech at the UNESCO Philosophy Forum, 1996.

———. *Objectivism, Realism, and Truth*. Cambridge: Cambridge University Press, 1991.

———. "Philosophy and the Future." In *Rorty and Pragmatism: The Philosopher Responds to His Critics*, edited by Herman Saatkamp Jr. Nashville, Tenn.: Vanderbilt University Press, 1995.

———. *Philosophy and the Mirror of Nature*. Princeton, N.J.: Princeton University Press, 1979.

———. "Pragmatism as Romantic Polytheism." In *Pragmatism and Religion*, edited by Stuart Rosenbaum. Urbana: University of Illinois Press, 2003.

———. "Religion as a Conversation Stopper." In *Philosophy and Social Hope*. New York: Penguin Books, 1999.

———. "Solidarity." In *Philosophy and Social Hope*. New York: Penguin Books, 1999.

———. "Trotsky and the Wild Orchids." In *Philosophy and Social Hope*. New York: Penguin Books, 1999.

Rosemont, Henry. *Rationality and Religious Experience: The Continuing Relevance of the World's Spiritual Traditions*. Chicago: Open Court, 2001.

Rosenbaum, Stuart. "The Constitution, Metaphysics, and Abortion." *Journal of Church and State* 43 (Autumn 2001): 707–23.

———. "MacIntyre or Dewey." *The American Journal of Theology and Philosophy* 19, no. 1 (January 1998): 35–59.

———. "Morality and Religion: Why Not Pragmatism." In *Pragmatism and Religion: Classical Sources and Original Essays*, edited by Stuart Rosenbaum. Champaign: University of Illiois Press, 2003.

———. "A Note on the Impossibility of Rationalizing Desire." *The Journal of Value Inquiry* 18 (1984): 63–67.

Roth, Robert. *Radical Pragmatism, An Alternative*. New York: Fordham University Press, 1998.

Russell, Bertrand. *A History of Western Philosophy*. New York: Simon and Schuster, 1946/1977.

———. *The Problems of Philosophy*. London: Oxford University Press, 1912.

Ryan, Alan. *John Dewey and the High Tide of American Liberalism*. New York: W. W. Norton & Co., 1995.

Saatkamp, Herman, Jr. *Rorty and Pragmatism: The Philosopher Responds to His Critics*. Nashville, Tenn.: Vanderbilt University Press, 1995.

Santayana, George. "Dewey's Naturalistic Metaphysics." *Journal of Philosophy* 22 (1925): 673–88.

Scanlon, T. N. "Moral Theory: Understanding and Disagreement." *Philosophy and Phenomenological Research* 55, no. 2 (1995): 343–56.

Singer, Marcus G. "The Ideal of a Rational Morality." *Proceedings and Addresses of the American Philosophical Association* 60, no. 1 (1986): 15–38.

Sleeper, R. W. *The Necessity of Pragmatism*. Champaign: University of Illinois Press, 2001.

Smith, Alexander M. *The No. 1 Ladies Detective Agency*. New York: Anchor Books, 2001.

Stack, George. *Nietzsche and Emerson: An Elective Affinity*. Athens: Ohio University Press, 1993.

Stephenson, James. *The Language of the Land: Living among a Stone-Age People in Africa*. New York: St. Martin's Press, 2000.

Stout, Jeffrey. *Democracy and Tradition*. Princeton, N.J.: Princeton University Press, 2004.

Stuhr, John. "Democracy as a Way of Life." In *Philosophy and the Reconstruction of Culture: Pragmatic Essays after Dewey*. Albany: The State University of New York Press, 1993.

Thayer, H. S. *Pragmatism, the Classic Writings*. Indianapolis: Hackett Publishing Co., 1982.

Tillich, Paul. *Systematic Theology*. Chicago: University of Chicago Press, 1973.

Watson, James. *The Double Helix*. New York: Scribner, 1998.

Welchman, Jennifer. *Dewey's Ethical Thought*. Ithaca, N.Y.: Cornell University Press, 1995.

West, Cornel. *The American Evasion of Philosophy*. Madison: University of Wisconsin Press, 1989.

Westbrook, Robert. *John Dewey and American Democracy*. Ithaca, N.Y.: Cornell University Press, 1991.

Williams, Bernard. *Ethics and the Limits of Philosophy*. Cambridge, Mass.: Harvard University Press, 1985.

Wilson, Edward. *Consilience*. New York: Vintage Books, 1999.

———. *On Human Nature*. Cambridge, Mass.: Harvard University Press, 1978.

Wolf, Susan. "Moral Saints." *The Journal of Philosophy* 79, no. 8 (1982): 419–39.

Yevtushenko, Yevgeny. "I Would Like." In *Almost at the End*. New York: Henry Holt & Co., 1987.

Index

About the Author

Stuart Rosenbaum is a professor of philosophy at Baylor University.

Breinigsville, PA USA
15 April 2010
236202BV00002B/19/P